MW00448152

BOOKS BY JOHN G. HALL

Majoring in The Minors: A Glimpse of Baseball in a Small Town
(1996; second editon 2000)

The KOM League Remembered: Images of Baseball (2004)

Mickey Mantle: Before the Glory (2005)

MICKEY MANTLE

BEFORE THE GLORY

By John G. Hall

Copyright © 2005 by John G. Hall.
Printed in the United States. All rights reserved.

ISBN 1-58597-317-3

Library of Congress Control Number: 2004118215

A division of Squire Publishers, Inc.
4500 College Boulevard
Leawood, KS 66211
888-888-7696
www.leatherspublishing.com

For my first and only wife, Noel, who allowed me to spend

five years of our married life putting this book together ...

and to the members of the Baxter Springs Whiz Kids,

Independence Yankees and Joplin Miners for sharing

their insights about their teammate, Mickey Mantle.

Contents

In the years just after World War II, the life of a baseball player setting out in the minor leagues is a hard
road to travel. Mickey Mantle's love affair with the
game begins almost at birth and is nurtured through
games played in vacant lots and backyards of a dusty
mining community. Other entertainment is centered
on the radio and live bands playing Saturday nights.
In this period the community is exposed to some of
the "star" bandits of the time, including a visit one
day by an escaping Bonnie and Clyde.

The Mantles' genealogy is traced two centuries to the
coal fields of England. In 1848 Mickey Mantle's great-
great-grandfather moves his family to Missouri. The
family takes up farming in the central part of the
state, a welcome relief from the mines. About 1899,
some of the Mantles, including Mickey's grandfather,
Charles, move to Oklahoma, planning to farm near
the town of Adair.

Farming income is supplemented by a bit of rum running during Prohibition. The Dust Bowl days of the 1930s take their toll on the family economically and psychologically. Tired of trying to scratch a living from blowing dirt, Mickey's father, Mutt, hears of opportunity a few counties away, in the mining industry their ancestors had fled by coming to America.

In 1935, Mickey Mantle, nearly four years old, departs his native Spavinaw for Ottawa County, Oklahoma, in the Tri-State mining region. Life in the mines is dangerous, with injury, illness and frequent deaths assailing the miners. Tensions exist socially between farmers and miners, and a labor strike shortens tempers even further.

Life in the small town is hard for Mickey, his family and friends. Discipline is strict and certain, chores always to be done. But there also is play, abiding loyalty and love at home, as well as in the community of hard-working people who face hard times with relentless determination. And there is perpetual concern for the development of sound character in the local youth.

Mickey Mantle's father begins playing baseball for a local mining company team, as a means of exposing Mickey to the game. In 1942, Mickey, nearly 11, plays for his first team, a kids' club at Douthat, Oklahoma. His mother, also knowledgeable of the game, frequently quizzes her son at home about baseball strategy and fashions some home-made sliding pads for him.

studded lineup. Area scouts representing professional baseball teams begin to take a look at the young man from Commerce. The author examines the still-repeated local legend that Mantle, while playing for the Whiz Kids, hit an amazingly long home run into Spring River at Baxter Springs.

Some of the significant early baseball figures who influenced and nurtured Mantle's maturing baseball skills and his lifelong devotion to the game are discussed. Mickey's innate shyness begins to give way to a love of pranks that his peers enjoy so much. A tryout for a college football scholarship fails, keeping Mantle on the path to a baseball career.

A wide variety of friends, fellow baseball players and adults affected Mantle's early years. They range from lifelong friends to brief but significant acquaintances, from serious-minded future business executives to the more fun-loving good old boys, from the playfully profane to the profoundly pious.

Professional scouts and team officials jockey for the inside track when it is decided that young Mickey Mantle is worth an initial contract as soon as he graduates from high school in the spring of 1949. The infighting between the suitors is given a close look in the days leading to Mantle signing to play his first season of professional baseball, for $1,500, which includes a $1,150 bonus.

Foreword

By Merlyn Mantle

Long ago, Teresa Brewer recorded a song with and about my husband entitled, "I Love Mickey." When he was in his final hours on this earth I went in to his hospital room with a prepared letter I had written. Although the contents of that letter are personal, I can say that "I Too Loved Mickey," as did millions of baseball fans, in their own way.

Since Mickey first entered baseball there have been many books written about his on- and off-the-field exploits. Some of the books were very accurate while others somehow told a story of his life that didn't always report names, places and events in a factual manner.

As a young lady growing up in Picher, Oklahoma, I knew very little about the young man living a few miles south at Commerce. There is much about Mickey's family background and early baseball early years of which I was totally in the dark until I got to know John Hall, the author of this book.

Mr. Hall and I have visited in my Joplin, Missouri, home, toured a microfilm library and conversed by telephone many times in uncovering information about Mickey's early days at Commerce High, as well as his time with the Baxter Springs Whiz Kids. It was great fun to find out things that I had never known and then in turn being able to share them with my sons.

The author has done a great job in researching the history of the Mantle family back to England and bringing to light things I never knew, as well as finding photos of the Mantles as far back as the 1800s in Missouri.

In this book Mr. Hall interviewed former teammates of Mickey's with such teams as Douthat, Oklahoma, of the Gabby Street Pee Wee League, the Baxter Springs, Kansas, Whiz Kids of the Cardinal Junior and Southeast Kansas Ban Johnson Leagues and two of Mickey's minor league teams, the Independence, Kansas, Yankees and the Joplin, Missouri, Miners.

This book tells the compelling story of my late husband from the perspective of his buddies while growing up in the Cardin, Whitebird and Commerce communities of Oklahoma. Many of the revelations in this book fascinated me, since they are glimpses into the life of a young man that predate — in some instances, by a decade — our meeting each other.

The author has captured the essence of growing up in the harsh environment of the mining area of Northeast Oklahoma. Many of the fathers of young men and women went off to the lead and zinc mines to earn enough money to put food on the table and clothes on the backs of their children. My dad also started in the mines, but due to a mine-related injury, went to work in the family-owned lumberyard and escaped the harsh fate of many a miner.

There was little time for few other things except work. One of the diversions from the harshness of the mining life was a weekend baseball game or two. Miners like Elven "Mutt" Mantle took the time to share his love of the game with his eldest son and my future husband. In fact, Mutt got the message over to Mickey so forcefully that I can honestly say that "Baseball was my competitor" during our life together.

For those of you who idolized my husband as a baseball player, I highly recommend this book. It is a glimpse of his early life as seen through the eyes of the young men who used to come over to play with Mickey and eat a few meals cooked up by his mother, Lovell. Through the pages of this book you will see what shaped Mickey into becoming the hero of millions. This is truly the best account of the early life of my husband. I trust that you will enjoy *Mickey Mantle: Before the Glory* as much as I have.

Introduction
The Metamorphosis of a Book

For many reasons Mickey Mantle was never a baseball hero of mine. He played for the wrong Kansas-Oklahoma-Missouri (KOM) League club — Independence, Kansas — and he became a member of the New York Yankees, for starters.

I had seen Mantle play a couple of games at shortstop for the Independence Yankees against my Carthage, Missouri, Cubs in 1949. Just a few things which stuck out in the mind of a nine-year-old batboy were that Mantle couldn't throw the ball very straight from his position at shortstop to the first baseman, whether it was Nick Ananias or Bobby Gene Newbill. The other thing about the 17-year-old shortstop was that he got to first base faster than anyone else in the park.

Eight years later I had graduated from Carthage High School and was attending a trade school during the summer of 1957 in Kansas City. A bunch of us guys, living in a rooming house on Troost Avenue, would trudge through the humid Kansas City evenings to Memorial Stadium and watch whatever team was in town to beat up on the hapless A's.

One evening the Yankees were the opposition with all their stars. I remember looking at Mickey and thinking how much bigger he was than when he played for Independence. He was not as large in appearance as Mel Allen's radio account of him in World Series games made him out to be. Television was not the staple in many homes in Carthage, and what was seen on most screens appeared more like a whiteout condition in a

Midwestern snowstorm.

Even as late as 1957 baseball fans knew the Yankees still viewed Kansas City as their Triple A affiliate, even though they carried the designation of a major league club. Kansas City had been the Blues when they were the Yankees' farm club in the Triple A American Association. However, acquiring the American League franchise from Philadelphia, the Kansas City A's performed the same function as the Blues had done for years, feed the Yankees with some good talent. Arnold Johnson, owner of the A's, didn't have a lot of money, so he would take Yankee outcasts like Bob Cerv, and team him with Irv Noren and Gus Zernial to form one of the slowest outfields in the game.

Watching a mid-summer night game between the Yankees and A's, my thoughts went back in time to the KOM League. Harry Craft was managing the A's in 1957, having been with many of his young charges all the way from Class D Independence up through Class C Joplin, Missouri, to Double A Beaumont, Texas, and Triple A Kansas City. Craft may have suspected that Mantle, Lou Skizas, Bob Wiesler and Steve Kraly, whom he had guided as a first- and second-year manager in the lowest of minor league classifications, would all follow him into the American League. However, he had no way of knowing that he would be on the other side of the field managing the opposition.

Skizas had re-united with Craft by 1957 and Mantle was in the outfield for the Yanks. Ralph Terry, like Mantle, also from a small northeast Oklahoma town, Big Cabin, was on the Kansas City roster that year, honing his skills to eventually be called back up by the Bronx Bombers. Terry, again like Mantle and other notable players from this part of the country, had played with the Baxter Springs Whiz Kids just across the state line in Kansas. Terry made the team in the final year that Walter A. "Barney" Barnett managed it before his death on November 1, 1952. Mantle had played in three games in 1947, plus the All-Star game, had a full season in 1948 and appeared in four games in 1949.

The northeast quadrant of Oklahoma always seemed near the "end of the earth" to me. My aunt Bertha and uncle Bob Thompson lived in a little hamlet just east of Big Cabin called Pensacola. It had a two-pump gasoline station in front of the general store, which also served double duty as the United States Post Office. That little country store was a forerunner to the convenience stores of today.

Big Cabin was indelibly etched in my mind from my earliest recollection since my first cousin's husband — a full-blood Cherokee Indian — had been murdered there back in the early 1940s. The family tale had always been that Andy Locust, a fine amateur baseball player and graduate of the Haskell Indian Institute in Lawrence, Kansas, had been killed just outside Big Cabin on his way to Vinita to purchase a set of new tires for his car. Family lore was that he had about $100 in his pocket and unknown road bandits murdered him.

I heard that story for a half-century before learning from Locust's widow that the circumstances of his death weren't that mysterious. She told of how her husband stopped by a roadhouse after receiving his weekly paycheck and was probably "hoodwinked" out of his money by a barmaid. When he protested too vociferously, two gentlemen whom my cousin claims probably murdered him to keep him quiet followed him out of the roadhouse.

She recalled that for many nights afterward a car went past her parents' house, where she moved with her two-year-old daughter, after her husband's murder. The occupants of the car appeared to be sending a message for the family to keep quiet and not to pursue the matter through the local law enforcement agency. She said that as she and her mother and daughter slept in the back room, her father would sit in the living room of the house all night with a shotgun on his lap. The family never took the case to court, for they didn't have the money necessary for a prolonged legal battle. Also, it was probably safer for all family members to remain silent.

To get to Uncle Bob's from Pensacola, it was necessary to cross one of the most rickety of wooden bridges known to mankind. When I traversed it with my mother, father and three sisters it was the consensus that our '39 Ford would go through the floor of the bridge and we would all be hurled to our death in the Grand River.

It was a great hunting and fishing area, one reason my dad always liked to go into that part of Oklahoma, at least once each year. It was a cinch that there would be food on the table after each fishing trip, for my dad and his friends always returned home with their limit of crappie or whatever it was they were fishing for at the time. As a young child I never liked the odor of fish. However, my aunt and uncle had a well from which they drew all their water. The water was high in sulfur content and to smell it was so odious that the odor of fresh cleaned fish was more tolerable.

Many years later Cliff Mapes, a Mantle teammate on the Yankees, was persuaded to move to that part of the country. This was because of the stories Mantle would relate to him about the great hunting and fishing in the Northeast Oklahoma area.

The Yankee-A's game I saw in 1957 was marked by one significant thing — Mickey Mantle and his hitting. Batting against left-hander Alex Kellner, he hit a couple of balls over the left field wall into the parking lot. There were two sounds: The crack of the ball on the bat and the "thud" when the ball came into contact with a car that was parked in the wrong place. Hearing the sound of horsehide on metal almost made me feel sorry for the defenseless automobiles.

A metamorphosis had occurred in Mantle from the time I had seen him in Carthage eight years before. He had gone from a drag-bunting, scatter-armed 160-pound shortstop to the best player in the major leagues and with power to hit home runs from either side of the plate further and more often than any of his peers.

Over the intervening years my interest in Mantle did not rise or fall. He was just another member of the Yankee dynasty. I was always a St. Louis Cardinal fan and didn't realize at that time Mantle had some of the same heroes that I admired as a boy: Enos Slaughter, Marty Marion and Stan Musial. While growing up, he had played the same imaginary games with his boyhood pals — Leroy Bennett, Nick Ferguson, as well as with his brothers Ray and Roy and first cousin Maxie — that my buddy Corky Simpson and I played when we were boys. He listened to the same radio station we boys in Carthage, Missouri, heard to tune in the St. Louis Cardinals games featuring Harry Caray and Gabby Street at the mike, KGLC, 910 on the dial in Miami, Oklahoma, and enjoyed the same "sing through nose" country music that A. J. Cripe put out over the airwaves of the 5,000-watt giant, KOAM, in Pittsburg, Kansas.

Each time information was passed on to me in preparation of this book, I was amazed at some of the things my family and I experienced about the same time in life as did the Mantles. This is NOT a comparison of my baseball skills or athletic ability with Mickey Mantle. But I was intrigued by the recurrent coincidences:

- At the time Mickey was receiving penicillin for his osteomyelitis (1947), my dad was in the hospital and none was available. Mickey was in Children's Hospital in Oklahoma City and got the drug. My dad was in McCune Brooks Hospital in Carthage, Missouri, and didn't get it. He died.

- Mickey's ancestors moved from Missouri to Oklahoma. My Harrison/Hall clans moved from Oklahoma to Missouri.

- Mickey's mother worked in a blue jean manufacturing plant in Commerce, Oklahoma, after Mutt Mantle's death. After my father's death, my mother worked her fingers to the bone at Smith Brothers overall factory in Carthage.

- Mickey hurt his leg in the 1951 World Series and wound up eventually being treated by Dr. Daniel Yancey in Springfield, Missouri. I received multiple injuries to my left arm on my 12th birthday, which fell on Thanksgiving Day of 1951. You guessed it. I wound up being treated by the same Dr. Yancey.

- Mickey Mantle and I could both swim… like a rock.

- One of Mickey's best boyhood friends was born in Missouri (Carthage) and moved to Commerce. One of my best boyhood friends was born in Oklahoma and moved to Missouri. Mickey's pal was two years his senior and my best pal was two years my senior.

- Mickey could hit from either side of the plate. I could get hit from either side of the dinner plate depending which of my sisters I was irritating at mealtime.

- Mickey had brothers by the name of Ray and Roy. I had uncles by the same names.

- Mickey's dad died when he was 40 years old. Mine, too.

- Mickey had an aunt by the name of Thelma. Likewise here.

- Mickey went to work for his uncle Emmett at the Safeway grocery store in Picher, Oklahoma, bagging groceries in 1945. I started bagging groceries for Safeway in Carthage in 1956.

- Mickey's aunt and uncle lived at Spavinaw, Oklahoma, near where lived an aunt and uncle of mine.

- Mickey's mother made him and his buddy their first pair of pull-up sliding pants. My mother made my buddy and me our first authentic major league jersey. She was an embroiderer at the Big Smith overall factory. My buddy's shirt had the Phillies logo on the front; mine, the Cardinals.

- Mickey's best friend settled on the western United States coast. So did mine.

- Mickey's mother lived to be 92. My mother is 90 and going strong.
- Mickey died at age 63. I've now reached that age. Whoa there!! I think this has gone far enough.

Mantle's career bloomed, faded; he went into retirement and then the Hall of Fame. There were always the stories and rumors of the kind of friends he kept and the distasteful things that he did in his life during and after his baseball career, but that was never an interest to me.

One evening, in the spring of 1989, I was living in Round Rock, Texas. My wife informed me that Mantle was going to be on the radio with Larry King. I said something to the effect, "Big deal." For unexplainable reasons she kept urging me to call in and ask him a question. I couldn't think of one to ask for which I didn't already have the answer.

I knew that I would never get through on the line, but in order to pacify my wife I kept dialing and, lo and behold, I got lucky. I asked Mantle if the Joplin catcher in 1950, Cal Neeman, had also played with him at Independence in 1949. He proclaimed to a national radio audience that he never played with Neeman. That came as a shock; how could Mickey have forgotten such a teammate?

Larry King jumped to the defense of Mantle's answer and informed me that the person I had in mind was Bob Nieman. Furthermore, Mantle said that Nieman was an old Major Leaguer on his way down and he was actually the Carthage first baseman during the 1949 season. (That would have really been a surprise to Bob Speake for he held down that position with Carthage.) I attempted to inform King and Mantle that the only other Nieman who played in that area and era was Elmer "Butch" Nieman of the Topeka Owls. However, as I attempted to refresh Mantle's memory of Nieman and set the record straight for King, I was unceremoniously cut off.

Nearly six years passed. The next thing that brought Mantle into my awareness was the announcement that he needed a liver transplant. Like most other sports fans I followed his final days with a certain level of interest and a great amount of sadness. I was driving between Des Moines, Iowa, and my home in Columbia, Missouri, the morning of his transplant. That trip and Mantle's surgery took precisely the same amount of time.

As the news of Mantle's inevitable demise was made known, a number of his old Independence (Kansas) Yankee teammates called to find out how they could get a card to him. The year before, I had begun publishing a monthly newsletter for and about the Kansas-Oklahoma-Missouri League's former players, managers and others once associated with the now-vanished minor league in which Mantle had first played professional baseball in 1949. I had addresses for him in New York and Dallas, where a few copies of the newsletter had been sent but I was sure he never saw any of them and figured that none of the cards that would be sent to those addresses would ever get to him.

When the bad news came, I was at the computer when my son came downstairs around 2:00 a.m. on August 13, 1995, and said, "Mickey Mantle died."

Mantle's last days were very sad to the guys who knew him as the fun-loving kid from Commerce, Oklahoma, who had more talent in every aspect of the game than any of his teammates at either Independence or Joplin possessed.

Late in his life, a very old looking, frail and dying man had stood before the national media and proclaimed, "I'm no role model." But, at that point Mantle became one to me. By then, I was no longer the Yankee-hater who had developed that animosity during my formative years. Mantle, being a part of that Yankee dynasty, had been lumped together with the group. Guilt by association, I suppose.

Amazingly, after the death of Mantle, I was besieged by newspaper and radio sources to give my views on his career. I truly felt unqualified for the task, but related what insights I had about the "Commerce Comet" from what had been shared by many of his former teammates from the minor league Independence Yankees.

In the early days of writing the KOM League newsletter I always steered clear of "featuring" Mantle, since I felt everything that could have been written about him had already been published. Moreover, most former Class D minor league players never received much recognition for their careers on the farm teams of some major league organization. Thus, I concentrated on them.

Time passed swiftly. Four years after Mantle's death the telephone rang. The voice on the other end said, "I'm Tom Gott. After Joe DiMaggio's death I got to thinking about Mickey Mantle. You know, there was never a factual book written about Mickey that talked about what a great kid he was. All the stuff I have seen deals with all the things that sell books." Gott had known Mickey on a very personal basis, for they were teammates and roommates on the 1950 Joplin Miner club, and consequently did all the

MICKEY MANTLE

things together that young men do.

Gott, who batted in front of Mantle for the entire 1950 season, believed that Mickey had no idea how talented he was at that point. He recalled that Mantle never lost a foot race in any exhibition he ever entered. Gott found it incredible to think that the fastest players the Yankees could line up against Mantle he would leave in the dust by the time the 100-yard dash was three-quarters completed. "He had the body of a person who worked out on weights but never did such things," Gott recalled.

Few things in life come as great revelations. However, just days before Gott's call I, too, had the same thoughts but didn't act on them. When Gott called I said something to the effect, "I knew someone was going to call and come up with the idea for a book about Mickey." However, I never dreamed that I would be asked to write it.

In July of 1999 Gott, then living in Quincy, Illinois, proposed that we "round up" the old Joplin Miners of 1950 and invite them to my house in Columbia, where they could record their recollections about that season, especially of a young and fun-loving "Superman" in a boy's body. I was honored on one hand and scared to death on the other to have been selected to take on such a writing foray. Before thinking through the ramifications and difficulty of such a task I agreed to assist the group in honoring Mantle's "breakout" year in baseball.

The Joplin Miners who made the trip to my home or were contacted by telephone and letter and freely provided their personal reflections of Mickey included Gott, Bob Wiesler, Steve Kraly, Cal Neeman, Cromer Smotherman, the late Alvin Long, David Waters, Lou Skizas, Lilburn Smith, Al Billingsly, Carl Lombardi, Dale Hittle, Jerry Buchanan, Len Wiesner, Dick Fiedler, the late Frank Simanovsky and Dan Ferber. These fellows were the former teammates who saw Mantle blossom into a complete ballplayer and to a man knew he was "head and shoulders above the rest" and destined for greatness.

Of all the books ever been written about or by Mantle I have read only a couple from cover to cover. Many of his friends have related that they didn't like most of them. So, with the initiation of this project I decided the focus should be on the person Mickey Charles Mantle truly was, particularly as the product of parents who were determined to raise good children. I determined the best course would be to do what others have not done, or done very thoroughly: document Mantle's early days and his brief minor league career; the days, in short, before fame overtook him. This is not to imply that the stories about Mantle's big league days were false. However, my objective from the beginning was to write a book about such things as the Baxter Springs Whiz Kids, chores around the home, the certainty of punishment for misdeeds, administered at the hand of loving but attentive parents, back yard baseball and the development of character. My focus would not be on Mantle's big league career — and not what allegedly happened on the bed-springs of a hotel in some American League city.

After the death of Bob Dellinger, the editor of my first book, *Majoring in The Minors*, a history of the KOM League, I inherited his library. In his collection were a number of books about Mantle. Thinking of the proposed book that I was to write about Mantle, I sat down to read one of the inherited books. This was just four days short of the fourth anniversary of Mantle's death. I read it from cover to cover in one evening. Looking at that book and its stories scared me to death. I knew that I didn't have the literary skill to duplicate such a work. The writers of all the Mantle books were very gifted.

However, as I read, I became appalled at the lack of facts as well as the mistakes regarding historical and geographic references. For example, the book talked about Bob Weisler. I looked in my billfold and there was a check from him, spelling his last name W-i-e-s-l-e-r. The book in question mentioned that Mantle played at Joplin with Tom Cott. I knew it was Gott. The names of towns in Oklahoma were spelled wrong (McAllister instead of McAlester, and such).

There was the story of Mickey hitting a home run in Carthage, the night that that Chicago Cubs affiliate had signed Rogers Hornsby, Jr. The version of that incident claimed Mantle hit a line drive that Hornsby, Jr. lost in the lights and it went for a home run. That story was garbled from the "git-go." First of all, the Hornsby boy was named William. He had joined the Carthage Cubs from the Mattoon, Illinois, team of the Mississippi-Ohio Valley League three weeks before the night Mantle hit the homer. Second, Mantle's line drive was "lost in the lights" because Mantle hit the ball at Carthage's Municipal Park stadium above the 80-foot light towers, most of which were located on the field of play. The ball was so high and airborne so long that Hornsby had no way to judge where it was or where it would finally descend from ebony skies. He did what was referred to as a "maypole dance" and when the ball came down from the stratosphere it found a resting spot on his forehead.

The mistakes — mostly minor ones, some not — in that book began to give me some confidence that what I lacked in literary skill I might be able to make up in factual accuracy and correct spelling. More important, my reading also raised questions as to whether some of the other "facts" in the book — and others about Mantle — were accurate.

Merlyn Mantle, Mickey's widow, was approached about the project. She agreed to meet with Lilburn Smith, Tom Gott and this author to discuss it. During that first visit with Merlyn, I became aware of books about her late husband lying around her large living room in Loma Linda, a golfing resort home on the southwest outskirts of Joplin. I asked Merlyn if she felt the books about her late husband were all factual and represented his true feelings and recollections of past events. She replied, pointing to a book on the coffee table, "This guy came to our Dallas home with the manuscript. Mickey threw a fit," Merlyn recalled. She explained that the writer had Mantle using the word "ambivalent" in describing a certain individual. "Mickey said, 'Hell, I don't even know what the word means.' So, Mickey with the help of his attorney, Roy True, sat down and basically re-wrote the thing." As Merlyn recalled, it was a rather long and heated rewrite and she heard it all from the safety of the kitchen as True and Mantle "straightened out history."

After plowing through the book that Mantle and True had edited, I began to see what Gott had meant when he first called me. Maybe there hasn't been a definitive work on Mantle after all, and almost certainly not about his first 20 years of life. When readers are finished with this book they might say that's still true; however, any mistakes will be honest ones (if such things exist).

Between the initial writing of this book and the current time, other books have been written about Mantle. I still haven't seen much written about the baseball side of Mantle's life from 1940 to 1950. Whatever positive or negative things have been attributed to him, he was foremost a dedicated baseball player — he would have had to have been in order to play with the pain he endured since his sophomore year of high school. The greatest compliment any teammate can pay a comrade is that he is "a team player." More than once I heard "Mickey Mantle was a true teammate," from the guys with whom he played for the Baxter Springs Whiz Kids, the Independence Yankees and the Joplin Miners.

I am deeply indebted to many people. Every member of Mantle's family who was contacted gave information freely and candidly, and topped off that generosity with more photos than could be wedged into this book. Hopefully, with all the material that was shared, this book will provide the reader with never-before-seen glimpses into the life of a fun-loving kid honing his skills on his way to the big show.

In addition to numerous members of the Mantle family and their relatives, this book was made possible by the splendid cooperation and encouragement of Mantle's boyhood pals, high school classmates and teammates from the Douthat, Oklahoma (1942) and the Baxter Springs teams in the Gabby Street, Pee Wee, Cardinal Junior and Southeast Kansas Ban Johnson leagues (1947-49) and, in professional baseball, the 1949 Independence Yankees and the 1950 Joplin Miners.

Likewise invaluable were extensive contemporary press accounts from, in Missouri, *The Joplin Globe, The Joplin News Herald* and *The Carthage Evening Press;* in Kansas, *The Independence Reporter, The Baxter Springs Citizen, The Coffeyville Journal* and *The Hutchinson News;* and, in Oklahoma, *The Miami News-Record.*

1

Setting the Scene

Between the end of World War II and the outbreak of the Korean conflict was, in my opinion, the golden era of minor league baseball. From 1946 through 1949 there didn't appear to be anything on the horizon that would cause the small towns of America in the range of 10,000-30,000 citizens to give up on their professional teams.

The Class D and C minor leaguers gave older players from 21-25, just back from the "Sands of Iwo Jima" and the Battle of the Bulge the chance to resume baseball careers that had been interrupted at a very young age. Some came home with mental and physical injuries too severe to resume baseball at any level but for those who could, the lower classification leagues provided them the opportunity.

Interspersed with that group of war heroes were young boys fresh out of high school who were sure that their fame would be established not in towns like Independence, Kansas, or Joplin, Missouri, but in places where Babe Ruth, Ty Cobb, Walter Johnson and Bobo Holloman made theirs. Right? Well, not quite. Not all went to the Hall of Fame as did Ruth, Cobb and Johnson. There was always room in the world for guys like Holloman

Principal Towns in the
Tri-State Lead and Zinc District

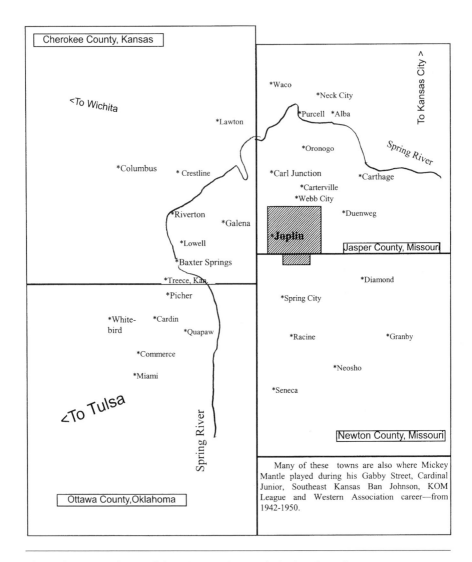

This is the principal part of the Tri-State Zinc Land District of Southeast Kansas, Southwest Missouri, and Northeast Oklahoma.[1]

---

[1] Author's map based on materials from the George A. Spiva Library, Missouri Southern State University, Joplin, Missouri.

to emerge on the scene, toss a no-hitter, win two more games, drop seven and suddenly go into baseball oblivion.

Fame and fortune were not synonymous in the baseball world in the era before the Korean conflict. Back then baseball was played for the love of the sport. Contract disputes in Class D or C leagues usually hinged on a hassle over a $10-a-month raise. Seldom was a holdout successful in his effort, for there was always another phenom on the horizon to take his place.

In the year preceding the attack of South Korea by the communist regime of North Korea came one such phenom from the lead and zinc mining area of northeast Oklahoma, ready to conquer the baseball world The area in which Mickey Mantle was raised was the Tri-State Mining District (also called the "Joplin District"), which covered some 1,200 square miles of southwest Missouri, southeast Kansas and northeast Oklahoma. Mantle played baseball in all four of the district's counties: Jasper and Newton in Missouri; Ottawa County, Oklahoma; and Cherokee County, Kansas.

As a ten-year-old kid, Mantle played his first organized games in Ottawa County, at Douthat, in 1942. After a halt during the World War II years, he played with Cherokee County's Baxter Springs Whiz Kids from 1947-49, including many games on the home diamonds of teams located in the Cardinal Junior League's Jasper County towns of Carl Junction, Webb City, Alba and Purcell and, in Newton County, Seneca, whose team, the Indians, included a guy with whom Mantle later became close friends in professional baseball, Joe Dean "Red" Crowder.

Mantle's hometown was Commerce, Ottawa County, where he played high school baseball, as well as football and basketball, plus countless informal backyard or vacant lot baseball games. His first year in professional baseball, 1949, he played for the Independence Yankees in Kansas, a few miles west of the four Tri-State counties. Among other teams in the league were the Miami Owls of Ottawa County and the Carthage Cubs of Jasper County. By 1950 he still was in the Tri-State, living at home in Ottawa County when his new team wasn't on the road, driving up with his dad to games each evening in Joplin, Jasper County.

Mantle knew this area and its residents about as well as everyone in this part of world got to know him. There was a mutual admiration society between the young slugger and those who cheered him in his baseball venture.

In 1803, the Tri-State area was part of the Louisiana Purchase and was generally an unexplored wilderness. Most of the region's European settlement and lead mining were in Missouri, especially southeast Missouri.

Moses Austin, a visiting Virginia miner, was one of the first to note ore deposits in the Tri-State District, doing so around 1798. However, the area remained a "howling wilderness," inhabited by hunters, trappers and Indians until 1819-1820. In 1819 Henry Schoolcraft, the explorer who discovered the source of the Mississippi, reported from the future Tri-State that he had mined lead, smelted it and made himself some bullets. If it was that easy for one man to conduct the mining and refining operations, then the ore must certainly have been of a pure and superior quality.

Few mining operations were documented before the Civil War. There were a few camps located in southwest Jasper County and in Newton

Chat piles currently appear as miniature reminders of the past. This pile once reached over 500 feet into the heavens. Over the past half-century erosion has moved the lead and zinc residue into underground water supplies and on to surrounding yards of the citizenry.

County. The two counties were identified at different times with the Union and with the Confederates. These shifting allegiances resulted in multiple battles that ravaged many towns and destroyed most of the original mining camps.

After the war, mining began in earnest. People began to move to the district to join the farmers already there. Unlike other mining areas in the United States, most "immigrants" to the Tri-State came from long-settled parts of the young nation — particularly Illinois, Indiana and Kentucky. Through the boom time decades of the 1870s to 1940s, the people of the Tri-State were a generally stable population whose ancestors were virtually all United States citizens going back to the early days of the nation. As historians Arrell Gibson[2] and George G. Suggs, Jr.[3] would point out, this stability and "ethnic American" makeup of the people would have important influences on the nature of the mining industry itself and the role that the Tri-State miners played as nationally recognized "strike busters" during the rise of organized labor in the 1920s and 1930s.

As production stepped up and wealth increased in the latter decades of the nineteenth century, life in the area became as wild and colorful as anything seen in the more famous "gold rush" in the West. By 1872, speculators, gamblers, "women of disrepute," "moochers," ruffians and the other "usual suspects" who flocked to boomtowns had descended on Joplin. As one local resident (Dolph Shaner, quoted in Gibson, 1972, p. 34) put it: "...there was no officer to call to keep the peace. The hoodlums, bad men and drunks took advantage of such a condition. They showed no respect for decency. Shooting at all hours was a pastime. The drunks lay around all the streets. There was no jail in which to place them and no officer to make the arrest. Saloon fights and street fights were common and there were a few fatal shooting scraps. A saloon or two closed at noon Sunday but most of them never closed. Women did not feel safe to be on the streets day or night.

Though some "law and order" was brought to the Joplin area by the end of the 1870s, the boomtown atmosphere persisted for decades. Though there was an opera house and a theater, there were also scores of saloons and a not a few "bawdy houses." Banking, shopping and celebrating the latest

---

[2] Gibson, Arrell (1972). *Wilderness Bonanza: The Tri-State District of Missouri, Kansas and Oklahoma.* Norman, OK: University of Oklahoma Press.

[3] Suggs, George G. Jr (1986) *Union Busting in the Tri-State: The Oklahoma, Kansas, and Missouri Metal Workers' Strike of 1935.* Norman, OK: University of Oklahoma Press.

ore strike filled the streets of Joplin on Saturday night. From 1850 to 1950, the lead and zinc production in this area was worth more than a billion dollars, stoking the flames of all the small businesses (both legitimate and those "of ill repute") located in the area.

By the mid-1890s, mining camps had sprung up all over Jasper and Newton counties and were beginning to "spread west." Rich new deposits in Ottawa and Cherokee counties were discovered. The ready availability of streetcars and, later, automobiles made it possible for the Tri-State miners to live in one community and work in another. People moved readily among the three states, and often "commuted" to work. This mobility led to identification with the district rather than with any particular state.

The 1930s was a pivotal decade in the district, for as in the rest of America, the Depression changed some aspects of life. While there were some hard times for miners and their families, the Tri-State district offered the opportunity to farm and keep a couple of head of livestock for food and milk. When a mine's ore veins were tapped out and the location shut down, the miners could individually prospect in other areas while farming to feed their families. Historians speculate that this ability to be more easily self-supporting than other groups of miners in other parts of the United States led to a greater sense of independence, less hopelessness and a decreased willingness to give up self-determination to organized labor. The attempts of outside agents to bring organized labor to the Tri-State resulted in extreme resistance and bloodshed on more than one occasion.

By the 1950s, mining operations in the Tri-State were winding down. The high-grade ores had all been taken, leaving only lower grade minerals that were more costly and complex to mine. Even so, Gibson (1972) noted that, as of 1950, unmined reserves contained enough zinc to make 20 million automobiles, 650 million sheets of galvanized roofing and almost 12 million miles of barbed wire. There was lead enough for 11 million storage batteries and 18.5 million gallons of paint. The Eagle-Picher Company, one of the few companies that have remained in production until the present, is able to derive germanium and cadmium from the ore.

After 1950, the price for locally produced lead and zinc went down as well. The federal government wished to stockpile munitions metals and drew up long-term contracts with South American and other foreign producers. Eventually, the imports and development of new mining areas sounded the death knell for large-scale mining in the Tri-State.

The legacy of the Tri-State miners today lies in the "industry" of wide scale efforts to reclaim the land and clean contaminated waters in the district. In an online publication of the Geology Extension of the Kansas Geological Survey, it was reported that in the early 1990s U.S. Bureau of Mines " … studies identified more than 1,500 open shafts and nearly 500 subsidence collapse features in the Tri-State. A total of 599 mine hazards were found in and around Galena, Kansas, many of which were concentrated in an area known as "Hell's Half Acre."[4]

Environmental Protection Agency personnel and local citizens filled in these hazard areas in 1994 and 1995, and reclamation efforts continue. Cleanup of lead and other mineral contamination of waters in the Tri-State area also continue to the present day.[5]

Mickey Charles Mantle was born at Spavinaw, Oklahoma, just south of the Tri-State, on October 20, 1931, and moved four years later to Ottawa County. He would become a legend of the game. His heroics, as a member of New York Yankees, have been well chronicled. His ascension to baseball's Hall of Fame was deserved. But greatness had to await a testing period in baseball's minor leagues. Mickey, a son of a miner and farmer, Elven "Mutt" Mantle, played one year each at the Class D and C levels. Such experiences make or break young ballplayers. Many of them find that they can't make the grade in the professional ranks and head into other fields of endeavor.

Mantle's early days in the KOM League at what then was the sport's lowest level, Class D, almost had him convinced he was not cut out for professional baseball. He had a confrontation one evening in Independence, Kansas, in full view of his teammates. Mutt had come up to see Mickey play. He was hitting about .221 at the time. He confided in his dad that he couldn't hit the pitching in the KOM League.

As Bob Mallon, his roommate, recalled, "Mutt called Mickey a spineless little so-and-so." The apartment house at 405 South 10th Street in

[4] "Lead and Zinc Mining", Geology Extension of the Kansas Geological Survey. Retrieved 17 May 2002 at http://www.kgs.ukans.edu/Extension/ozark/mining.html.
[5] "Tri-State Mining District—The Jasper County Superfund Site Project,"presentation published by HQ Environmental Division, U.S. Army Corps of Engineers. Retrieved 17 May 2002 at http://hq.environmental.usace.army.mil/minutes/p03.pdf .

Independence where many of the players were residing, was the scene of the encounter. Mallon remembered that Mantle's twin brothers, Ray and Roy, were also along with their dad. Mutt advised Mickey he could pack and get in the car and go back to Commerce if he didn't have the desire to play the game. However, his dad told him that when he got home he would have to work in the mines.

Mutt's psychology was not lost on his eldest son. Mallon said, "Mickey thought about the alternative for a couple of seconds and decided to give it another shot."[6] Maybe Mantle also recalled that his dad never drove over his self-imposed speed limit of 30 miles per hour and didn't want to make that slow journey back to the southeast that night.

One of Mickey's old Baxter Springs Whiz Kid teammates went to visit him during his early days with the Independence club. Nick Ferguson recalled, "Donnie Dodd and I took a bus up there. When I saw Mick I knew he was homesick. He begged me to try out for the team because he wanted someone around who he knew."[7]

The early days of Mantle's professional baseball career were not pleasant or productive. He played his first game on June 14 and by July 17 was hitting a meager .226. His roommate, Mallon, recalled that Mantle used to lie in his bed at night and worry that the Independence club would cut him before the remainder of his bonus for signing his professional contract came due. Had he not lasted through July he would have forfeited $750 of the $1,150 bonus.[8]

An important part of Mickey Mantle's growing-up years in Commerce lay in the area's radio stations. Heard locally during daylight hours were stations based in each of the three states: Miami (KGLC) and Tulsa, Oklahoma (KVOO); Pittsburg (KOAM) and Coffeyville (KGGF), Kansas; and Joplin, Missouri (KFSB). The nation's big 50,000-watt, clear channel stations didn't bombard the paint off the garage doors until after sundown. Entertainers in the mid-part of the 20th century used their radio shows to reach a wide audience. Then they would parlay that "fame" by playing at dances throughout the towns and villages of the Midwest. Most of the dance bands went out on Saturdays to play an evening benefit at some municipal building or high school.

---

[6] Mallon.

[7] Nick Ferguson.

[8] Mallon.

One of the most popular country and western swing bands of the late 1940s was Bob Wills and the Texas Playboys. Wills originally started out in Fort Worth, Texas, as "Bob Wills and the Light Crust Doughboys." Burrus Mills employed Wills and his band. W. Leo "Pappy" O'Daniel, who owned

The Bob Wills band in a photo taken by Walter Madson in 1937 at Tulsa, Oklahoma. Wills is the man on the left in the front row. Suspenders, white shirts and ties were much in vogue in that era.[9]

Burrus Mills, used the band to provide the entertainment in his successful campaign for governor of Texas. O'Daniel's radio exposure started a political career that would take him to the Texas governor's mansion in 1938, and in 1941, he'd beat out a young Lyndon Johnson in a U.S. Senate race.

By the 1940s Wills was a regular on Tulsa's KVOO. That station, even in the daytime, sent enough of a signal into Commerce that it could almost be picked up on the No. 8 washtub that served as the family bathtub. So ran an often-heard expression among folks those days. Wills went into the service during World War II and brother Johnny Lee took over, basically running

[9] Photo from the Don Steele collection, Joplin, Missouri.

the show through 1958. Many of the people who thought they were listening to Bob were actually hearing the song renditions of his brother.

Johnny Lee Wills traveled many times to Joplin to perform at the Memorial Hall, and often Bob would make the trip with him. Jerry Waldrip of KKOW (formerly KOAM radio in Pittsburg) recounted a story that Bob Wills liked to tell about meeting a young man while on his way to a Joplin appearance.

Waldrip recalled that Wills told him about seeing this kid sitting along Highway 66 each time they went through Commerce, Okla. The boy would always wave as Wills and the band passed by in their large sedans. One day Wills stopped and introduced himself to the young admirer. The boy in turn obviously was awe struck to meet a man who had put "Faded Love," "San Antonio Rose" and scores of other songs onto the hit list of that era.

During that brief meeting the boy asked Wills if he could go to Joplin with him and see the performance. Wills advised him to ask his parents for permission and the next time the band was scheduled for a Joplin appearance he would meet him at the same spot where they were then talking. The date and time was agreed upon and the kid got parental consent. A few weeks later the Wills troupe including such performers as his brother Johnny, Leon McAuliffe, Smokey Dacus, Leon Rausch[10], Tommy Duncan and Eldon Shamblin, were on their way to Joplin. Upon reaching Commerce, they spied the young boy in his finest attire, eagerly awaiting their arrival. Mickey Mantle.[11]

Mantle had probably never ridden in such a vehicle in his life — a Chrysler stretch limousine. Guy Crow, Whiz Kid batboy, recalled seeing that large vehicle go past the ballpark many times with the bass fiddle strapped on top. The young men would wave as the Playboys passed and the band would honk their horn and wave back in return.[12] Thus, on Mantle's trip into Joplin that Saturday evening, he was being chauffeured by the best guitar and fiddle players of the era. In order to pay his way, the boy volunteered to help set up the equipment for that night's performance. So for one night Mantle was a member of the Bob Wills troupe and was truly a "Playboy" for a day.

---

[10] On the east and west side of of Billings, Missouri, highway signs welcome travelers to the home-town of Leon "Rauch."

[11] Jerry Waldrip.

[12] Guy Crow.

Upon many return trips to Tulsa, the Wills band frequently stopped in Commerce. About the only place for late-night travelers to stop for a meal was the Black Cat Café there, one of the few all-night eateries between Kansas City and Tulsa. The place was recalled by one Tulsa newspaper reporter as an eatery that "welcomed many famous names to its doors. The late Avery Wilbur, zinc wealthy rancher who lived west of town, brought several guests including Buck Jones and Will Rogers" to the Black Cat.

The newspaper article continued by saying that "Bob Wills and his band frequently patronized the cafe while traveling between engagements. It was a conspicuous place on U.S. 66."

The article added that when Mickey Mantle was a local high school star in the late 1940s, he frequented the Black Cat Café to sip drinks with his pals. "He is a wonderful boy," said the café's owner. "And his dad, Mutt, used to drop in, too, but for a beer or two. He was the man who made 'Mick' a player and it's too bad he couldn't live to see him at his best."

The same article also referred to a vividly recalled memory around Commerce, a visit in 1934 by the notorious outlaw couple Bonnie and Clyde. On April 6, 1934, immediately following the murders in Grapevine, Texas, of two highway patrolmen, Bonnie Parker, Clyde Barrow and Henry Methvin were on the run. Sighted near Texarkana, Arkansas, they crossed the Red River and entered Oklahoma at a time when heavy rains had been battering the area for days.[13]

Their Ford had become stuck in the mud, so Barrow and Methvin tried to flag down a passing motorist at gunpoint. The driver accelerated to safety and notified authorities about the outlaws. Commerce Police Chief Percy Boyd and Constable Cal Campbell went to the location to investigate, and exchanged gunfire with the outlaws.

The sixty-three-year-old Campbell fell with a bullet in the heart, and Boyd, in his thirties, received a head wound and immediately surrendered. Barrow and Methvin then flagged down a truck driver and at gunpoint forced him to liberate their car from the mud.

When the truck driver looked inside the car, he had noticed Parker calmly smoking a cigarette and a bloody, subdued Chief Boyd. Barrow told the trucker to warn the law to back off or the captured police chief would be killed. Barrow gave Boyd a new shirt to replace his bloody one, then began

---

[13] *The Tulsa Tribune*, 1963 (otherwise undated): "It was the Hangout for Everyone." Clipping from a Nick Ferguson scrapbook.

driving around the countryside. During his ordeal on the road with the Barrow gang, Boyd struck up a conversation with the outlaws, bringing up subjects such as the Grapevine murders.

Barrow denied any involvement in the killings and Parker expressed her dismay at being dubbed a "cigar smoking gun moll." She wanted him to tell the public that she didn't smoke cigars. "Nice girls don't smoke cigars," she explained. At a stop near Fort Scott, Kansas, near the Missouri border, they bought a newspaper and read about the abduction of Chief Boyd, and also learned of the death of Constable Campbell.

After a carefree picnic in the woods with their captive, Boyd was released nine miles south of Fort Scott, 18 hours after his capture. Seventy-five miles to the south in Coffeyville, Kansas, a large search party was scouring the area looking for the elusive Barrow gang."[14] As is widely known, Bonnie and Clyde escaped that day but were gunned down in a lawmen's ambush in Louisiana seven weeks later.

Just a few short years after making his memorable trip with the Wills band, Mantle returned to Joplin, riding the bus of baseball's Joplin Miners. He came to make his mark on the Western Association and in so doing impressed baseball experts so much they envisioned him as the next great superstar on the Major League scene. He did not disappoint. He became the idol of American youth, his the most prized of all photos ever to appear on a Topps Baseball Card, the heir to Joe DiMaggio's throne and enshrined in the Hall of Fame.

14 Website, "Frank R. Ballinger's Bonnie & Clyde's Hideout," February 2004, "Campbell Killing," http://texashideout.tripod.com/Campbell.html.

2

The Mantle Migration:
From England to Missouri

On January 22, 1805, George S. Mantle came into this world in the town of Hopton Wafers, Shropshire, near the border with Staffordshire. At that point in time baseball wasn't even a word. From those humble beginnings George could never have imagined that 145 years later a great-great-grandson would burst onto the scene to become one of the most popular athletes of the 20th century. The prospect of that descendant earning his sports reputation in the United States wouldn't have seemed possible, for George and his family before him were part of a long line of coal miners from Wales, Shropshire and Staffordshire.

The Mantles worked the mines around Brierley Hill in the heart of the old coal mining and iron smelting area near Birmingham. According to Mantle family historian Harold Mantle, "That area was called 'Black Country,' probably because of the dirty air and soot all over everything."[15]

---

[15] Harold Mantle, "The Mantle Family History," unpublished manuscript, undated.

In 1848, George, his wife Maria (Scriven) and their five children sailed from Liverpool toward the "new world" with the hope of a better life in the United States. George and Maria had been married at the Tipton Parish church near Brierley Hill on June 16, 1828. According to family records cited by Harold Mantle, "The marriage was witnessed by William Mantle (possibly a father, brother or cousin) and all three made their mark in the register book. They were illiterate, which wasn't too unusual for that time and station in life. They were about as far from royalty and coats-of-arms as you can get. I guess you'd have to say the old-time Mantles had 'true grit'!"[16]

Although the census of 1841 in England listed George and Maria as illiterate, another family historian, Hallie Mantle, took exception to that finding. She wrote, "I have seen a journal in which George wrote his income expenses and other data. I also found a copy of a very nice, informative letter, which was written to a grandson when Maria was past 60 years old. She had misspelled a couple of words (names of people—a common error), but she wrote a wonderful letter—better than many college grads can do."[17]

"True grit" must have been what saw the Mantles through their long journey to the Untied States. Had they known what lay ahead, they might have chosen to stay in England. George then was 42 years, his wife Maria, 37. The children were John Edward, 17; George Jr., 15; Joseph, 13; Maria, 10, and James David, 7.[18]

The patriarchal lineage of Mickey Mantle:[19]

George S. Mantle
Born: 1805, Brierly, England
Died: June 9, 1879, Osage County (Vosholl), Missouri

James D. Mantle
Born: May 10, 1841, Linn, Missouri
Died: September 30, 1930, Linn, Missouri

---

[16] Ibid.

[17] Hallie Mantle, untitled, unpublished Mantle genealogy, 1990. This is a collection of oral history and charts.

[18] Staffordshire, Stourbridge, census of June 10, 1841. The family evidently resided at 100 Selsdon North, Kwingswindord Parish, District 24. George's occupation was listed as "stonegetter."

[19] From the genealogy files of Hallie Mantle.

Charles Edwin Mantle
Born: October 27, 1883, Linn, Missouri
Died: September 6, 1944, Spavinaw, Oklahoma

Elven Charles "Mutt" Mantle
Born: March 16, 1912, Adair, Oklahoma
Died: August 12, 1952, Denver, Colorado

Mickey Charles Mantle
Born October 20, 1931, Spavinaw, Oklahoma
Died: August 13, 1995, Dallas, Texas

The voyage across the Atlantic was arduous and filled with peril. Sailing is exactly what they did. Their vessel, the *Sailor Prince*, was dependent on the winds in order to take them to their new world. Hallie Mantle, the foremost historian of the George S. Mantle wing of the family, tells of how the Mantles faced death on many fronts. There were the inevitable storms as they sailed westward and there was the constant problem of the lack of adequate drinking water. When the water got undrinkable, vinegar was placed in the supply just to make it palatable.[20]

On the days that the winds calmed and the sailboat was dead in the water, the Mantle women got out their washtubs and did the laundry. During one washday a large storm descended on the mariners and the tubs were washed overboard. That ended the laundry tasks until the family arrived in the United States.

The Mantles touched dry land at New Orleans, Louisiana, after two months on the high seas. From there they boarded a riverboat and headed north up the Mississippi River. At St. Louis, Missouri, they ended their journey. In time, the men found work in the coal-mining region of the city now known as Tower Grove Park.

Getting established in the new country took a couple of years. Longing for a life not consumed with the harshness of mining, George heeded the spirit of the cry of Horace Greeley and in 1851 he and his family, headed some ninety-five miles west of Tower Grove to the beautiful rolling hills of Osage County, Missouri.

Osage County had been established in 1842. Linn, the county seat, was

---

[20] Hallie Mantle genealogy.

attractive to many people because of its strategic location on the Missouri Pacific Railroad line, which made travel to St. Louis to the east and the capital city of Missouri, Jefferson City, a few miles to the west, convenient.

Records of the Mantle family in Osage County are not complete. A couple of major fires at the Courthouse in the past 150 years meant that not all the deed and census records were available. It appeared, however, that the family survived a cholera epidemic that ravaged the populace about the time the Mantles arrived. Many of the early inhabitants of the Linn Free Cemetery wound up there as a result of the outbreak. The Mantles also appear to have survived the ravages of the Civil War in their part of Missouri. The Confederate general Sterling Price led his army through Linn, intent on destroying a Union recruiting and training center in the nearby village of Medora.

The Mantles managed to eke out a living raising their own farm products and keeping enough cattle to provide milk and beef. No doubt, they found farming a much more agreeable way of life than mining. However, two of their sons, Joseph and George Jr., decided instead to mine coal in the Troy, Illinois, area for the rest of their lives.

The Mantles were religious folks who had embraced the Primitive Methodist faith in their native England. Whether it was a religion born of conviction or of some convenience is unknown but the George S. Mantle family had lived across the street from the Primitive Methodist Church in Brierley Hill. One of the Primitives' basic tenets of faith was that of doing good deeds. Each time their congregations came forth to praise God it was done with testimonials as to the good deeds they had done the preceding seven days. They were expected to recite how many sick people had been visited, the number of poor being fed and any other act of kindness they had shown their fellow man the past week. Each of the testimonials was recorded in a ledger. The Primitive worshippers took the Epistle of James to heart, which proclaimed, "Faith without works is dead." They were in direct opposition to Martin Luther, who had proclaimed that book of the New Testament to be "an epistle of straw."

The Primitive Methodists were called "dissenters" and "non-conformists" because they didn't belong to the Church of England. Robert Mantle, another family historian, wrote, "Under the rules in effect at that time a couple had to be married by the official church, the Church of England, but they could be baptized by any church." In his research he reported, "I found the marriage records of George and Maria, but no baptism records for the children." The religious tradition may not have been passed down through the family tree but at least the proper marriage laws were adhered to through the history of the Mantle family all the way down and including Mickey Charles, nearly eight decades later.[21]

In Missouri, the Mantles appeared to have remained as faithful members of the Primitive Methodist religion until 1865, when many of them joined a group known as the Whearso Saints. There is a sign on a church building in Linn that now reads," A Branch of Reorganized Church of Jesus Christ of Latter Day Saints. Organized June 1865 at Whearso [in an Osage County town renamed Vosholl] moved here 1894. Land donated by Joseph and Maria Bourgeret."

In 1849, a year after the George Mantles had left England, his brother, Charles Mantle Sr., also had moved to Osage County. Charles Sr. lived out his days farming in the Vosholl area. He died June 9, 1879. He was buried on his own land in a picturesque gravesite that included large upright tombstones surrounded by a wrought iron fence. A few decades later the property changed hands and the new landowner, a farmer, knocked down the fence and shoved the tombstones into a nearby creek, according to family historian Hallie Mantle. The principal historical and genealogical groups in the "Show Me" state have recognized Miss Mantle, born in 1914, as the leading Mantle historian. Hallie and her older sister Myrtle, born in 1911, moved into the house their father built in 1911. Both have lived there nearly an entire century.

James David Mantle, Mickey Mantle's great-grandfather, and the youngest of George S. and Maria's five children, apparently never joined the

On the west side of town lies the Linn Free Cemetery. Scattered throughout that final resting place for many early settlers of Osage County, Missouri, are several burial plots with the name of Mantle inscribed.

Whearso Saints. In 1869 David purchased some land from the George Vaughn family in Osage County, where he remained until around 1918. By age 22, he was married to Elisa C. Moore in Linn.

---

[21] Robert Mantle.

David and Elisa lived in other small towns in Osage County, including Vosholl, located northwest of Linn. Vosholl was nothing more than a post office and general store, run by one person who lived on the premises. The town got its name from Judge J. W. Vosholl, who had served as prosecuting attorney in Osage County from 1891 to 1895 and then as a state representative from 1910 to 1914.

A family photo from 1893 of the Mantle clan shows David as the eldest present. He was a justice of the peace in Linn for 32 years. The family notes compiled by Hallie Mantle describe him in this manner: "He was known as Esquire David Mantle. He was usually called Squire David Mantle, since there were two other David Mantles in the area. As Justice of the Peace, he united many in marriage, served as a judge in some court trials and was a busy man. He was very sober and serious and had no time for foolishness. He had eleven children who grew to maturity, and 54 grandchildren."[22]

The Mantle family photo taken at Linn, Missouri in 1893. <u>Front row:</u> Thomas, Mrs. Elisa Mantle (mother of the flock), Charles (Mickey's grandfather), David Mantle (patriarch of the family) and David Jr. <u>Back row:</u> Edward, Mose, William L., Richard, Ann, Robert, Elizabeth and Ellen.[23]

Every year or two for 20 years after David and Elisa were married; a new child arrived, until one shy of a dozen had their feet under or near the dinner table. Among these was Charles Edwin Mantle, Mickey's grandfather, born on October 27, 1883, at Linn.

---

[22] Hallie Mantle genealogy.
[23] Photo courtesy of Hallie Mantle.

In early 1911 Charles married Mae Clark, a native of Eureka Springs, Arkansas. On March 16, 1912, Elven "Mutt" Mantle was born. Following were the births of Eugene "Tunney," born June 15, 1913; a daughter, Thelma Louise, born on October 24, 1914, and, Emmett Dale, born on February 27, 1920.

This is the first known picture of Mickey's dad, Elven Charles "Mutt" Mantle. It was taken in the fall of 1912.[24]

The Mantle migration to the newly established State of Oklahoma was made by covered wagon most likely in the late 1890s. There is some speculation as to why they left Missouri for the Land of the Cherokees. Conventional wisdom would lead most to believe they went out to farm on land more suitable for raising row crops and cattle. However, Miss Hallie, the family historian, believes the cause for the trek south by southwest from Osage County was involved more with religious beliefs than anything else. There is no record that David or Elisa Moore Mantle ever joined the Whearso body of believers; likewise, Charles Edwin and Mae Clark Mantle.

Even though it was by now approaching the 20th century, the mode of travel by wagon train into pre-statehood for Oklahoma was not entirely safe. Robert Mantle, a St. Louis native, who also had researched the genealogy of his family, told of an account of the wagon master who took the Mantles from Linn to Spavinaw, Oklahoma. The wagon master, in his diary, wrote of the great number of new settlers who were being attacked and robbed by bands of marauding Indians. He wrote, according to Robert, that the wagons on which the Mantles were riding were spared because their passengers included two Indian ladies who had married into the Mantle family.[25] Another member of the Mantle family, Mark, of Columbia, Missouri, had never heard the account of the wagon train incident. When asked about it, he became quite intrigued, for he recalled going through old family files and seeing names of some Indians who had married some of his great-great-great-uncles. The brides were Osage Indians.[26]

[24] Ibid.
[25] Robert Mantle.
[26] Mark Mantle.

Hallie Mantle disputes the account that any of the Mantle men were married to Indian ladies but did concede that other members of that caravan into Oklahoma could have had Indian wives.[27]

There is a reel-to-reel tape on which John Edward Mantle — Mickey's great uncle, born in 1867 — recounted family history to Hallie before his death. He knew the entire story of the move from Missouri to Oklahoma.[28]

Hallie stated that some of the cousins had heard Mickey's great-uncle tell the story of the trip from Missouri to Oklahoma. Those kinfolk are Joy and husband Levi Mantle who reside in southern Arkansas.

According to Levi and Joy, both in their eighties, Uncle "Ed" John Edward Mantle, was sixteen years the senior of his brother, Charles Edwin—Mickey's grandfather.[29] When John Edward struck out for Oklahoma he was insistent his brother Charles come along for he feared the young man would drink too much if left alone in Missouri.[30] Joy claimed, "Uncle Charlie could drink just as much in Oklahoma as he could in Missouri, and did."

According to the story John Edward shared with the family, the Missouri leg of the trip ended at Seligman, Missouri which is on the state line just north of Pea Ridge, Arkansas. John Edward claimed in his oral history that it was the last civilized place he saw during the rest of the trip into the Adair, Oklahoma area.

John Edward, Charlie and the rest of the group made the trek in two wagons. One of the wagons was purportedly a wide one and the other narrow. They were pulled by mules and for most of the journey those making the trip walked. John Edward said the wagons were always at a severe angle due to the steepness of the terrain.

The account of that trip also stated Charles shot a turkey as they entered Oklahoma and it served as a well-appreciated meal. However, the trip took its toll on man and beast and after crossing into Oklahoma from Arkansas one of the mules fell over. A group of cowboys came down the road and saw

---

[27] Anecdote heard in interviews; however, it wasn't verifiable through the genealogy records of Hallie Mantle.

[28] Hallie Mantle.

[29] Joy and Levi Mantle.

[30] The reference to leaving Missouri at the town of Seligman and knowing the Mantles departed to Oklahoma from Linn, Missouri indicates the caravan most likely traversed the Butterfield Overland Stage route. That part of the trail started at Tipton, Missouri, some 40 miles west of Linn and the terminus was Fort Smith, Arkansas.

the predicament the Mantle clan faced. The cowboys asked if they had any pepper sauce on the wagon and the Mantles were able to fill that request. The cowboys took two bottles of the hot stuff and forced the mule to consume it. After that he got up and didn't stop until he found water according to the tale.

The cowboys got into a discussion with the Mantle party and inquired what they planned to do when they arrived at their destination. The Mantles responded that they were going to write a letter back home to Missouri and let the family know they had made it. One of the cowboys replied, "Letters, there's no need for education in Oklahoma. The only letters you need here is 'letter go' and 'letter rip.'"

With the move, the Mantles left behind not only Missouri but also the religious beliefs most of the family had embraced. From the accounts of the life of Mickey Mantle's parents, Mutt and Lovell (Richardson) Mantle, and of those who knew the family best, there isn't any indication that the Mantles who went to Oklahoma ever formed a relationship with any organized church.

The Mantles never intended to go to Oklahoma to do anything other than farm. However, the cruelties of drought, drought and more droughts sent many Okies either toward California or to any job they could find within the surrounding area. The lead and zinc mining operations that sprang up in the late 1800s were at their peak by the 1920s in what was called the Tri-State mining region of Northeast Oklahoma, Southwest Missouri and Southeast Kansas. It was the only way most men could find a way to put food on the table for their families.

3

Life in a New Land: Oklahoma

Spavinaw, Oklahoma, was typical of most small towns of Northeast Oklahoma in the first few decades of the 20th century. Lives were spent working on small farms or in the small shops and stores of the community. Most of the inhabitants had migrated from the surrounding states of Arkansas, Kansas and Missouri after the Sooner State had been admitted into the union in 1907.

Hard times befell the Charles Mantle family after they arrived from Linn, Missouri. Shortly after the birth of the fourth child Emmett in 1920 at Adair, Charlie's wife Mae passed away.

The Mantle men of that era did not remarry when their wives passed away. Family historian Hallie Mantle recalled, "When it became impossible for [Charles] to care for all of his children, Uncle Ed and Aunt Ida took little Emmett into their home and raised him in the town of Pryor, Oklahoma." Charles managed to care for Mutt, Eugene and Thelma but realized he couldn't take proper care of little Emmett. Hallie said she and her older sister Myrtle always had a soft spot in their hearts for Emmett. "When the Mantles returned for family reunions in Linn, we felt sorry for

Emmett because he was a little boy without a momma," she said.[31]

One day while Charles was at work, Emmett, still living with his father, and Eugene went out to the barn. It was a very cold day and the two boys were in need of heat.They got some combustible material together with which to build a fire. They obviously succeeded, for they burned down the barn in the process, said Max Mantle, Eugene's son.[32] Whether this was another indication that Charlie couldn't properly look after young Emmett or not, soon thereafter he was sent off to be raised by his aunt and uncle.

From 1904 to 1935 the Mantles farmed and Charles' four children grew into young adults. Charles also worked in a local grocery store as a butcher to make ends meet, Max recalled.[33]

In 1930, Charlie's oldest son Elven, then 18, met and fell in love with a 26-year-old divorcee, Lovell Thelma Richardson-Davis, seven years divorced and the mother of a daughter, Anna Bea, and a son, Theodore. Mutt had been dating Thelma's sister, Dulsa Annie, two years his junior. However, when he spied the young divorcee, Mutt began dating Lovell and they were soon married. By October 1931, their small family had grown to three with the birth of Mickey Charles.

Lovell's parents, Charles and Annie Laurie[35], were Methodists, he a deacon.

However, the religious influence didn't always take hold of their nine children.[36]

The Richardson boys' occupation was bootlegging moonshine whiskey, according to Max Mantle. He recalled that they were big, strong and mean boys — all over six feet tall and weighing more than 200 pounds when that was large — and you didn't mess with them. They were like the guys you see in the movies who were rough and tumble, Max said.[37]

---

[31] Hallie Mantle.

[32] Hallie Mantle.

[33] Ibid.

[34] Photo courtesy of the Hallie Mantle collection.

[35] Annie Laurie Thomas Richardson, born April 2, 1879, at Peace Valley Grove, Arkansas, died December 27, 1967, at Gravette, Arkansas.

[36] In order of birth, they were Jesse, born October 15, 1894, at Cleora, Okla.; Mary Odessa, June 27, 1896; Claude Lorene, June 14, 1898 (Claude had to be tough with a middle name of Lorene); Lee Owen, March 10, 1899; Lester Lewis, April 10, 1901; Cleora, died December 20, 1950, Spavinaw, Okla.; Lovell Thelma, February 12, 1904, Ketchum, Okla.; Luther Charles "Luke," July 28, 1910, Ketchum; Dulsa Annie, February 9, 1914, Pensacola, Okla.; and Blanche Ardith, December 2, 1916.

[37] Max Mantle.

Charles Richardson was a "shirttail" politician, according to his grandson, Jim, and ran the road crew for Mayes County. It was a means of making a living for his family and ensured that his sons would be gainfully employed.

The hot steamy days of 110-plus-degree Oklahoma weather during the Dust Bowl years made young men yearn for a number of things, not the least of which was some good beer and whiskey. Jimmy Richardson said that his uncles looked forward to Saturday nights when they washed their necks, put on a clean shirt, headed to one of the two bars in Spavinaw, drank until they got drunk, then had a reason to get into a fight. Usually, they had managed to finish up each evening poking their friends and enemies wherever their inebriated punches happened to land. They always had Sunday in which to get back in shape for the grueling work they faced the following week.

It surprised Jimmy Richardson that his uncles didn't drink themselves to death or get killed in a barroom fight. He recalls that they all died of lung cancer, probably, he said, from cigarettes.[38]

Max Mantle and Jimmy Richardson have conflicting reports of the Richardsons; function in Oklahoma's illegal — and thriving — alcoholic beverage industry. Max recalled them as bootleggers; Jimmy says they just consumed the alcohol on their Saturday night forays since there was not much else to do in a small town.

According to Richardson, John McCall was the kingpin of Spavinaw. He owned and operated a package liquor store more than a half-century before such a thing was legal in Oklahoma. The "store" was a small white building across the street from the Sportsman's Club.

The Sportsman's Club was an establishment where even 3.2 percent beer couldn't be sold legally at the time in the state. Later on during Prohibition days, a sort of beer was sold in Oklahoma, called, "near beer" or "pale beer." Its total alcohol content was one-half of one percent. The pale beer that made its way into Northeast Oklahoma was produced in St. Joseph, Missouri. What made it "drinkable" was the addition of grain alcohol which the locals added, about an ounce to each bottle of beer. When the liquor control agents showed up in Spavinaw, the white envelopes with the payoff came out of the cash register and the agents, after examining the contents, would declare, "There isn't any alcohol here." The slogan in that area, known to every man, woman and child, was "there is no law in Spavinaw."

---

[38] Jimmy Richardson.

Spavinaw's location was strategic, in that anything the natives desired that was illegal or taxed too high was accessible in nearby Missouri. Mr. McCall was a forerunner of the "Dukes of Hazard." He had some souped-up cars that could outrun any law enforcement vehicle in the area. All booze, cigarettes or anything illegal or highly taxed in Spavinaw came out of Bagdad Corner, a wide spot in the road just outside of Joplin, Missouri. That place is not known to many residents of this era but the youngsters of the 1930s and 1940s recall it well. Val Greenwood of Joplin said, "If you go down Schifferdecker Avenue across Shoal Creek and turn right on Apricot Road, that is old 166. Go west about two or three miles and you will go down a little dip and make a left turn and you are on Bagdad Hill," which overlooked Bagdad Corner.[39]

Joplin was notorious during Prohibition days as supplying much of the booze that flowed in a wide and deep river into Oklahoma, as well as to the speakeasies of Kansas City. Young people such as Joan Haney Getter formerly of Iola, Kansas, recalled how the cars of the 1930s would travel through her hometown on either U.S. 69 or 54 highways on their way to their Kansas City destinations. The cars hauling the hooch were always identifiable by authorities, since the weight of the load would cause the cars' trunks to ride close to the ground. The Allen County sheriff and Iola police would arrest the occupants, shoot up the cars, the put the vehicles on display for all the local townsfolk to see. This demonstrated how the local authorities were diligent in upholding the Prohibition laws of that era.[40]

When the supply of "firewater" ran low in Spavinaw, McCall would mobilize some of his employees, who would get into their souped-up automobiles and head to Joplin, Missouri. The one-way trip to Bagdad Corner from Spavinaw was about 70 miles. Frequently, the return trip was longer — on the occasions when the boys attempted to "shake the law" on those unpaved red clay back roads of Eastern Oklahoma. The trips were usually made on the weekends, since the Richardsons had day jobs during the week. The "whiskey running" was just a way to add a little non-taxable income and to ensure there was something to drink after working all day on their road building jobs.

There wasn't much room left for error in McCall's planning. It was always possible that when the authorities took out after his illegal loot that

[39] Val Greenwood.
[40] Joan Haney-Getter.

the long arm of the law would prevail. Thus, McCall had another car that acted in the role of a "blocker." Leaving nothing to chance, the driver of the blocker car had to be fleet of foot. McCall had a young Indian lad who filled that job description to the letter.

When lawmen would spot a low riding car on a dusty back road in Eastern Oklahoma, it was a cinch that they would be in hot pursuit. The price McCall paid for doing business was that he had to sacrifice the blocker car, for it would be impounded after each chase that the driver had to abandon it. The Indian lad was never apprehended in those foot chases.[41]

The adventures of getting alcohol to retail distribution points at times seemed almost tame compared to patronizing such outlets. Max Mantle recalled that until one memorable evening his father was known as Eugene. That evening he walked into one of the two bars in Spavinaw to get Luke Richardson, Lovell Mantle's brother, out of there. Mantle said it was illegal for a white man to be in the place.[42] Jim Richardson remembered that it was not illegal for a non-Indian to be in that bar, just not very smart.[43]

When Eugene found out that Luke Richardson was in that bar, he took his sister Thelma's husband, Orville Holt, with him to extract Richardson from that establishment. With the propensity of the Richardson boys to drink, then fight, it wasn't going to be a fair battle with only one member of the clan in the bar that evening. Orville's nickname was "Grab,"[44] and that's what he and Eugene did when they found Richardson. They were walking backward dragging him out of harm's way when one of the Indian patrons jumped Eugene. Eugene, standing about five feet, ten inches tall and weighing less than 200 pounds, had a lot of the physical characteristics that his nephew Mickey would develop a couple of decades later. With Richardson being held by Eugene's left arm, Eugene landed a right hook to the eye of his attacker. The blow knocked the poor Indian's eye out. From then on, he was called "Tunney" after the great boxer of that era, Gene Tunney.[45]

The time of the Mantles' stay in Spavinaw came to an end in 1935, when grubbing around on earth parched by years of drought had taken its toll. The name Spavinaw comes from the French words *cépée vineux,* meaning wine-colored saplings. The reference was to the town's groves of young red

---

[41] Richardson.

[42] Max Mantle.

[43] Richardson.

[44] Perhaps as in "grab holt," a corruption of the ruralism "to grab hold of something."

[45] Max Mantle.

oak trees. But those namesake groves, and many others, were now in dire straits. Although the the Dust Bowl onslaught was centered a couple of

Eugene B. Mantle was the first of Mickey's uncles to die due to mine-related diseases. The robust youngster wasted away to just over 100 pounds at the end of his short 34 years of life.[46]

hundred miles to the west of Eastern Oklahoma, the effects of insufficient rainfall in the Midwest for three to four years of the 1930s were severe, too much for the Mantles to endure. Thus, the 22-year-old Mutt and his 30-year-old wife Lovell decided to relocate elsewhere to take on the challenges of eventually raising seven children.

Never could Mutt and Lovell have dreamed that in less than a half dozen years the part of the world where they had met and married would become an "Oasis in Eastern Oklahoma." Had they known what lay ahead for the economy of the Spavinaw area and the many jobs that would be created, they would probably have remained to work on the Grand River Dam construction and lived out their days enjoying the sportsman's vast paradise that developed with the dam's completion in 1940.

Spavinaw had become important to Northeast Oklahoma in 1921 when a bond issue was passed to build a small dam and run a 55-mile water line from there to Tulsa. But the project, though a boon to Tulsa, had little effect on the economy of the Spavinaw area. By October 11, 1922, the specifications for the project had been drawn up and within just two years President Calvin Coolidge sent a telegraph message signaling that the water was supply was to be turned on.[47]

As the Dust Bowl days burned on, some civic leaders of Northeast Oklahoma began to pin their hopes for relief on building a dam on the Grand River. The original intent was to provide the Cherokee Nation, which

---

[46] Photo taken by author in July 2003 at the Daughters of the American Revolution Cemetery in Miami, Oklahoma.

[47] "Clear & Cold, Pure As Gold; How the Waters of the Spavinaw Came Down to Tulsa," Tulsa Metropolitan Utility Authority, Community Affairs and Planning Section of the Department of Public Works, City of Tulsa, Okla., 1995, pp. 1-16.

was located in that part of Oklahoma, with electricity. But, leaders saw, it could do even more — provide a reliable source of water for agriculture and provide a significant boost to outdoor recreation.

The project was the brainchild of a couple of graduate engineering students, Harry and Bert Holderman. Like the dry-land farming the Mantles had undertaken, the concept of selling a huge dam to the folks with the money was no simple task. Trips to Washington were never very fruitful. But in a stroke of brilliance, local leaders put the project onto the front burner one day when, during the 1936 presidential campaign, Washington came to Oklahoma.

An enterprising Vinita, Oklahoma, visionary, George Schaefer, had the foresight to propose a city ordinance, and get it passed, requiring any presidential train passing through the city to stop. As fate would have it, President Franklin D. Roosevelt's caravan soon rolled into Vinita one day and, as required by the new law, had to stop. The president was greeted with a banner strung along the north end of the depot which read, "Let's Build Grand River Dam."

FDR thanked Vinita people for arranging the unscheduled stop, and said he would see what he could do about funding the dam. With the help of U.S. Representatives Wesley E. Disney and W.R. Holway, funding was approved in September 1937. A month later, engineers Holway and Heufer began surveying and engineering. Massman Construction of Kansas City was the prime contractor, and construction began in December 1938.

Unbelievably, especially considering the equipment of the day, the dam was completed in 20 months. The final openings in the dam (under arches seven and eight) were closed in March 1940, and Grand Lake was full by the end of that summer![48]

After his family moved away from Spavinaw to Cardin, some 40 miles to the north, young Mickey Mantle returned to his native town a number of times when his mom and dad went back to visit his father's sister Thelma and her husband, "Grab" Holt.

Jim Richardson recalled during one visit that Mantle, still a kid, took his brothers and cousins for a drive. The journey included a ride up a winding

---

[48] Rusty Fleming, publisher, *The Chronicle of Grand Lake*, Spavinaw, Oklahoma, newspaper website, December 2002.

hill to the top of the dam site. The dam was 3,500 feet long and 55 feet high. Mantle wondered out loud how fast a car — the car he was driving, for instance — could go downhill while in neutral. The new lake was being pumped at the rate of 24 millions gallons a day into a flow pipe that was 60 inches in diameter. However, when Mantle started the descent, that much blood was going through the heart and veins of each of the passengers in the car he was steering.

According to Richardson, the people back in Spavinaw could hear the tires of that car squall as it careened down the side of the hill, rapidly gaining speed as it went. At the foot of the hill all were emotionally spent except the driver. Mantle thought it was a barrel of fun. Richardson recalled that had Mickey's mother found out about the stunt, she would have used up a switch on his tail.[49]

On their visits back to Spavinaw, the Mantles easily could see what the Grand River dam and the new lake at Spavinaw were coming to mean to their old hometown. But a few years back, when they felt they could go on no further there and no other choices in view, they made the move to Cardin, where jobs were plentiful and the wages enough at least to support their growing family by mining.

---

[49] Richardson.

4

Farmed Out: From Spavinaw to the Tri-State

On moving day in late 1935, Lester Richardson loaded up his sister Lovell her two children by the previous marriage, Anna Bea and Theodore, Mutt, Mickey and Grandpa Charlie Mantle in his old pick-up truck and headed north to Cardin, Oklahoma. It was up to Lester because the Mantle family had no transportation of their own. After depositing the Mantles in their new home, Lester went back to Spavinaw and got his family. Mutt found employment immediately with the Eagle-Picher Mining Co. (the largest in the area, based at nearby Picher) as an ore bucket loader at the Blue Goose mine.

Eagle-Picher was one of the largest mining companies in the world and operated the world's largest lead and zinc mill. Others operating in the Tri-State were called At Last Mining Company, Baby Jim Mining, Big Chief, Bigham, Big Elk, Black Cat, Birthday, Sonny Boy, Skelton, Liza Jane, Eleventh Hour and Incas.

Blue Goose, part of the Eagle-Picher empire, averaged taking 200 tons of material per shift from the earth. The mine was located southwest of

Cardin, toward Commerce, a couple of miles away.

Located in the Tri-State mining area where Oklahoma, Missouri and Kansas join, Picher, Oklahoma, was in its "hey day," a thriving metropolis of 30,000. Lead and zinc were "king" until some years later another discovery was made in New Mexico. Almost immediately the Tri-State mining towns like Cardin, Picher and Commerce were being abandoned for the more glamorous "young girl" on the block, uranium. The mines around Picher were stripped of equipment, loaded on trains and trucks and were on their way to Grants, New Mexico. Since the early 1950s the small towns of the Tri-State mining area have passed into near oblivion in some instances and totally in others.

But in those early days, when the Mantles arrived, the Tri-State's mining towns had colorful names[50] that beckoned one and all to come and work in the mines and get a steady job. Any man who applied for a job was hired, so long as he wasn't a foreigner or black. There was no physical examination or background check. The work was hard, dirty and dangerous beyond belief but it would at least provide food and shelter for a man's family.

Each day, seemingly without exception, there would be the sound of a wailing siren and the little white ambulance would be on the way to some mine with an intriguing name such as the Blue Goose, to pick up mining's latest casualty. Years later, this still was a vivid memory for Johnny LaFalier, recalling his early days as a student in the Picher school system.

Death was the constant companion of a miner. Each resident of the little towns hearing those sirens would hold their breath until they determined which way the "death wagon" was headed. If it went in a different direction from where their family member was working they heaved a sigh of relief. If it went in the direction where their loved one was working, they waited anxiously until learning the name of the latest fatality.[51]

The annual *Dixon's Oklahoma-Kansas Mining Directory*,[52] which listed all operating mines, carried ads at the top of each page which indicated just

---

[50] For example: Afton, Belmont, Ben, Black Hawk, Blue Goose, Burch, Cardin, Century, Columbus, Commerce, Dawes, Dotyville, Eastside, Fairland, Ferial, Fivemile, Four Mile, Golden Road, Grand River, Hackerville, Halfway, Harland, Hockerville, Joplin Junction, Kellyville, Keltner, Kema, Lincolnville, Mallabury, Max, Miami, Mills, Mineral Heights, Moreville, Narcissa, North Miami, Oak Grove, Ogeechee, Ontario, Oseuma, Ottawa, Ouray, Paradise, Picher, Pooler, Prairie City, Quapaw, Saint Louis, Scammon Hill, Smallwood, Surles, Tar River, Traber, Wealand, West Seneca, Whiting, Wyandotte and Zincville.

[51] Johnny LaFalier.

[52] Reprint of a 1926 edition.

how dangerous the job of mining was: "Ambulance Service—Phone 800—Free Lung Motor Day or Night—Hall Undertaking Company—Lawrence Hall, Manager. Miami, Oklahoma" and "Picher Hospital—American Hospital Phone 86. Picher, Okla."

Local newspapers from Miami, Oklahoma, on the southwest of the Tri-State, to Webb City, Missouri, on the northeast almost every day carried the names of men who had eaten their last supper with their wives and children the previous evening.

Those families who didn't lose their men to accidents in the mines lost them later because of mine-related maladies. Of Charles and Mae Mantle's three sons, a short life due to mining-related diseases was their fate. Eugene "Tunney" died at 34 on August 6, 1947, in Commerce; Emmett Dale, also 34, on November 13, 1954, in Tulsa; and Elven "Mutt," 40, in a Denver, Colorado, hospital on May 7, 1952, while undergoing experimental treatment for Hodgkin's disease.

The mining towns were not easy places to live and work. The air was always full of mine tailing dust when the winds came sweeping across the plains. The men filled their lungs beneath the ground with the mine residue and the children and the wives of the miners consumed it above ground.

Getting out of the mines was not an option unless there was promise of work elsewhere. Many a mother or father who brought their young families to extract the ore from the earth would look into a coffin of a premature death of a young man and cry out in anguish, "I brought my family here for a better life by working in the mines and the mines killed them."

Most escapes were thought of in terms of physical getting up and moving somewhere else. Years later, in a letter to the editor of the Tulsa newspaper, a former resident of the Tri-State, recalled life there with anything but fond nostalgia. Dean Sims[53], who grew up in the Picher region during the peak mining years in the 1930s, recalled it as a time when pollution was just another big word and dangerous jobs in the deep ground were the norm.

Lead poisoning resulted in cases of mental retardation and other severe problems, Sims wrote. And even if some of the parents had known their children's mental slowness was the result of lead poisoning, it likely would not have mattered.

"Folks were just plain mean," Sims went on, "from all their difficult circumstances. I witnessed a lot of suicides, like chug-a-lugging a bottle of

---

[53] Dean Sims, letter to the editor, "Inside Picher and Tar Creek," *The Tulsa World*, Jan. 5, 2003, p. G-2.

carbolic acid that burned out all the throat. Toddlers were pulled lifeless from drill holes all the time, after falling in upside down or standing up. Death was always nearby, even at the old Whitebird School, where cars whizzed by recklessly and the students were crossing streets without help."

Emmett Mantle had escaped the mines and gone to work for the Safeway grocery at Pryor, Oklahoma, while still in high school. By the end of World War II he had become manager for Safeway in Picher. While in Picher, during his mid-twenties, Emmett lived with his older brother, "Tunney." As store manager, he resorted to a little nepotism and hired his young nephew, assigning him the duties of a grocery bag boy. Thus, placing groceries into a paper sack was one of Mickey Mantle's first paying jobs.

Thelma, Mutt's sister, never left the family homestead near Spavinaw. She died at 75 in 1989.

In addition to death, disease and illness related to work in the mines, the industry also had a grievous, almost obscene, effect on the Tri-State's environment. Every eight hours, three to four hundred tons or more of lead and zinc ore were taken from the mines. Not all of this was marketable. Hills — almost mountains — of chat, debris from the hunt for saleable minerals, loomed over the region. Rancid water seeped from the mines into Tar Creek and other streams, often running the color of blood.

The chat pile at the Big Mill between Commerce and Cardin rose five to six hundred feet into the air. At night the lights of Parsons, Kansas, some 60 miles away, could be seen.

Many a man sought distraction from the harshness of mining. The main recreations were women, booze and baseball. Some conquered all three. Many of the different mining crews had their own baseball teams. Mutt and Eugene "Tunney" played for a team in Cardin before Mickey was old enough even to recognize a baseball. The miners played many "beer games" in that era, wherein it was that the losing team would pay something like 60 percent or even 100 percent of the occasion's beer.

There wasn't much drinking around the Mantle home. Delbert Lovelace recalled that the extent of Mutt's drinking was limited to a couple of beers on Saturday night at the Black Cat Café.[54] Mickey Mantle's boyhood friends, high school teammates and all the guys he played with through his time with the Independence Yankees, his first professional

---

[54] Delbert Lovelace.

team, don't recall him drinking or smoking.[55]

The Mantles' move from Spavinaw to Cardin came at a very turbulent time in the relations of mining industry employees with the heads of the lead and zinc industry. George G. Suggs, Jr. chronicled that era in his book.[56] He wrote, "Throughout the twenties and thirties, the Tri-State Mining District of Oklahoma, Kansas, and Missouri was the world's leading producer of lead and zinc concentrates. Traditionally, the Tri-State had been a nonunion district, but in the early 1930s the International Union of Mine, Mill, and Smelter Workers organized seven locals there. Unable to gain recognition from the mining and milling companies as the exclusive bargaining agent for the district workers, union officials called a strike in May, 1935, a strike that completely shut down mining and milling operations and left thousands of men unemployed in the midst of the Great Depression."

Since Mutt Mantle found immediate employment upon arriving in Cardin in 1935, the strike had been settled by that time. The post-strike environment into which he brought his young family was still colored to some degree by animus, as Suggs described: "Already suffering from a host of chronic social and economic ills, Tri-State workers and their beleaguered families were forced to endure additional hardships because of the shutdown. The walkout of the metal workers failed to generate a great deal of national interest, although their strike was as tempestuous as the more publicized walkouts elsewhere. Like the others, it provoked mass demonstrations, a back-to-work movement, military intervention by the national guards of two states, the emergence of a strongly supported company union, subtle and overt intimidation of the striking workers, destruction of property, a bloody shoot-out and brawls between antagonists in the dispute, charges of communist leadership, and federal intervention under the pro labor laws of the New Deal. The strike involved thousands of workers and dramatic episodes of violence, but it was largely ignored by the news media because of the physical remoteness of the district and the labor unrest then occurring in more populous industrial centers."

Jimmy Richardson recalled that he was 11 months old at the time of his family's move to Cardin. The Mantle and Richardson men worked at the Blue Goose mine together and Jimmy and Mickey formed a close relationship that

---

[55] Bob Mallon.

[56] Suggs, George G., Jr., *Union Busting in the Tri-State: The Oklahoma, Kansas and Missouri Metal Workers' Strike of 1935* (Norman: The University of Oklahoma Press, 1986).

saw them get into some scrapes — some they could get out of, others that were resolved only by the switch Mickey's mother used on their rear ends.

Literally overnight, the Mantles went from an economy of agriculture to one of mining. There was a real difference in the people each occupation attracted. By most accounts, the farmers didn't like the miners coming in and taking the land. The miners and farmers saw each other in some respects as competitors, and in another sense as folks who shouldn't be trusted.

The farmers were more conservative in their approach to life. They planted the seed, tilled the ground and prayed to their God in formal religious services twice on Sunday and once in the middle of the week that their crops would be spared drought, hail and pestilence so that they would have food on the table for the entire year. The miners were more fatalistic in their approach to life. Death was their constant shadow. Mine cave-ins were the norm. Pressed to extract from the earth as much lead and zinc as possible during a shift, the miners often took great risks in order to bring in another ton of ore per shift in order to make another dime a day.

This 1946 photo shows Mutt Mantle on the far left end of the back row. Due to page limitation, the entire photo cannnot be seen. However, due to the camera used for capturing the work force of the Blue Goose mine, Mutt was able to leave that pose and run to the right end of the photo, where he is captured once again. He wasn't a twin, but Ray and Roy at home were.

This is a continuation of the photo. The photo hangs on the wall of the Pastime Pool Hall in Picher, Oklahoma. The proprietor, Orville "Hoppy" Ray, allowed this author to take these photos with a digital camera. While Mutt is on the left side of the previous photo, he is also the third man from far right in back row. [57]

The miners and farmers both worked equally hard but the miners as a group viewed life as a fragile commodity, so that when the men left the mines they played hard and drank in many cases just as diligently. The Mantle family saw in the men of this era much early death, the result of the lung diseases caused by the minors being exposed to the dust in the deep shafts that were not always well ventilated. Coal miners in other parts of the country knew that when the canaries which they took into the shafts with them lost their song and started teetering on their perches, it was time to head to the surface. Some made it. The lead and zinc miners didn't have canaries to warn them of impending doom and the miners developed silicosis from the coating of the lungs caused by the flint rocks' dust. In min-

---

[57] Photos courtesy of Orville "Hoppy" Ray.

ing areas where the natural stone was lime rock, the disease was not as much of a problem. Silicosis was called "rocks in the box" or "the miners con," according to Guy Crow, who served as a batboy for Mickey's last non-professional team, the Baxter Springs Whiz Kids. Crow was familiar with the mining industry, since his father worked for Eagle-Picher, both in the Tri-State area and later in Galena, Illinois.[58] When the miners came down with spots on the lung, Eagle-Picher medical authorities verified it and the company in turn wrote out a severance check for $1,800 and sent the diseased miner on his way. That was the last the company had to do with an employee who had literally given it his life's breath.

There were three good things to be said about the mines, from the men's point of view. They provided jobs, were cool in the summer and warm in the winter. Many a young person can remember seeing their fathers wear long underwear the year 'round.

One of the earliest incidents Jimmy Richardson recalls occurred just after the Mantle and Richardson families had moved to Cardin, when he and cousin Mickey were around four years old. Mickey always had a dog from the time he was a small boy. According to Richardson, every time the dog wet on the floor Mickey's mother would make him get a mop and clean up the mess. Richardson said that he was told later in his life that every time he would see Mantle coming to the scene of a new spill, he sang, "Here comes Mickey with a mop on his back."[59]

Evidently, Mantle was a sociable tyke. According to Denna Brown of Tulsa, Oklahoma "My grandmother, Nellie Brown, used to tell of Mickey Mantle coming to see her. The Mantles lived next door to her in Cardin before moving to Commerce. As she was sitting in her porch swing, he'd come up to her and say 'Brown, put your legs together, I want to sit in your lap.' I don't know whether it happened or not, but she always told it for the truth."[60]

The Mantles first lived at 3rd and McGee Streets in Cardin. On a rare warm day in November of 2002, Johnny LaFalier was the personal escort of this author as he pointed out the significant places in Mickey Mantle's early life. A photo was taken of the vacant lot where the house where Mantle first lived upon arriving from Spavinaw used to stand. As the subject of this

---

[58] Guy Crow.
[59] Richardson.
[60] Denna Brown.

book, both are now gone.

As LaFalier pointed out other places of interest a motorist pulled alongside his car, having recognized him. LaFalier told his friend that he was showing his passenger some of the places where the Mantles lived in the mid-1930s. The elderly gentleman said, "Well, you will have to go down Stringtown Street, for the family lived there after moving from the 3rd and McGee location." This was news to LaFalier, who throughout our interview clearly was knowledgeable about the Mantle family's time in Cardin and vicinity.[61]

The roads in Cardin today are much the same as they were in the 1930s—unpaved. There are few streets that run more than a block or two. The roads end where the chat piles begin. All around the city are vestiges of the mining that raped the 1,200 square miles of Northeast Oklahoma, Southeast Kansas and Southwest Missouri during the last half of the 19th and the first half of the 20th century. The area is bleak beyond imagination and could easily be the backdrop for a movie depicting the Earth after a nuclear holocaust.

PHOTO COURTESY OF JACK VONMOSS

This is the Whitebird, Oklahoma baseball team during a game at Cardin in 1940. Left to right: Jay Hemphill, Johnny Hemphill, Eugene "Tunney" Mantle, Hayden Brown, Leonard Brown, Ed VonMoss, Paul Townsend, Thurman Townsend, Winford Richardson, Elven "Mutt" Mantle, Roy Heatherly, and the little boy in front is Jack VonMoss.

[61] LaFalier.

5

Ottawa County in the 1930s

The culture and values of the small town and the farm — the rural surroundings where the Mantles lived while Mickey was growing up – by all accounts had much to do with the formation of his own values and personality. After the family moved from tiny Spavinaw, they lived the rest of Mickey's youth in the villages and on the small farms of Ottawa County, Oklahoma. After Spavinaw, there was even smaller Cardin. They lived in at least two places there before moving to Commerce, living there before moving to a farm which Mutt operated for a Commerce doctor, Frank Wormington, for two years. The family also lived on a small farm at Whitebird, west of Cardin. Commerce, population 2,400 in the 1940s, was the largest of the towns in which the family lived.[62]

The farming done by miners in Ottawa County usually did not fully support a family. Cows, chickens and a few pigs were a means to ensure that

---

[62] U.S. census figures: Spavinaw wasn't large enough for an official census until 1940, when the count was 255. Cardin likewise didn't merit a census until 1920, when 2,640 were counted. This dropped to 437 in 1930; then, no censuses until 1980, when 172 were counted, 22 more than in 2000. Douthat has never had a census.Ottawa County's population peaked in 1920, at 41,108. Population was around 36,000 when the Mantle family moved there and was 33,194 in 2000. The county seat and largest town in 2000 was Miami, 13,704, down from its peak of 14,237 in 1980.

there was enough food and milk on the table for a family of nine, as was the case with Mutt and Lovell.

Jimmy Richardson recalled that when his cousin lived in Cardin he enjoyed taking out the garbage, because he loved burning stuff in the trash pile. Jimmy figured his cousin Mickey would grow up to be a fireman. One day the sparks got on to some dry grass and nearly burned down the outhouse. Richardson recalled that Lovell and Mutt had a dish pan with a hole in it positioned near an outside hydrant. Mickey tried to fill it up with water and run as fast as he could to douse the fire. By the time he got it to the fire only a couple of drops of water were left. The fire grew menacingly close to the outdoor privy. Finally, Mutt saw what was going on came out of the house and extinguished the fire, then, in the interest of fire prevention, warmed the seat of Mick's britches.[63]

Such punishments, or the persistent prospect of them, were not unusual in the household. This was not a spare-the-rod family. There was considerable attention paid each day to the behavior of each of the Mantle children and justice was as swift as it was certain, lest a child be "spoiled."

Having enough food to last the year 'round was another continual concern in such a low-income household, and during depressed economic times. And getting groceries didn't always involve a trip to the grocery store. Leroy Bennett[64] recalled that while the Mantles lived at Whitebird he witnessed a hog-killing. He never got over the power in the arm of Mickey's Grandpa Charlie. Fifty years later, the memory is still vivid for Bennett of seeing Uncle Charlie taking one swing at a hog and splitting its head wide open. Being able to do that with only that single swing made Bennett a

The Whitebird home of the Mantles has long vanished. Only a vacant field and a lot of memories by the surviving members of the family can restore the images of kids growing up in innocence and adults working hard just to survive.[65]

[63] Richardson.

[64] Leroy Bennett.

[65] Johnny LaFalier led this author on a tour of the Mantle homesites in November 2002.

believer in the old man's power. After the hog was deceased, it was scalded, then dressed out. The stench was overwhelming, Bennett said.

In each rural site where the Mantles lived, they had milk cows. Mickey milked every morning. A lot of his friends attributed the strength in his wrists to doing all that milking. One would have to be on guard when Mickey was milking, according to Nick Ferguson[66], because he could squirt a person in the face halfway across the barn. Jim Richardson recalls that Mickey used to take target practice by squirting the stream of milk at the cats, who by nature hang around dairy barns.

One day when the Richardsons were visiting the Mantles, the boys decided to go out to the barn. Mickey, Jim Richardson and his little brother, Don "Hook," were messing around with a calf when it occurred to Mickey that his life's vocation might be in the rodeo promotion business. He coaxed little Hook to get on the calf and ride it like real rodeo performers ride bulls. When Hook was placed atop the calf he would immediately slide off. After Hook slid off a few more times Mickey and Jim decided to strap Hook on by tying both his legs together under the calf's belly. Up that point, things were going well. However, the calf didn't like having a rider and began bucking and making a beeline for the barn door. As the calf bucked its way out of the barn, it came close to decapitating young Hook on the top of the door sill.

When asked if Mantle's mother or dad ever found out about the incident, Richardson replied, "No, for she would have given us both a beating."

Richardson's most vivid memory of Whitebird had nothing to do with baseball but a whole lot to do with Mickey's one day disobeying his mother's warnings about swimming. Despite her son's constant begging to let him go swimming in one of the old mine pits nearby, his mom always replied that he couldn't go until he learned to swim. That just didn't make much sense to Mickey, for he couldn't figure out how he could learn to swim without practicing.

After one admonition to stay away for the water, Richardson said, "We got on our bikes and slipped off and went anyway." Mickey paddled around in the water of a mine pit a few hundred yards east of this home for a while. Suddenly, he jumped out of the water, exclaiming "Let's get out of here." Richardson said he looked up and spotted Mrs. Mantle coming down the railroad tracks dragging little Butch[67] along behind her.

---

[66] Nick Ferguson.

[67] Larry Mantle was known by his nickname, Butch.

The boys, wet clothes and all, jumped on their bicycles and headed for the power plant — further to the east, away from the Mantle home and the "swimming pool." Mickey found some old newspapers lying around the railroad tracks. He grabbed them and stuffed them into the seat of his pants. Richardson asked what he was doing. Mickey replied, "I'm going to get a whippin' and this will help lessen the pain."

When Mrs. Mantle caught up with the boys, who by then had reached the power plant, she started in on her son. Her weapon was a tree branch, commonly referred to as a switch. Richardson wasn't interested in interfering in a family affair and he readied to make his exit. As he was starting to head off toward home on his bicycle, Mrs. Mantle pointed the switch in his face and said, "You're not going anywhere 'cause you're next." He recalls that Mrs. Mantle wore out the switch on Mickey's rear end and he escaped her wrath that day.

On the 80th birthday of his Aunt Lovell, Richardson and his wife were visiting with her and the whipping story came up once more. Mrs. Mantle told Richardson that the only reason she didn't "whip his ass" that day was that she wore herself out on Mickey. She said, "You know you deserved a whipping that day and I may just have to give you one yet to make up for it." Richardson said that she didn't say it to be funny, she meant it.

Whenever Mickey would sneak off to go swimming with his buddies, as he did often, according to Leroy Bennett, he had a standard cover-up explanation for his eyes being bloodshot because of the old mine shaft water's impurities. Bennett said when Mickey's mother would ask her son what was wrong, Mickey would shrug it off by saying he had been playing baseball on the alkali field, another local source of mining's poisoning of the Tri-State environment.[68]

All of the Gabby Street Pee Wee League games were played on this field at Picher, Oklahoma. Johnny LaFalier surveys the site where young Mickey Mantle played his first organized games.

[68] Bennett.

Max Mantle recalled that Mickey never did learn to swim but while playing for the Baxter Springs Whiz Kids a job that seemingly required this skill was secured for him. Max had a difficult time telling the story because of laughing but said, "They got Mickey a job that summer at the local swimming pool as a lifeguard. Fortunately, no one got into any trouble. If anyone would have needed help they would have drowned."[69]

The Mantles had been transported from Spavinaw to Cardin by the Richardsons since they had no means of transportation. After working awhile in the mines, Mutt remedied the situation. One day when the Mantle twins were still very young Mutt loaded the boys on a wagon pulled by two horses and they headed to Afton, Oklahoma, nearly 20 miles away, where Ray recalled his dad traded that team for a used Buick La Salle. If Mutt drove at the speed his sons always accused him of driving, then the trip from Afton back to Whitebird was probably not faster than the trip earlier in the day to buy the vehicle. Ray recalled that the family trips from Cardin to Spavinaw was a half-day affair for his father to drive that 40 miles.

And Lovell didn't drive much faster, herself. One Sunday, Mutt and Lovell invited Ferguson to join them on a trip to Spavinaw to visit with the Holt family — Mutt's sister Thelma's people. When Ferguson and Mantle weren't playing baseball they were doing something together. Shortly after their arrival, Mutt complained of a headache and dizziness. Lovell announced that everyone must get in the car for the sudden return to Commerce. She also announced that Mutt wasn't fit to drive and that she was going to do it. Everyone was shocked because Lovell had never driven in her life. Ferguson recalled that Mickey sat in the back seat laughing his head off all the way home continually repeating, "Mom, at some point you are going to have to shift it out of first gear."[70]

On the Whitebird farm was a small pond inhabited primarily by frogs, turtles and perch. Ray Mantle[71] recalled that his twin brother Roy and Mickey decided they were going to go out to that pond and catch a stringer of perch. Various old anglers had told them that the surest way to lure the fish was to spit tobacco juice on the hook before putting on the bait. Ray said that they got hold of a package of Beech-Nut chewing tobacco. Neither Mickey nor Ray wanted to do the honors, so they convinced Roy to do the

[69] Max Mantle.
[70] Ferguson.
[71] The Mantle offspring from the Elven and Lovell union were: Mickey, Ray, Roy, Barbara and Larry.

"chewing and spitting." Ray didn't recall if they caught a "mess" of fish for supper but did remember that Roy was much worse for the experience. He and Mickey dragged their brother home and in Ray's words, "He was sicker than a bulldog."

When Mickey and his pals Ferguson and Bennett weren't working, going to school or playing other games, if they were not playing baseball they were practicing the game. When the Mantles lived at Whitebird Mutt built a small backstop next to the barn. He and "Grandpa" Charlie would throw tennis balls to the three youngsters. Mutt threw right and Charlie left-handed. Early on, Mickey's father was determined that his son be a switch-hitter.

Mutt taught other fundamentals, as well. Quoting the cliché, "you use what you have," Rex Heavin claimed that Mutt taught Mickey how to slide. The base usually consisted of something that there was plenty of on a farm, a pile of manure. Heavin said when Mantle did a belly slide he would get back up smelling like the base, and the base smelled like what the cow had dumped there not too long before.[72]

Jimmy Richardson, Leroy "Pee Wee" Bennett, Nick Ferguson and Max Mantle all had first hand glimpses into the formative years of Mantle. Bennett recalled that there weren't many modern conveniences in Commerce back then. Sewer systems were never available to all residents.[73] The infrastructure philosophy of that era was let it run into the creek or sink a hole in the ground and from there it will drain down into some mine shaft. Jimmy Richardson[74] said that Commerce used to dump its raw sewage into a creek. Things went well until the creek would back up and the "Baby Ruth candy bars" would float on the water right back to town.

Thus, Nick Ferguson's grandfather performed a very essential service in town, operating the "Honey Wagon."

For sure, none of these fellows ever thought that their pal Mickey Mantle would rise to the stature of a baseball player honored in the Hall of Fame at Cooperstown, New York. More pressing in their minds was finding a way out of the gloom of the Tri-State mining area; each would do almost anything to escape the fate of their fathers, uncles and brothers. The young men who played hide and seek, coffee can basketball and baseball games using a tennis ball or cork from the end of a thermos bottle saw Mickey as a fun-

---

[72] Rex Heavin.
[73] Bennett.
[74] Richardson.

loving runt of a kid who would probably someday work in the mines.

None of the boys who hung around the Mantle house recall seeing much of either Mickey's step-brother Theodore or step-sister Anna Bea. By the time Mantle was in his teens both Bea and Theodore had gone out on their own. One of Mantle's pals did recall that Mickey helped Theodore out later in life when he would get in a "bind." In fact, most of his friends recall that Mantle was generous to a fault. Merlyn echoed that same idea in this manner. "Mickey's biggest fault was that he worked himself to death and gave it all away. When I asked why he did it he replied because I want to."

The Mantle house was a beehive of activity year-round. Basketball, football and/or baseball were always on the sports agenda. Ferguson remembered that Max and Ronnie Mantle, first cousins and sons of Eugene "Tunney" Mantle, lived across the alley from him. Ferguson remembered Tunney was a great man and a good catcher for the mining clubs before he took sick from the mines.[75]

One day the whole gang, Mantle included, were playing football. Max tried to tackle Ferguson and hit his tooth on Ferguson's shoe heel. It knocked the tooth out but no one ever said anything to Ferguson. It was just part of the risk of playing at full tilt, the Mantle custom. There was no lawsuit or any expectation that one family would pay for the injury suffered by the neighbor's child.

Max recalled it was not in Mickey's nature to give up. He was always the leader in games and strived for excellence. He and his pals played baseball and other games on the chat piles — the mining residue that came from the lead and zinc excavation. Max said Mickey was a couple of years older than him and twin brothers, Ray and Roy. Max vividly remembered that Mickey was fond of playing a game called "outrun the shot," for the lack of a better term. Another thing Mickey was known for, according to his first cousin, Jimmy Richardson was the use of nicknames. He recalls that Mickey was fond of referring to Ray and Roy as Rachael and Rose.[76]

The contest consisted of Mickey closing his eyes and counting to ten. Max, Ronnie, Ray and Roy were then told to run as fast as they could in those ten seconds. They were to get as far away from Mickey as possible due to what was coming. At the count of ten, Mickey would run after his brothers and cousins with a loaded BB gun. At that point they were fair game.

---

[75] Ferguson.
[76] Richardson.

Max said Mickey could run, re-cock and shoot with accuracy without a hitch. The designated target was the rump of each of the boys. As Max now tells it, with a smile on his face, "Mickey seldom missed."

Max surmised that when he, his brother and his twin cousins got a little older they would be faster. Thus, by the time Mantle counted to ten they would be a lot farther away from him and less likely to be hit in the rear with those "rear end stinging BBs." However, the logic didn't take into consideration that Mantle sped up his count and was up to ten before the boys got any farther away from him than they had before. And, with advancing age Mantle also gained foot speed, too.

As for baseball, the boys of Commerce had plenty of guidance and inspiration from the adults. Influences beyond even the significant ones offered by their fathers and other older men of the community — the mining teams, especially — were looked to. The men whom Ferguson recalled playing for the adult mining teams were Mutt Mantle, Bob Montgomery and Guy Froman, probably the most experienced player of the adult mining teams. Froman played professional baseball from 1921 until 1932,[77] then in 1933 joined the Eagle-Picher Mining Co. team in Ottawa County playing for it until 1946, when he became the manager of the Miami, Oklahoma, team in the newly formed Kansas, Oklahoma, Missouri League.[78]

Froman, born in 1902, lived to age 92, was the chief of the Peoria tribe and a friend of Jim Thorpe, the legendary Sac and Fox athlete and fellow Oklahoma native who often would bring a barnstorming baseball team into Northeast Oklahoma. Mrs. Froman said she shared a laugh with Thorpe the day he told them a movie was going to be made of his life and the actor selected for the role was Burt Lancaster.[79]

Mutt was an average player but he was great in Mick's eyes, Ferguson said, and Mickey's desire to please his father contributed decisively to the young man's early dedication to the game.[80]

Also looked up to were the men who coached the boys in organized leagues —Pee Wee and Ban Johnson baseball. And after World War II, there

---

[77] Guy Froman's career: 1921-22, Coffeyville, Kansas, Southwestern League; 1923, Oklahoma City, Western League; 1924-25, Hamilton, Ontario, Michigan-Ontario League; 1926, Syracuse, New York, International League; 1927, Topeka, Kansas, Western Association; 1928-29, Shawnee, Oklahoma, Western Association; 1930-31, Danville, Illinois, Three-I League; 1932, Springfield, Illinois, Three-I League.

[78] John Hall, *Majoring in The Minors* (Stillwater, Okla.: Oklahoma Bylines, Inc., 1996), pp. 32-33.

[79] Ibid.

[80] Ferguson.

was professional baseball nearby from which to take inspiration and renewed dedication. Ferguson said a special influence on him from the local minor league team at Miami in 1946-47 was Bill Chandler, a shortstop. That was the position Ferguson played for the Whiz Kids until Mantle arrived on the scene.

Ferguson especially enjoyed going to the Miami games when the Ponca City Dodgers were in town. Ponca City had a heavy-hitting and slick field-ing shortstop in 1947 by the name of Dimitrios James Baxes. He led the league in home runs and also in holding the attention of young Ferguson. He studied Baxes' every move in order to learn how the position should be played. Some twelve years later Ferguson's belief in the talent of Baxes was borne out when his childhood hero appeared on the Major League scene for the Cleveland Indians and later with the Los Angeles Dodgers. That was the same Jim Baxes who had a step-daughter who married the crooner and actor, Dean Martin.[81]

Not only the men of the community contributed to the boys' develop-ment in baseball, the women, at least some of them, including Mickey's mother, helped, too. Lovell was an excellent seamstress and made the mem-bers of Mickey's "inner circle" their first "pull-up" sliding pants.[82]

In time, many of the young athletes of Ottawa County discovered that organized sports could have an unforeseen benefit. In a place where inside plumbing was a rarity and baths were limited to twice a week, in a good week, the occasional after-game shower was an exciting discovery for the young men. Especially if there was hot water. Even though Commerce had natural gas, water heaters were still a luxury. Thus, in many homes, water was heated on top of the kitchen stove, then dumped into the old galva-nized tubs that also served as horse and cow watering troughs for many a Midwest farmer.

One should not assume that after each bath at home the water was changed and a fresh batch of hot water added. The trick of bathing as a member of a large family was to be the first one in the tub; that was when the water was the hottest and the cleanest.

Poverty and hard times were the norm for many of the Tri-State's young men of the time. One young friend of Mickey Mantle, Rex Heavin, recalled,

---

[81] Ibid.
[82] Ibid.

"Our family was so poor that we could never pay attention and that we would climb over the gate to save wear and tear on the hinge."

Heavin wasn't bemoaning the fact that just his family was devoid of a lot of the things that the current generation sees as essentials. "All the kids in town were poor," he said. "We lived in a shack, and the Mantles didn't have a whole lot more. We played baseball for fun and diversion."[83]

In the eyes of their parents, significant side benefits to the diversion of baseball and other sports was that they reduced the boys' time and inclination to sin. In the Bible Belt of Oklahoma in that era, there was a handful of things that would ensure you a certain trip to Hell if you embraced them, including smoking, drinking, dancing, going to pool halls and consorting with wild women. (In this generation, only about 20 to 40 percent of those things considered to be absolutely damning in Mantle's boyhood would be considered mortal sins.) Ferguson recalled that when he, Bennett and Mantle went off someplace for the afternoon to play baseball, they would have to promise Mrs. Bennett that they wouldn't go around the local pool hall. And, if they did, they had to make sure her son Leroy didn't join them.[84]

[83] Rex Heavin.

[84] Ferguson.

6

Douthat: The First Innings of Organized Baseball

Not playing baseball never was an option for Mickey Mantle. Mutt wanted his son to be like Mickey Cochrane, and had named his first son after that great major league catcher. Mickey Mantle's first contact with any kind of organized baseball came through watching his father and his uncle Eugene "Tunney" playing for the Whitebird mining baseball team in the late 1930s. Mickey, not yet 10 years old, was always at their games. And, of course, he played an endless succession of baseball in backyards and on the chat fields of Ottawa County.[85]

Exposing his son to the game was one of the reasons that motivated Mutt to play for the local mining teams. He was committed to lead by example as well as word. While, by most accounts, Mickey thought his dad was a great player, fellows like Nick Ferguson, one of Mickey's boyhood chums, recalled that Mutt was "average" at best.[86] Mickey's first cousin, Jim

---

[85] Ibid.
[86] Ibid.

Richardson, echoed that judgment.[87] Harry Daniels, the talented pitcher of the Tri-State, said that the reason guys like Mutt never had a chance to develop their game was there was very little equipment and very few organized teams where the youth of his generation could learn to play the game.[88]

Ray Mantle recalled that it was fun growing up watching his brother Mickey and dad always in some type of competition. He told of a ride he made one day with his twin brother Roy, Mickey and their dad. Ray remembers that Mickey and Mutt were fussing about who was faster afoot. Mutt pulled over to the side of the road, got out of the car and took off his shoes for a foot race with his son. "Mickey took off and left Dad 'in the gravel,'" Ray recalled.[89]

The first organized team for which Mickey, 10 years old, played was a team at nearby Douthat, Oklahoma in 1942. Douthat is located at the south edge of Picher and just north of Commerce. Also in the league were two teams from Picher, plus squads in Kansas at Treece and Baxter Springs. Mantle caught quite a bit of the time, Ferguson said. No doubt because his major league namesake had been a catcher. His most enduring memory of Mantle's catching was how much bigger the chest protector was than the kid behind the plate.[90]

Not much remains in Douthat today, with the exception of the Baptist Church, located a block west of this sign, and a few mobile homes. Most of the property has been condemned due to the lead and zinc contamination.

It was there that Mickey joined up with Delbert Lovelace, Nick Ferguson, Leroy Bennett and others to play in the Pee Wee Division of the Gabby Street League. The league derived its name from the former big league catcher and

[87] Richardson.
[88] Harry Daniels.
[89] Ray Mantle.
[90] Ferguson.

manager Charles Evard "Gabby" Street, by then a resident of Joplin, Missouri. The "Old Sarge," as he was affectionately called by famed broadcaster Harry Caray when Street was the color announcer for St. Louis Cardinals network, had set up a sizeable number of teams that played in Joplin and a few small, Northeast Oklahoma and Southeast Kansas towns.

In 1942 all the league games were played in the ballpark in downtown Picher, where, according to several who played on that field, the earth opened up one day and swallowed everything around it. Another mine cave-in casualty.[91]

Bennett recalled the first time the guys ever saw their names on an official baseball document. It was a little scorecard from the first game they played in the Gabby Street League. Scored in pencil, the card to this day is still readable and quit a nostalgic bit of memorabilia that Bennett can point to and say, "Mantle and I started out together."[92]

Though Mutt was a soft and seldom-spoken man, when he opened his mouth, his son listened. And his teaching was to be heeded by Mickey regardless of whether he was present at one of his games. One day in 1942, Mutt was not there when a game started, for his shift at the Blue Goose mine was not complete. He arrived at the game awhile later without Mickey's knowledge. When Mickey's turn at bat came he stood in from the right side against a right-handed pitcher. Of all the things he ever did to displease his father, that incident ranked near the top — particularly after all the backyard batting practice Mutt and Grandpa Charlie had thrown to Mickey.[93] The Douthat team won the league title that summer. As a reward, Street came down from Joplin to speak at a banquet for the team. Ferguson recalled, "Gabby regaled us with stories, like when he, after several misses, caught a ball dropped from the top of Washington Monument. He showed us his right hand with every finger and thumb at right angles. What a mess. We all went 'wow,' would our hands look like that if we continued to play ball?"[94]

The Douthat manager,[95] Jess "Redneck" Lovelace, saw something in his young catcher, Mantle, that maybe some others were overlooking. According to Delbert Lovelace,[96] "Dad told people back then that someday

[91] LaFalier.
[92] Bennett.
[93] Ferguson.
[94] Ibid.
[95] Delbert Lovelace.
[96] Ibid.

the Mantle kid would play ball for somebody." Redneck meant by that that Mantle would play the game at the professional level.

Lovelace recalled knowing from the first, back in 1942, that Mantle was different. He was precocious in his technical knowledge of the game, much in the manner of a child who can play a violin or piano at five years of age. Mantle instinctively knew the game, Lovelace said. Even as a pre-teen, if a runner was on third with less than two out and a long fly was hit into foul territory, he would yell at the outfielder on his team not to catch it. The rest of the guys wouldn't have a clue as to why Mantle was telling them that under those circumstances, according to Lovelace. "Of course, we found out later that Mantle was attempting to keep a run from being scored against our team," Lovelace said.

Not only were parents supportive of the young boys' interest in baseball, Lovelace recalled that professional players from nearby minor league teams would often even visit their games and practices. During the summer of 1942, He recalled that a pitcher for the Joplin Miners team of the Western Association, showed up at one of his Pee Wee League games in Douthat. Bill Davis, according to Lovelace, was playing catch with the Douthat boys. Lovelace got a terrible bruise on his hand from the encounter. "It was so bad it abscessed," he moaned, seeming still to feel the pain sixty years later. What he didn't realize at the time was that Davis had been summoned back to Joplin for the 1942 season and was working his way back into shape at the expense of some "young and tender hands." By 1947 Davis was down in Miami, Oklahoma, pitching and managing his KOM League troops to the pennant and playoff championship. Many of those same Douthat boys frequently returned Davis's visit, shagging baseballs during Miami's batting practice.

7

The World War II Years: Backyard Baseball

It appears that after the 1942 Gabby Street Pee Wee League season, Mickey Mantle and his teammates did not play organized ball again until 1947,[97] though Mantle may have begun playing for Commerce High School in the spring of 1945 when he was in the ninth grade. The school yearbook lists him as having played baseball but doesn't specify which seasons. However, he is listed as having played football his junior and senior years (the seasons of 1947 and 1948) and basketball all four years before graduating in the spring of 1949.[98]

Nevertheless, during the war years Mickey and his friends, particularly Leroy Bennett and Nick Ferguson, reveled in nonstop activity around the Mantle home on Quincy Street in Commerce.[99] Both Ferguson and Bennett, who practically lived with the Mantles, were in need of an older male role

[97] Based on the recollections of several of Mickey Mantle's contemporaries who were interviewed.

[98] Yearbook, Commerce High School, which also commented about Mickey Mantle: "They're great pals, he and his baseball jacket."

[99] This was one of the many places the Mantles lived while in Northeast Oklahoma.

model, and Mutt filled the role willingly and ably. Ferguson had moved to Commerce as a young man from the Southwest Missouri town of Carthage. By that time his father was not around. Bennett's parents were not in good health. (His mother died just after he graduated from high school and his dad died during Bennett's senior year in high school of a mine-related disease.) Mutt Mantle thus served as a father figure to more than just his offspring. Mickey, his brothers, plus Ferguson and Bennett were usually playing out in the yard when Mutt arrived home each night in his dirty clothes and mud-laden boots. To the delight of the boys, Mutt never failed, regardless of fatigue, to stop and play pepper or work on the fundamentals of such baseball essentials as turning the double play and switch hitting.

Ferguson used to get up early each morning and wander over to the Mantle home. He remembered the household routine this way: Mrs. Mantle would put a fresh box of Wheaties on the table and Mickey, Ray, Roy, Larry and their sister Barbara would eat every flake in that day's box. Ferguson, recalling the times he would get invited over for supper, said the meal always consisted of brown beans, corn bread, fried potatoes and something else that was special: he could still see Mickey's mother taking onions and cutting then into quarters and placing them in a bowl. "Each person at the table had their individual onion and each consumed it as if it were an apple," Ferguson related, with tears in his eyes. He said some at the table would use their onion quarters to scoop up the beans.[100]

Another of Mickey's childhood friends, Bill Mosley, said his fondest memory of a meal with the Mantles was that, "Lovell cooked a great pot roast."[101]

The topic of conversation at each meal was always the St. Louis Cardinals game, if the Redbirds had played that afternoon. Ferguson recalled that, "Mrs. Mantle, while doing her housework, would listen to the Cardinals on the radio and then recap the game for the family over dinner."

When the boys weren't playing games in the Mantle backyard, the only flat surface available was a nearby alkali field where mine sludge had been drained, creating a smooth surface. Whenever the wind blew, most of the guys would be red-eyed from the dust created and Mantle seemed to suffer from that more than any of the fellows.

The youngsters played all available sports in grade school and continued those games after school and on the weekends. Ferguson recalled, "When

---

[100] Ferguson.
[101] Bill Mosley.

the weather would not permit playing outside (and believe me, it had to be very bad to keep us inside), we would hang a small basketball hoop over a doorway and Mickey, Ray, Roy, Leroy and I would play. We also played cards or Monopoly a lot. Also, we devised a couple of baseball games played with dice or marbles for inside entertainment. Mickey did not have the patience for the inside games though, not enough action."[102]

During the summer afternoons, Ferguson recalled, they used to go out in the yard and play, often turning to versions of baseball where, in their imaginations, each of them represented their favorite major league team, batting in order as a representative of each team member. Mantle's favorite team was the Boston Red Sox; Bennett rooted for the St. Louis Cardinals; Ferguson liked the New York Yankees.

The games were played with a broomstick and tennis ball. A ball hit to the shed on the ground was a single, against the side of the shed on the fly was a double, atop the roof was a triple and clearing the structure was a home run. As each boy came to bat, he hit right- or left-handed depending on who they had listed on their lineup cards that day for the Cardinals, Red Sox and Yankees.

When the Mantles lived on the Whitebird farm the last couple of years Mickey was in high school Mickey and his cousins[103] used to get a bag of lime and mark off a number of baseball fields in various sizes. The version of baseball played in these games was dubbed "corkball." "Those cork ball marathons started at daylight and lasted until the sun went down," according to Bennett.[104] The ball was the plug found in any thermos bottle used in that era. The cork would "dance" even better than a tennis ball. Its movement was even harder to hit than when Mantle later faced the noted knuckleball artist, Hoyt Wilhelm, upon arriving in the Major Leagues, Bennett said.[105]

Max Mantle recalled the first time Mickey ever saw the guys playing with the cork. He exclaimed, "You guys are crazy." Max said the cork had to be taped so it wouldn't fall apart after being hit a couple of times. The way the pitcher held the cork determined what it did as it approached the batter. Throwing it small end forward caused it to drop like a sinker pitch; if it was

---

[102] Ferguson.
[103] The cousins were Max Mantle and Jimmy Richardson.
[104] Bennett was included in the corkball game.
[105] Bennett couldn't recall Wilhelm's name.

thrown sideways it would rise. No matter how it was thrown, Max said Mickey couldn't hit it.

There was nothing that set young Mickey Mantle apart in talent, in the eyes of his teammates and young friends, several of them agreed years afterwards. That would come later.

Many years after the last pitch of corkball had been thrown, Mantle escorted New York Yankees teammate Billy Martin out to the Whitebird farm to show him where he was raised. According to Max Mantle, who was with the ballplayers that day, Martin was astonished. He looked at the old farmhouse and exclaimed, "You lived in this? This thing isn't fit to live in. If anyone ever tells me they had it tough growing up I am going to tell them about this place." At another point, Max said, Martin said of the Mantles' old Whitebird home, for $100 they could buy the place.

Mantle took Martin over to the horse trough and said, "Billy, this is where we took our baths in the summer time." There stood a small shed — the one that had served in the 1940s as the basis for determining a corkball double from a homer[106] — located between the house and the horse trough in which long ago the boys would change clothes as part of an evening bath. Mickey told Billy that the trough had to be emptied and refilled afterwards so that the horses wouldn't be drinking the soapy water left from a half dozen or so young men taking baths.[107]

It was in the fall of 1945 when Mickey Mantle returned to organized sports, when he entered Commerce High School as a ninth grader. He may have gone out for football that season; it is known he was on the 1945-46 basketball team and, possibly, that spring of 1946, on the CHS baseball team. Mantle's boyhood pals and cousins agreed that Mickey was not scholastically inclined. Bill Mosley, the football quarterback for the Commerce Tigers in his and Mantle's senior year, said, "We were just jocks."[108] However, what Mantle lacked in the pursuit of book learning he made up for on the gridiron, basketball court and on the baseball diamond.

---

[106] This is not the same shed that is often cited as being on Quincy Street in Commerce.
[107] Max Mantle.
[108] Mosley.

Mickey Mantle (front row, far right) was not the "specimen" that would define an athlete in his sophomore year in high school. Nick Ferguson (front row, third from far right) was a constant figure at the Mantle home.[109]

[109] Photo courtesy of Nick Ferguson.

8

Commerce High School
and a Near-Amputation

It was 1947 before Mantle is known to have returned to an organized
form of baseball, and it was almost a miracle that he did. His love of
football almost ended everything. Mantle injured his ankle during football practice in October 1946, his sophomore year,[110] and for too long the
severity of the injury was underestimated.

When it became clear that something was seriously wrong with
Mantle's leg, he was taken to American Hospital in Picher, an Eagle-
Picher Mining Company facility. He was a patient of Dr. D. L Connell,
who said the leg might have to be amputated. Lovell yelled, "You ain't
taking his leg off," according to Max Mantle's memory of the story handed down through family conversation about his cousin's injury.[111] Jim
Richardson, Lovell's nephew,[112] recalled that Mutt nixed the idea of any
possible amputation by telling Dr. Connell, "There isn't any place in the

---

[110] Ferguson.

[111] Max Mantle.

[112] Jimmy was a son of Lester Richardson, Lovell's brother.

world for a one-legged man."[113] Jimmy Richardson said that the night the doctor suggested amputation, his dad came home and remarked to his mother, "Mutt just did something I don't think I could have done."

Max Mantle said, "My wife worked at the Picher hospital as a nurse's aide for a couple of years during high school. Doctor Connell told her that while Mickey was there with the bad leg, one of the things they tried to get rid of the infection was putting maggots in the infected area, a last resort cure before amputation."[114] Richardson recalled that some of the medicine administered to Mantle at Picher was sulfur tablets. Mantle confided in his cousin that he always threw those out the window when the nurse left his room. Richardson said he went out one day to take a look to verify Mantle's story and "the ground was covered with pills."

When the maggot and sulfur treatment didn't have any positive effect on Mantle's condition, Mutt and Lovell decided to take him to Children's Hospital in Oklahoma City, where medical care was provided for people who didn't have the financial means to afford the high cost of medical care that Mickey's case called for at the time.

Upon arriving in Oklahoma City, the Mantles were told that the condition of their son's leg required immediate treatment. For 19 days he took a penicillin shot every three hours. "Prior to that time," Max said, "he was sickly and a runt. He usually had 15-20 boils on his body at all times." After a few anxious weeks, the leg began to respond well, and the family returned home to Ottawa County, the Wormington farm, where they had moved the year before.[115]

Upon Mickey's arrival back home, Max noticed an immediate change in his cousin. Not only had the penicillin saved Mickey's life, but the shots seemed to have cured the boils and his appetite had improved. He began to gain weight.[116] Richardson said, "Mickey was a runt for a long time. In the seventh and eighth grades Commerce had a midget basketball team. To qualify, a boy had to be five foot-two or less and weigh less than 90 pounds. He didn't have any trouble meeting those requirements."

Nick Ferguson recalls, "Even while limping badly Mantle still played basketball during the 1947 and 1948 seasons and could knock down the out-

---

[113] Richardson.
[114] Max Mantle.
[115] The Dr. Frank Wormington farm.
[116] Richardson.

side shot. I spent the winters of 1947-1948 in California and when I returned to Commerce in the spring of 1948 Mickey looked like a different person. He had gained at least 30 pounds up to 160."[117]

The high school coach at Commerce the year that Mantle was first hurt was Al Woolard, who didn't believe the injury was serious. Woolard moved over to Nowata, Oklahoma, for a short time and then went to Lawrence, Kansas, where he established a dynasty in Kansas high school football. From the 1960s through the 1980s he coached many a great football player, including Hall of Famer John Hadl.

Mickey Mantle's return to organized baseball in 1947 occurred when Northeastern Oklahoma A&M football coach Red Robertson was coaching a Ban Johnson League team at nearby Miami. After spending the last few years making do with corkball, alkali fields and sliding into bases of dubious composition, Mickey and his buddies welcomed the change. The field at Miami may have been the first real baseball diamond they stood on since 1942 at Douthat.

Mickey, still weakened by his hospitalization at Picher and then Oklahoma City, was able to play only a few games. The 1947 Miami team was about the only one on which Mantle played while growing up that he was not teammates with Lovelace, Bennett and Ferguson. Lovelace was playing American Legion ball that year at Columbus, Kansas. Later that year, however, Mickey was able to play four games for the Baxter Springs Whiz Kids, based just across the state line in Kansas, and the next year he and his old pals again were on the same team, at Baxter Springs.[118]

One advantage of playing in Miami for Mantle was that there he could spend a lot of evenings getting in the way of young men who were playing baseball professionally, for the Miami Owls, a team in the Class D KOM League.

As was the custom of baseball teams, the pitchers who were scheduled to pitch that evening ran wind sprints and shagged baseballs in the outfield. Young Mantle would come out on occasion, accompanied by one of his dogs. Jim Morris, a Miami Owl pitcher, and some of the other Miami players didn't always appreciate having some kid in their way. They would snatch the glove from the young man's hand and toss it over the fence. Since

---

[117] Ferguson.
[118] Delbert Lovelace.

the nearby Neosho River always posed a potential flood risk, the board fences didn't go all the way to the ground. There was space for Mickey's dog to go beneath the fence and retrieve the glove. This became the dog's duty.

Four years later, Mantle was in Joplin after having played in the World Series after his first year in the major leagues. Speaking at a luncheon, he commented on his early life at a luncheon hosted by Joplin restaurateur Red Wilcoxsin. He mentioned his fondness for the Miami Owls and said that "Jim Morris used to be my favorite pitcher until he threw my glove over the fence."[119]

---

[119] Jim Morris, interview at 1998 KOM League reunion.

9

1947: The Baxter Springs
Whiz Kids

Being a faithful fan of his father's and uncle Tunney's Whitebird mining baseball team resulted in Mickey Mantle taking his first step towards baseball stardom and immortality. For the games at Cardin also were attended by a man who was to play a key role in Mantle's development in baseball.

Barney Barnett who lived in Baxter Springs, Kansas, a town located just across the state line from Ottawa County, was one of those unsung heroes of baseball, the men who love the sport so much they devote all available time to the game for free. Their compensation is, simply, being part of baseball.

Barnett's non-playing involvement in baseball had started in the early 1930s when he managed the Joplin Boosters of the Joplin, Missouri, City League. Lloyd Shafer, who played on that club was quoted as saying, "Our league all-stars once defeated the American League All-Stars in the early '30s."[120] By the late 1930s Barnett's mining career had led him into Southeast

---

[120] *The Baxter Springs* (Kans.) *Citizen*, April 27, 1981.

Kansas, where he managed the Vinegar Hill-Barr Miners, a company base-ball team[121] just outside Riverton. In 1944, Barnett founded the Baxter Springs Whiz Kids team for local youngsters and managed it eight years until his death in 1952. His Whiz Kids were near-legends locally. Dave Newkirk, who made it as far as the Kansas City Athletics spring roster for a couple of years in the mid-1950s, put it this way: "The Whiz Kids were a way of life during those years. More of us wanted to play baseball for Baxter Springs than play football for Notre Dame, and believe me there were a bunch who wanted to follow Johnny Lujack."[122]

The 1947 Baxter Springs Whiz Kids. Back row: Mickey Mantle and Dick "Hog" Barnett. Seated, left to right: Bocky Myers, Bill Crow, Nick Ferguson, Jim Bowers, Wylie Pitts, Bill Johnson, Leroy Bennett and Calvin Mishler.

The Baxter Springs Whiz Kids team photo was traditionally taken with a Nilex 35 millimeter camera that scanned from left to right. The team photos were usually 8 X 22 and not conducive for entering into scrapbooks. Thus the Whiz Kid team photos in this book are split images. This photo is intriguing since the player on the far left of this photo and the one on the far right of the next picture is the same person.

[121] Company team.
[122] Dave Newkirk.

The second part of the same photo. <u>Back row:</u> Ben Craig and Barney Barnett. <u>Front row,</u> left to right: Guy Crow, Jim Kenaga, Jim Vaught , Bob Steele, Charles "Frog" Heavin and Bocky Myers.

Though Mickey Mantle is known to have played baseball several seasons at Commerce High School, the sport was not given much local attention. It is known that Mantle was a player to be reckoned with in games with other high school teams. Cousin Max Mantle said that during Mantle's high school career he was walked almost every time he went to the plate.

But if high school ball was given short shrift in that part of the country in the 1940s, the Whiz Kids were a different proposition altogether. And it was Mantle's play for this team that won him the attention of professional baseball scouts. The Whiz Kids' history was remembered [123] by one of its players, Calvin Mishler, the largest boy on the team, who played first base most of the time. Barnett's teams started out in the Gabby Street League in 1944, four years after the league's founding, and fielded a team for three seasons.[124] The competition included Treece, Kansas, and the Oklahoma teams of Douthat, Picher East Side and Picher West Side. When the Whiz Kids reached the upper age limits for that league, Barnett moved his team into the Cardinal Junior League in 1947. When the upper limits of that league's age class was reached then he moved them over to the Southeast Kansas Ban

---

[123] Calvin Mishler.

[124] The Whiz Kids were affiliated with the Gabby Street League in 1944-46, the Cardinal Junior League in 1947-48 and the Southeast Kansas Ban Johnson League in 1949.

Johnson League in 1949. In 1947 the league had been comprised of Columbus and Baxter Springs, Kansas, along with Alba, Carl Junction, Webb City and Seneca, Missouri. In 1948 Joplin, Missouri, and Galena, Kansas, entered the league.

The Whiz Kids were named, according to Wylie Pitts, after a nickname given the University of Illinois' basketball team. In 1942 and 1943, Andy Phillip, Jack Smiley, Gene Vance, Ken Menke and Art Mathisen formed the nucleus of the basketball team at Illinois, which, in time, became known informally as the Whiz Kids. They were ranked No. 1 in the nation but after their final regular-season game, the entire team entered the war effort. This still was on Barney Barnett's mind when, in 1944, he formed his first junior baseball team, Pitts said. After the war, incidentally, Phillip, Smiley, Vance and Menke returned for the 1947 season and helped the Illini to a second-place finish nationally.[125]

Calvin Mishler recalled when Barnett had taken the Whiz Kids to St. Louis at the end of their season in 1948. He recalled eating at the famed Diamonds restaurant on old Highway 66. Diamonds was the main eatery on the road between St. Louis and Baxter Springs. The team drew a lot of attention in the restaurant because of the Whiz Kid jackets they wore, Mishler said.[126] Guy Crow also remembered this occasion.[127]

In addition to getting to know Mantle at the Cardin games, Barnett had seen him compete in the Gabby Street Pee Wee League, many times in "pickup" games and in a few games earlier in 1947 when he played for Red Robertson's team in Miami. During the summer of 1947 Barnett installed Mantle, then age 15, as a short-term member of the Whiz Kids. Mickey played just four games that year for the Kids; he still was on the mend from his leg injury and hospitalization and unable to be an everyday player. Nonetheless, this was the beginning of something big.

---

[125] Wylie Pitts.
[126] Calvin Mishler.
[127] Guy Crow.

There would be "meat on the table" thanks to a stringer of channel catfish taken from the Neosho River west of the Mantles' Whitebird, Oklahoma, home. From left to right are Ray, Mickey, Barbara and Roy Mantle. Somewhere along the way someone wrote in the names of the Mantle clan.[128]

---

[128] Photo courtesy of Nick Ferguson.

PHOTO COURTESY OF JIM RICHARDSON

This is the last photo taken of the Mantle children. It was at the cemetery in Miami, Oklahoma, when their mother, Lovell, was laid to rest in 1995. Six months later Mickey passed away in Dallas. Left to right are: Ray, Larry "Butch," Barbara, Roy, Mickey and step-brother Theodore Davis.

Both Rex and Charles "Frog" Heavin were Whiz Kids before Mantle arrived on the scene. Rex remembered the first time the Whiz Kids saw Mantle. "He was young, didn't have any power and didn't have the look of magnificence." But Barnett had seen Mickey play both junior baseball and around men's town teams, Rex continued, and wanted him on the Whiz Kids team.[129]

On July 20, 1947, Mickey Mantle played his first Whiz Kids game. It was the championship game of the first half of the Cardinal Junior League season, and was played at Carl Junction, Missouri. Sunny Jim Walters, who owned a candy manufacturing company in Joplin, sponsored the Carl Junction team. In Mantle's debut with the Whiz Kids, he played left field and got one hit in five at-bats. That turned out to be his best day of the season; he was hitless in his next nine times at bat in three later games with Baxter Springs (excluding the Cardinal Junior League All-Star game).

---

[129] Heavin.

By the time Barnett got Mantle on the Whiz Kids team, the mode of uniform had changed. Mantle came along just one full season after Barnett discarded original New York Yankee uniforms that he had acquired when he established his first Whiz Kids team. It was unfortunate Mantle never got to play for the Whiz Kids when they wore those old uniforms. It would have set up one of the greatest trivia questions of all-time—"When did Mickey Mantle first wear a New York Yankee uniform?"

PHOTO COURTESY OF CALVIN MISHLER

This is the Baxter Springs Whiz Kids team. This photo was taken in front of Barnett's residence in 1944 in Baxter Springs. Left to right: Bill Crow, Sonny Helms, Charles "Frog" Heavin, Dean Cannon, Calvin Mishler, Cecil Crow, Barney Barnett, Guy Crow (kneeling), Ben Craig (not wearing a Yankee jersey), Jack Moore, Dick "Hog" Barnett, Bob "Bocky" Myers and Elmer Weaver.

The highlight of the season came on August 1, when 1,500 fans from all over the district showed up to see the Whiz Kids play the league's all-star team. *The Baxter Springs Citizen* reported, "The Whiz Kids were all suited in new uniforms and made a fine appearance. The suits were light gray with black and gold socks."[130] Mantle wasn't in the starting lineup; he entered late in the game and had one hit in two at-bats. On the opposing team was another future major leaguer, Kenny Boyer.

Two years later, Boyer and Mantle signed their first professional contracts on the same day. Both played their final non-professional game (in

---

[130] *The Baxter Springs Citizen and Herald*, August 7, 1947.

the Ban Johnson League) opposing each other. They never faced each other in an official game until the 1964 World Series, when the fields of competition had switched from Baxter Springs, Kansas, and Alba, Missouri, to New York City and St. Louis, Missouri.

At the conclusion of the 1947 Whiz Kids season, a team photo was taken. Mickey was on hand that day and Barnett asked him to get into the picture with the rest of his teammates. He was hesitant for he hadn't played that much for the team that summer and he wasn't in uniform as were the other boys. However, after some coaxing, he stood behind the boys in uniform. In a second photo, taken moments later, Mantle was standing a little further back than in the first picture. He was a frail looking young man.

At the conclusion of each season that Barnett coached the Whiz Kids, he would take his team to St. Louis to watch either the Cardinals play the Dodgers or the Browns play either the Yankees or Red Sox. He walked a tight rope to ensure that his boys got to the see the major league team of their choice. At the end of the 1947 season, the Whiz Kids stayed at the YMCA in St. Louis located just across the street directly beyond the centerfield wall of old Sportsman's Park.

The trip to St. Louis each year was a "project" that started with the first game of the Whiz Kids' season and lasted until the season finale. At each game a hat was passed to take up collection for the season-ending trip. Concession sales money was also used to help finance the trip. Many times there wasn't enough money raised to get all the boys up to St. Louis and Barnett would dig a little deeper to ensure that all of his young ballplayers got their annual two-day trip.[131]

This photo was taken in 1947 front of the St. Louis YMCA, located just behind the centerfield wall at Sportsman's Park. The Cardinals were hosting the Brooklyn Dodgers and their rookie sensation that day, Jackie Robinson. Standing: Bill Crow, Cecil Crow, Dick Barnett, fellow in background not identified and Ben Craig. Kneeling: Nick Ferguson, Bob Myers and Mickey Mantle.[132]

[131] Mishler.
[132] Photo courtesy of Nick Ferguson.

Barnett's generosity wasn't derived from great wealth. Though he was a supervisor (usually called a "ground boss") for the Eagle-Picher at its Foley Mine, he was by no means rich. He gave all that he could for the cause of baseball because he loved the game and he loved kids. His going the extra mile was appreciated by his young charges then and probably more in later life as they reflected upon him in their twilight years.

PHOTO COURTESY OF CALVIN MISHLER

This is a photo of Barney Barnett's crew in 1946. Pictured in front row, third from left, is Calvin Mishler. Even though the signs proclaim that the crew practiced safety, Barnett wasn't in the photo since he had been injured by a drag line that someone pulled while he was standing over it.

When the Whiz Kids would go out of town, Barnett always made sure the boys were given the very best possible. Nick Ferguson recalled that Barnett made it a point to take along an iced cold barrel of lemonade. "When the other team was drinking warm water we were having a cold drink," he said with a great admiration in his voice for his old coach.[133]

Barnett's house was always the place for kids to go for any of their needs at any time. He always told his team that whenever they needed a baseball, bat or glove they could go to his back porch and they were welcome to use anything that was out there. Calvin Mishler recalled that the offer was good

---

[133] Ferguson.

not only in the summer but every season of the year. Barnett was the living testament that "a rich man hath many friends." Richness, in his case, was in that he had so many friends, and many of them were the young boys he gave a chance to play the game of baseball and through those efforts they really did become the "Whiz Kids."

Although Mantle played in only four games in 1947, he was invited along to make the annual trek to St. Louis. The Whiz Kids all stayed in a single large room at the YMCA with cots strung out everywhere. Mishler recalled that the showers were stocked with paper towels on which to dry. Mishler laughed and said, "That was a remedy for disaster." As young men away from the restraints of home are prone to do, they decided to have some fun. They wadded up the towels and started a wet paper towel fight. Old Barney was lying on his cot attempting to recuperate from the long drive up to St. Louis. When the fight had gone on far too long he yelled out that enough was enough. One of the boys, Jim Kenaga, on the other hand, had not had enough fun and was ready to extend the melee a while longer. He had found a cloth towel and it was soaked when he heaved it at Barnett. That was one time he didn't call one of his young men "honey," his usual nominative of address for all his players.

Despite the dressing down, Kenaga wasn't through, however. The next day, Mishler went on, as the team was leaving for the short walk to the turnstiles at Sportsman's Park across the street, Kenaga spied some faults that creased the large rock base of the YMCA building, the cracks large enough for a person to insert his fingers and hands. Kenaga announced to his teammates, "I'm a human fly," then started climbing up the side of the building one boulder at a time. He had gone as high as the top of the first story before Barnett spotted him and "screamed" for him to get down. The "human fly" episode was the second time in a few short hours Barnett had refrained from calling Kenaga "honey."[134]

Kenaga's glee at getting on Barnett's nerves wasn't a new development in St. Louis. All during the 1947 season the young man hadn't relented. He succeeded particularly well during one game to the extent that the old manager used racial slurs against his young player. Mishler recalled that Barnett had a ritual at each ball game attributable to his chronically aching feet. He would wear regular shoes while in the dugout. But when the Whiz Kids

---

[134] Mishler.

came to bat he would put on his spiked baseball shoes and go out and coach third base. One night Barnett was having a hard time all around. His feet hurt worse than normal and the Whiz Kids were playing badly both at the plate and in the field. Kenaga, however, was having just another normal evening, figuring out how next to get on his coach's nerves. When Barnett took off his regular shoes and went out to coach third a bright idea came to Kenaga. He reached down and got enough dirt and sand to fill both of Barnett's shoes.

When Barnett came back to the dugout he picked up the regular shoes and without saying a word poured out the debris. Then he said, "The person who did this is a Dago, Wop, son-of-a bitch." Kenaga sat there with his angelic face on but Barnett wasn't fooled.[135]

Ferguson's most lasting memory of the St. Louis trip was not the water fight or the "Spider Man" antics of Kenaga. The Whiz Kids made the trip in eight hours by automobile, taking Route 66 out of Baxter Springs around midnight. When the weary team arrived in St. Louis they found at the early hour of 8 a.m. black people of St. Louis already starting to line up around Sportsman's Park to get right field bleacher seats in order to see their hero, Jackie Robinson, then playing his first year in the major leagues. In that era the seating was still segregated.[136]

Barney Barnett had a significant impact on young Mantle's career. At the close of the 1952 season he returned to Commerce after leading the Yankees to the World Series championship over the Brooklyn Dodgers. Barnett set up a contest at Joplin's Miners Park billed as "The Mickey Mantle All-Stars vs. The Cloyd Boyer All-Stars."[137]

[135] Ibid.

[136] Ferguson.

[137] Photo courtesy of Cass Barnett.

The game drew 5,000 fans and thankfully someone with the *Joplin Globe* took a photo of Mantle and Barnett. Three weeks later Mantle was attending the funeral services for his long-time friend and coach.

Mickey's numbers were as anemic as his health during the 1947 Whiz Kids season

PLAYER	AT BATS	HITS	RBI	AVERAGE
Holloway	5	2	1	.400
Steele	21	8	3	.381
Heavin	133	50	19	.376
Pitts	100	37	23	.370
Johnson	140	48	31	.343
Myers	81	22	18	.343
Vaught	31	8	4	.258
Ferguson	113	29	17	.257
Crow	93	23	10	.247
Mishler	120	27	26	.225
Bennett	125	28	16	.224
Bowers	18	4	2	.222
Craig	55	12	5	.218
Kenaga	10	1	1	.100
Mantle	14	1	1	.056

10

⚾

1948: The Commerce Comet Takes Off

In 1948 the Baxter Springs Whiz Kids reached the height of their popularity — or at least produced more ballplayers who were later known for athletic accomplishments at the college and professional levels than any of the other clubs Barnett produced. The Whiz Kids were competing in their final year of Cardinal Junior baseball that summer.

In order to get Mickey Mantle into the line-up to start the 1948 Whiz Kids season, Barnett had a trip to make to Illinois.[138] Eagle-Picher Mining, for which Mickey's father Mutt still worked, had decided to expand its operations into that state. During Mutt's "vacation" early that spring, he went to Galena, Illinois, to work on the construction[139] of a new mill in order to make some extra money. Mickey went along with his dad, probably on the basis of one of the popular sayings of that era, "If Arbie sees Obie, tell him Tex is hiring." In other words, the mining industry was

---

[138] Mutt Mantle was working his vacation that year to earn some extra money. Barnett went to Illinois to take Mickey home in order to prevent Mutt's losing a few days of work.

[139] Mutt Mantle was helping build structures that would enable the opening of the mine.

always looking for a strong back.

Guy Crow recalled that when his father,[140] Cecil Crow, was sent by Eagle-Picher to Illinois as the new mill's superintendent, Mutt was there also, looking around the area and considering the possibility of resettling in Galena. However, because of his eldest son's love for baseball and comfort level with the area he had moved to as a four-year-old child, Mutt decided not to uproot Mickey and the rest of the family.[141]

Many memories of the 1948 season were kept in a scrapbook[142] for more than a dozen years by Nick Ferguson. That season was one of transition, since Barnett had gifted players vying for the same infield positions. He had two shortstops, so moved Ferguson to second base and had Mantle play shortstop. Bill Johnson considered the Whiz Kids' brightest star, was moved to third base from his normal second base.[143]

Mickey is depicted in his junior class photo. Although he had originally autographed this photo back in his high school days, it appears that it has been traced over with a more modern pen.[144]

Teammates of Mantle's recalled that it was generally known that Barnett felt Mickey was a better right-handed hitter than left-handed, but in deference to Mutt, Barnett never said anything to Mickey about this during his tenure with the Whiz Kids.[145]

There are several versions of an event that was alleged to have happened during Mantle's only full season with the Whiz Kids, 1948. The story has appeared in print that in one game he hit a ball — perhaps even two — into Spring River, which flowed several hundred feet beyond the

---

[140] Guy Crow. His father helped transport the Baxter Springs Whiz Kids on road games.

[141] Guy Crow.

[142] The fate of this scrapbook is now unknown.

[143] Ferguson.

[144] Photo courtesy of Nick Ferguson.

[145] Ibid.

unfenced right field and center field at Kiwanis Park in Baxter Springs.

Delbert Lovelace played in every game for the Whiz Kids that year. When asked years later if he ever saw Mantle accomplish that feat, he paused for a moment, then said, "I don't want to destroy someone else's story; however, I was there all year and never saw him do it."[146] Guy Crow was the Baxter Springs batboy from 1944 through 1948. When asked about it, he said, "He did it in batting practice one day." However, according to Crow, "It went in on the bounce." Crow added that Dick Barnett, one of Barney Barnett's sons, used to hit fly balls to the outfielders during warm-ups and practices from the left field line, near third base. On one occasion he hit one into Spring River.[147] So perhaps, as memories failed over time, the ball hit by young Barnett during a warm-up session was linked to Mantle in a game.

The issue was one that Mickey fueled even in his Hall of Fame induction speech 26 years later. Mantle even upped the ante, from one homer to two. And each from a different side of the plate. Before a considerable crowd of his peers and fans, Mantle said at Cooperstown, N.Y., in 1974, "I hit three home runs that day. A couple of them went in the river – one right-handed and one left-handed."[148]

Clearly, during the writing of this book, the incident begged for some further research. Pulling into Baxter Springs one beautiful fall afternoon in November 2002, this author was on a mission to put the matter to rest in his own mind. The former Whiz Kid Calvin Mishler was contacted by telephone and asked if he would like to join the author at the ball park, and he came at once. He pointed out the exact spot where the old Kiwanis Park home plate once was located.

We then parked our pick-up trucks near where the right field line would have intersected the river.[149] Returning to home plate and looking toward the place where the playing field ended and the water began, our trucks parked there looked like toys, they were that far away. After some discussion Mishler, a man of over six feet in stature, and I decided we would both pace off the distance from home plate to the spot in center field ends at the river's edge and where lore has it that Mantle once crunched a home run. Or two.

Upon reaching the water's edge, Calvin called out "161." I grinned and

---

[146] Delbert Lovelace.

[147] Guy Crow.

[148] Mickey Mantle, speech, Baseball Hall of Fame, Cooperstown, N.Y., Aug. 12, 1974.

[149] This is based on the author's best estimate.

said, "160." So, figuring that each of our paces was about three feet long, we estimated the distance from home plate to the watery edge of center field was around 480 feet. A blow of such gigantic proportions hit by a five-foot, 10-inch-tall kid who weighed 155-160 pounds would have been tantamount to the tape-measure homer Mantle hit in Griffith Stadium some five years later in the major leagues against Chuck Stobbs of the Washington Senators.

Another former Whiz Kid, Rex Heavin, claimed years later that Mantle did hit one — not two — into the river at Baxter Springs. But it went into the river on one bounce. Heavin said he should know; he was the guy who made the pitch that Mantle hit. Rex said he was pitching for the Baxter Springs Cubs, another team in town that served as a sort of junior varsity for the Whiz Kids. Rex said the long home run was hit during a night game, not a day game as Mantle and others recalled.

Heavin said he had been instructed by his manager Johnny Fast that night to throw only knuckleballs to Mantle;[150] that odd brand of pitch is much harder for a batter to hit, and when he does, it doesn't go as far as a fast ball when struck. Both Heavin boys, Rex and Frog, had developed a good knuckleball. The year before, in 1947, when Mantle and Frog Heavin were on opposite teams, Frog was sent in by manager Fast to relief-pitch on just two days' rest. "I struck Mantle out," Frog said, "for he couldn't hit the knuckler. Anything else, he would have smashed."[151]

Mantle was so impressed by the Heavin brothers' knuckleball that he persuaded Frog and Rex to teach him how to throw it. Many a night in warming up along the sidelines before his earliest professional games in the KOM League and Western Association Mantle always wanted to show his teammates how he had mastered the pitch. By most of the accounts of the guys who caught him they could attest that the lessons provided by the Heavin brothers had been successful.[152]

In 1954 the New York Yankees signed Frank Leja to a large bonus and thus he was was placed on the Yankee roster. John LaFalier recalled, "Mickey called the rookie 'Jesse James,' since he felt he had taken too much of the Yankees' money." One thing Leja did with part of the bonus money, according to LaFalier, was purchase a catcher's mitt to use when he and Mantle

[150] Rex Heavin.
[151] Charles Heavin.
[152] Rex Heavin.

played catch. What he had learned with the Whiz Kids he was still perfecting as a member of the Yankees, throwing his knuckleball.[153]

Rex Heavin said the pitch Mantle hit into the river at Baxter Springs in 1948 was not the knuckleball ordered by manager Johnny Fast, but a fast ball. Fast leaped off the bench and, as Heavin told it later, "ran out to the mound and said, 'You little son of a bitch. Why didn't you throw him the knuckleball?'" Heavin claimed he told his manager there were some scouts watching the game and wanted to make Mantle look good.

Heavin added that his brother Frog, who was also there that night, "faintly" recalled him as being the guy who made the pitch that Mantle hit.[154]

So there the story stands. At least none of the aging witnesses claimed the ball bounced into Spring River into the mouth of a giant catfish, which then swam down the Mississippi to the Gulf of Mexico and then deposited it into the silt, where it produced hundreds of similar stories.

Visitors to the site where some have alleged that Mickey Mantle once (or twice) hit a baseball into Spring River are on perhaps more certain historical ground when reading a sign that stands nearby and advises: "On October 6, 1864 William Quantrill with 300 Guerilla Rebel Troops, forded Spring River nearby to attack Ft. Blair."

The late Calvin Mishler stands on a Civil War battle site; just a few feet behind him is the spot where Mantle purportedly hit two balls into Spring River.

Bill Mosley, one of Mantle's high school teammates, though he could not confirm the homer(s)-into-the-river story, did remember this most relevant anecdote. One afternoon in the fall of 1953, he, New York Yankee outfielder Cliff Mapes and Mantle decided

[153] John LaFalier.
[154] Rex Heavin.

they wanted to go up to Joplin to "have some fun."

The three men got into Mantle's car. On their way, within minutes they crossed the Oklahoma-Kansas state line and were in Baxter Springs. As the car was nearly out of the city limits, Mantle turned his head to the left and spied the old Kiwanis ballpark. The allure from his Whiz Kid days was too strong to resist. "C'mon, guys," he said. "Let's hit a few." Mantle had his trunk full of baseballs, bats and gloves, Mosley said. He informed Mosley that he was going to be the pitcher and that he and Mapes were going to be the batters. Mosley recalled vividly 50 years after the event the details of the impromptu Mapes/Mantle batting exhibition "I never saw balls hit that hard in my life. There I was 60 feet, six inches from home plate without a helmet. I could have been killed."

The logical question coming out of that conversation with Mosley was, "How many balls were hit into Spring River that day?" The answer came as no surprise, "None."[155]

What the members of the 1948 Whiz Kids recalled more certainly above all of Mantle's feats that year was a three-home-run game. Fortunately, documentation survives. The memorable feat occurred on Sunday afternoon, June 13, at Baxter Springs in a game against the Columbus, Kansas, Lions. The balls Mantle hit that afternoon got past the outfielders. Since there was no wall behind the outfielders to stop the ball, it could roll "forever," which is what happened.

The game pitted the ace of the Whiz Kids, Ben Craig, against Ted Atkinson, Columbus' top pitcher. Atkinson had been a member of the Whiz Kids in 1946 and would later sign a minor league contract with the New York Yankees. Despite those home runs, Mantle was not able to bring the Whiz Kids victory that day. His third homer came in the bottom of the ninth as Baxter Springs erased a 10-6 Columbus lead. However, Columbus scored two in the tenth inning to give the Baxter Springs a tough loss.[156]

Delbert Lovelace, in the lineup that day, recalled that a "hat passing" took place. In those days a particularly great feat on the diamond earned a player some much appreciated remuneration from the fans. A loud roar from the crowd erupted when someone gave up his straw hat for the purpose of "taking up an offering."

After Mantle's third home run, the hat came off some spectator's head.

---

[155] Mosley.

[156] *The Baxter Springs* (Kans.) *Citizen*, June 14, 1948.

When the hat had made its way through the old wooden bleachers at Baxter Springs it came back containing $75. That was quite a hefty sum for a kid whose father was a miner and didn't bring home that much money in nearly a month.

The news of the bonus traveled quickly, circulated probably by people in one or more of the towns in Oklahoma's Lucky Seven Conference, a high school league in which Mantle played football, basketball and baseball, and in which he was planning to play during his senior year, the 1948-49 school term. The Oklahoma High School Activities Association was notified that Mantle had forfeited his amateur status by accepting the $75. So he should not be permitted play any more high school sports, it was argued. The OHSAA ruled that Mantle must pay back the money or he would be ineligible for the upcoming sports season at Commerce High School. It didn't matter that he had hit the homers in Kansas and been given the money there.

Of course, by the time the case had been adjudicated the money was "long gone." The Mantles didn't have that kind of cash lying around the house or in a bank account. What finally happened to settle the matter, in the opinion of most the 1948 Whiz Kids interviewed later, was that was that Barnett led the campaign to help Mutt raise $75 to pay the restitution. Much if not all the money no doubt came from Barnett himself.[157]

Either Barnett recruited the best hitters in the area or after he got hold of a kid he made capable a stickman of him. On August 3, 1948, his Whiz Kids were in first place in the Cardinal Junior League and took on the best players from the other teams in the league. The Baxter Springs lineup against the league all-stars was:

Mickey Mantle	ss	.351	Nick Ferguson	2b	.378
Billy Johnson	3b	.368	Delbert Lovelace	1b	.483
Leroy Bennett	c	.354	Bill Pace	lf	.111
Bob Kurley	cf	.255	Jack Dorrell	rf	.280

Bob Steele, who had won five league games and lost none, pitched and the Whiz Kids won easily, 8-1.

The hitter with the highest average among the all-stars was Bennie Lee of Columbus. The all-star pitcher for that game was George Garrison of

---

[157] Lovelace, Ferguson and Bennett all surmised that this is probably what happened.

Joplin, who pitched during the regular season for the Alba Aces. In the return all-star game at the end of the season Garrison turned the tables on the Whiz Kids and won his own game with a grand slam home run, 10-9. It surprised no one that when the 1949 Whiz Kid season rolled around both Lee and Garrison were playing for Barnett's team.

Whiz Kid infielder Bill Johnson's most vivid memory of the 1948 season was the night they went to play arch-rival Columbus for the league championship. They won the game, then some of the boys decided to have some fun and headed for the Cherokee county fair nearby. The irrepressible Jim Kenaga was driving his father's brand new Plymouth that was equipped with a set of the newly developed low-pressure tires.

The three left the Columbus ballpark still wearing their baseball uniforms for there were no shower or dressing facilities at any of those ballparks. When Kenaga rounded the first curve his tires squalled, surprising Kenaga, who wasn't used to driving on low-pressure tires. Sitting right there was a Columbus policeman who immediately assumed Kenaga was speeding. Kenaga was issued a ticket for $10. He had $5 in his pocket, Johnson $3 and Mantle $2. They handed the money to the policeman and headed back to Baxter Springs. Their anticipated night of fun at the fair was dashed by the sound of tires on pavement and the reduction of the boys' treasury. There was no fair for them that night. Though they had just won the league championship that night, missing that fair was a great disappointment to each of the fellows and has remained one of the great memories in Billy Johnson's life.

Money was a constant worry for most of the families the Mantles knew throughout Mickey's youth. When the Whiz Kids played a game there was a second "game" also unfolding. While the baseball was in progress Rex Heavin and his brothers would keep one eye on the playing field and the other on the grandstand. Surveying the grandstand was conducted to determine just what person was sitting where in the old wooden bleachers. Rex said he and his brother Charles "Frog" would log that into their memory for use the next day. Early the next morning, he and Frog would go back out to the ballpark "at dawn's early light." Recalling the mental notes they had made the night before, they went underneath the grandstand in search of coins, bottles, cans, scrap metal or anything else they could find that could be sold. Who had been sitting where at the game was a guide as to the possible site of accidentally dropped coins.

On one of the scavenger hunts Rex found a brand new Rawlings baseball glove under the grandstand which he put to good use. He said it was the best glove he ever had in his life.

Another mental game that Rex played while participating in each Whiz Kids game was to note where all foul balls were hit out of the park during a game. After searching under the grandstand for items he might be able to sell, he would then go in search of baseballs that might have been missed by the "ball shaggers" in the darkness of the previous evening. Each baseball found was a "jackpot," for Barney Barnett purchased it for 50 cents.

One morning while out scavenging, Rex and Frog ran into Nick Ferguson and Mantle coming into the park to see if they could find anything under the grandstand from the previous evening. When Mantle spied Rex, he said, "Ain't no use for us to look. The Heavin boys have been here." Knowing that there wasn't going to be any loot to be found, Rex recalled that Mantle then looked at him and said "Rex, can you loan me a jitney? I'll pay you back later." In the common parlance of that era a "jitney" was a nickel. Heavin doesn't recall Mantle ever paying him back the jitney he loaned him that day.[158]

If a nickel was a lot of money to the Heavin boys, then paper money represented "tons of cash." Early one morning when the Rex and Frog had gotten up even before the rooster crowed, they made their normal post-game rounds. Having scoured the entire ballpark, they became thirsty and headed toward the water fountain. Frog spied something he had never seen before in all the scavenging he and Rex had done. On the ground, partially protruding from beneath Rex's shoe, lay a $5 bill. Frog developed a gregarious side to his personality in just seconds and told Rex to get his drink first. Being suspicious, Rex couldn't figure out what was going on and was very cautious before taking another step. After surveying the ground for a few seconds, he saw a "fortune" beneath the heel of his shoe.

Ferguson recalled, Mutt Mantle took him and Mickey to a tryout camp at Pittsburg, Kansas, sponsored by the St. Louis Browns late in the Whiz Kids season of 1948. Ferguson believed Mantle eventually would have signed with the Browns after he graduated from high school the following spring.[159] That recollection of a tryout camp fits the account of a *Joplin Globe*

---

[158] Rex Heavin.
[159] Ferguson.

story.[160] The newspaper announced there would be a tryout camp for young hopefuls from the four-state area that August 8. However, Ferguson said it rained all that day, so he and Mantle went back to Commerce. Mickey was frustrated that he hadn't been able to show the Browns what he had to offer, Ferguson said. He added that he was not interested at that point in signing a baseball contract, for he had recently moved to California and wasn't interested in leaving his family and heading back east, even to play professional baseball.[161]

Mantle and Leroy Bennett's time together ended with the conclusion of the 1948 Whiz Kid season. Mantle's academic endeavors could be characterized as "jock," Bennett indicated,[162] for Mickey didn't take them all too seriously. Rather, his dad had charted his path on the road to baseball glory. Bennett, however, took to academics due to his father's admonition never to enter the mines; anyway, Bennett had a desire to go to college. And along the way academic excellence was grilled into Bennett by a high school principal. Bennett chuckled, "When Mickey was practicing some sport I was taking courses in HAM radio which sparked my interest a few years later in electrical things."[163]

Members of the Baxter Springs Whiz Kids (1947-49):

Nick Ferguson, Leroy Bennett, Willard "Billy" Johnson, Guy Crow (batboy), Bill Crow, Delbert Lovelace, Buddy Ball, George Garrison, Joe Daniel, Duffy Harbaugh, Rex Heavin, Charles "Frog" Heavin, Calvin Mishler, Bob Steele, Bennie Maxwell Lee, Bocky Myers, Wylie Pitts, Bill Pace, Scoop Albright, Jim Bowers, Earl Holloway, Ben Craig, William Kerley, Jim Vaught, Wilber Kaiser, Mickey Mantle, Gene Lindeman and Jack Dorrell.

---

[160] *The Joplin Globe*, August 3, 1948.
[161] Ferguson.
[162] Bennett.
[163] Ibid.

11

Walter A. "Barney" Barnett, Sr. — A Major Influence

The Whiz Kids, always successful under Barney Barnett, usually played 50-55 games a year and would win 40 or more each season. The reason for the success was in the leadership of Barnett. He pushed, prodded and worked the team out every day that they didn't have a game.

His obvious devotion to his kids, and his appearance and manner endeared him to most of his players. Barnett was about as big as the first four letters of his last name. His manner of speech was appealing. and he dished out criticism in a memorable way: "Honey, why did you do that?" Calvin Mishler some fifty years later chuckled and commented, "Can you imagine him calling Mantle 'honey?'"

Usually, when he was giving a player that "honey" speech, Barnett would have the boy by the front of his jersey and be lifting him off the ground as he looked him straight in the eye. That figure of speech spilled over to his son Barney Jr., who years later still called everybody "Hon."

The Whiz Kids probably hit their peak during that 1948 season, as they added Mantle to their roster for the whole season. In time, it was not unusual for Barnett to add players to his Baxter Springs team who were not from that town. Naturally, this caused some resentment among local boys. Ben Craig, one of the original Whiz Kids, having joined the team in its maiden year of 1944, said years later, "That was an all Baxter Springs team before we started getting those guys from Oklahoma."[164]

And not only did Barnett try to add the best talent from the entire area, he also was not afraid to hone their already advanced skills by pitting his youngsters against adult teams. Barnett did more with baseball than just coach the Whiz Kids. He had a group of players he called "The Barney Barnett All-Stars," and he would schedule games with good semi-pro teams as far away as Bentonville, Arkansas. He supplemented the ranks of his all-star club with members of the Whiz Kids.

There also were numerous times when the Whiz Kids played under that name but added a "ringer" or two when they played teams outside their youth league. Former pros such as Bob Montgomery and Barney Barnett, Jr. would at times pitch for the Whiz Kids. Combined with the Whiz Kids' hitting skills, it was almost a sure bet they would win almost any time, even against teams with much older players. Mantle's development certainly was accelerated by playing at a tender age against players a notch or two above his age level.

When Northeastern Oklahoma Junior College at Miami started up its team in the late 1940s, they had a great deal of trouble finding anyone to play them. Barnett agreed to let his Whiz Kids play that college team.

In one of those games against the college team,[165] Mantle made a deep impression. The opposing pitcher was Max Buzzard of Seneca, Missouri, who by then had spent a couple of years in the New York Yankee system at the Class D level in both the Sooner State and KOM leagues. Although Buzzard hadn't been a pitcher in the minor leagues, he nonetheless had a good arm. Buzzard recalled "this kid" coming to bat for the Whiz Kids one day and batting from the left side since Buzzard was a right-hander. In his first at-bat "the kid" hit a homer over the right field wall. When Mantle came to bat again in the third inning he hit from the right side against Buzzard and cleared the left field wall with his second home run of the game. After that 14-5 loss to an amateur team, Buzzard said, he didn't doubt

---

[164] Ben Craig.
[165] This was against Northeastern Oklahoma Junior College.

Mantle's ability to play ball.[166]

Buzzard's memory was jogged back to late 1947. Due to his inability to hit the curve ball, the Independence Yankees thought he needed some further help and suggested he give up the professional game for a while and go over to nearby Yates Center, Kansas, and work on his hitting with Raymond "Rabbit" Powell. Powell was a nine-year big league performer in the early part of the 20th century, spending most of his career as an outfielder with the Boston Braves.

Instead of going for that hitting instruction, Buzzard went back home and played the latter part of the 1947 with the local Ban Johnson club in Miami, Oklahoma. He recalls that when the Miami club would head north to Pittsburg, Independence or Chanute, Kansas, they would always have a stop to make. Mantle would be waiting in front of the Cardin, Oklahoma, post office and would be picked up there for the trip to the scheduled game. Buzzard recalled that Mantle played right field and that he played center. Not being boastful Buzzard said, "There was a time I could have given Mantle a pretty good challenge in a foot race. With him in right and me in center, we controlled that part of the outfield pretty adequately."[167]

Mantle also began to establish himself as a fun-loving kid about this time. Accounts recalled years later by the members of the 1948 Baxter Springs Whiz Kids indicate that, while most kids naturally like to contrive fun for themselves, the "ringleaders" of the team, when it came to merry-making were Buddy Ball, Jim Kenaga and Mickey Mantle. Nick Ferguson recalled, "Although Mickey was a little shy around strangers, he loved to clown around a lot and had a great sense of humor. Check the 1948 Whiz Kids picture, where he put his glove on the wrong hand to make it appear he threw left-handed."[168] In the team photo, Mantle is seated next to Barney Barnett and sitting as straight as a string. His face had a "chessie cat" grin on it. He thought he was pulling off a good one.

Team photos were one way the Whiz Kids could express their comical side and record it for the ages. In two 1947 team photos in which Mantle appears there is an extra player in one. Those pictures were taken with motor-driven Nilex 35 millimeter camera mounted on a tripod. They could scan a large group of people or a wide vista, usually starting at the

---

[166] Max Buzzard.
[167] Ibid.
[168] Ferguson.

PHOTO COURTESY OF WYLIE PITTS

Mantle, seated second from far right, has his glove on his right hand to indicate he was a southpaw. Ben Craig, third from far left, was doing likewise.

left and moving right, so it was possible for a person to be in the photo more than once. In the 1947 Whiz Kids photo, Bob Myers is on both the far left and far right.

In the 1949 team photo, Jim Kenaga and Bob Steele were seated in such a spot that they were out of sight of Barnett. Barnett is shown in the middle of the group looking as though he could be the body double of Honus Wagner. About four players to his right sat Kenaga and Steele. They were holding hands. Protruding above Kenaga's belt buckle was a pistol. At first glance, the gun looks real. However, it was a toy pistol that Kenaga found going into the ballpark the morning the photo was taken.

Mantle's mischief was a bit subtler than that of Kenaga. He never duplicated Kenaga's Godzilla routine of the 1947 St. Louis trip. But Mantle could tell a "whopper" without cracking a smile. And both boys were gifted at practical jokes and generally gave Barnett a tough time and tested his patience to the limit.

12

Recollections from Mantle's
Early Friends and Associates

The early years of Mickey Mantle's life were touched by a number of
people whose influence contributed significantly to his development. His fiercely close-knit family was, of course, way ahead of others in this regard but others played significant roles, as well. Probably, in the
early going, Mantle was, after his family, closest to Leroy Bennett and Nick
Ferguson. That closeness was reflected in the trio's being known by their
friends as "The Three Musketeers."[169]

Leroy Bennett (the "smart one")

Leroy Bennett was more scholastically inclined than Mickey Mantle and
most of their other friends. So much so that he wound up with an appointment to the U.S. Naval Academy and also earned an advanced degree from
the Massachusetts Institute of Technology in Electrical Engineering.

---

[169] Nick Ferguson.

Bennett had taken to academics partly because of his dying father's admonition never to enter the mines and partly because he had been taken under the wing of a high school principal and a teacher who had recognized his intelligence and encouraged him to use his "smarts" to the fullest. All this was highly influential on him, but even without such advice, Bennett most likely would have gone to college anyway. He wanted to. A friend, Calvin Mishler, asserted that Bennett was "a brain" and without trying made straight As in all his classes.[170]

Mantle and Bennett were similar in their love of sports, but Mantle took it a few notches higher. One of Bennett's favorite photos is that of him and Mantle walking off the basketball floor at Commerce High School together. [171]

Bennett played the 1948 season with the Whiz Kids, and then went off to Oklahoma A&M (now Oklahoma State University). Overriding everything else in Bennett's life in this period, however, were the health problems afflicting his parents. His father died[172] during Bennett's senior year in high school at the age of 59 from silicosis that he had contracted by working in the mines. Bennett's mother's death in late 1948 interrupted his college studies for a year. However, at this point he had received an appointment to the Naval Academy.

At Annapolis, Mishler said, Bennett won a spot on the Naval Academy baseball team. Mishler quoted Bennett as saying, "I sat more than I played; however, I enjoyed it."[173] Regardless, Bennett lettered two years as a catcher. He looked back on those days with some pride, for he recalled, "I got to play on many of the Ivy League baseball fields, such as Yale, Dartmouth, Princeton, Cornell and a few others."

However, the single greatest benefit of being on the Navy baseball team was being allowed to eat with a college team and not the "grunts," his other classmates. Bennett said that the food given the athletes at Annapolis was worth any sacrifice it took to keep his grades up while playing baseball.

Upon graduation from the Naval Academy, he joined the United States Air Force. After military service, Bennett enrolled at the Massachusetts

---

[170] Mishler.

[171] Bennett.

[172] Leroy Bennett's mother died in late August 1948 and his father died four months later, that December. Leroy had enrolled at Oklahoma A&M University after his mother died, but after his father's death he dropped out for a semester.

[173] Mishler.

Institute of Technology, where he earned a master's degree in electrical engineering. He spent the next 38 years at Conoco's international head-quarters in Ponca City, Oklahoma.

After retirement, Bennett stayed in the "electrical" field — in a sense. He was an accomplished steel guitar player and began picking out the tunes he and Mantle had heard performed back in the old days by A. J. Cripe on KOAM radio from Pittsburg, Kansas, and Western Swing guru, Bob Wills, when he filled the airwaves from KVOO in Tulsa. One thing that Bennett stressed was that he didn't want anyone to think that he was an "egghead."[174] And he had a point. After all, not many "eggheads" play baseball and the steel guitar. Still, he did more than live up to that "brain" image his friends had of him long before.

Nick Ferguson

Leroy Bennett's two best buddies' real names were Mickey Charles Mantle and Jackie Leland Ferguson. All his friends knew Jackie Leland as "Nick."

Unlike Mantle, Ferguson never made it out of the Tri-State mining area by virtue of professional baseball, even though the Pittsburgh Pirates attempted to sign him and send him to their minor league team at Bartlesville, Oklahoma, in 1950. Had Ferguson accepted the Pirates' offer, he often would have been back in Miami, Oklahoma, playing in front of the home folks from Commerce. Both towns had teams that were charter members of the KOM League. Instead, Ferguson settled in Southern California and later lived two miles from Jack Murphy Stadium in San Diego. He became a longtime fan of the old San Diego Padres of the Pacific Coast League and later a big fan of the California League.

Being a Whiz Kid paid off for Ferguson in 1947. He had graduated from high school by then and was going between California and Oklahoma each summer. Barney Barnett, Jr., the son of the Baxter Springs Whiz Kids coach, had been drafted by the Chicago Cardinal football team straight of Northeastern Oklahoma Junior College at Miami. The Cardinals visited Los Angeles for an exhibition game with the Rams and Barney Jr. invited Ferguson to the hotel where the Cardinals were staying. Ferguson got to meet and visit with members of a professional football team, a big thrill to a young man who had seen very few football games beyond the high school

---

[174] Bennett.

level by that time of his life.

In 1951, at the beginning of Mickey Mantle's rookie season in the major leagues, Ferguson, by now a permanent resident of California, was reunited briefly with Mantle when the New York Yankees trained at Phoenix. Ferguson went over from California to see him. Mantle insisted that Ferguson stay with him. Bob Wiesler, Mantle's roommate, had to report for two weeks' national guard duty, so Ferguson moved in with Mantle for three or four "fun-filled days." Ferguson said, "Clint Courtney and Ernest Nevel were always trying to get me to sign Joe DiMaggio's name to the meal tab every time we went out to eat." Those two players then were on the roster of the Yankees' minor league team at Beaumont, Texas. Courtney had not yet had his "cup of coffee" in the majors, but the "aging" Nevel had made it to the Yankees for a "sip" the year before.

When the press started talking about Mantle's prospects of making the ball club, Ferguson heard Mutt Mantle telling a sportswriter, "Jim Brideweser might be a better prospect than my son." Ferguson knew that Mutt was a man of few words and also that he was not beyond "yanking the chain" of a newsman. Mutt was asked during the 1950 season if there were any more at home like Mickey. He replied that there was Ray, Roy, Larry and Barbara and, "she can throw like a boy."

Ferguson recalled that when the Yankees went to California for some exhibition games that spring they played in Los Angeles' Wrigley Field. He said that at Wrigley as well as everywhere else they played up and down the Pacific Coast, Mantle   bombed the ball and was building a reputation, as well as great expectations.

"I worked aircraft through the fifties," Ferguson said, "then 26 years for the U.S. Postal Service. Played sandlot baseball every Sunday year 'round in the fifties, played on one team with Don Larson, who would play the outfield in winter ball. Larson could hit as well as any pitcher all-time. I met Larson again when the Yankees came west on an off day to play a Roy Campanella benefit game in May of 1959. It was the largest crowd ever to see a baseball game at 92,000 in the L.A. Coliseum," Ferguson recalled fondly.

Also, he went on, the "secret word" was always beneficial in getting Mantle's attention when he later had throngs of admiring fans vying for his attention. Ferguson said, "When I would attend Yankee games, and in pre-game practice when all the fans were screaming Mickey's name, I would just call out 'Spavinaw' and he would know it was me and would come over and tell me how to get into the clubhouse. It was easy under Yankee manager Casey Stengel; a little more difficult under [Ralph] Houk," Stengel's successor. Ferguson saw Mantle for what he was, a small town boy who gravitated to the street-wise players with the Yankees. Instead of blaming Billy Martin for a lot of the problems that occurred at times during Mantle's baseball career, Ferguson believed Martin, in his way, may have been good for Mantle. As far back as his second year in pro baseball, at Joplin, Missouri, Mantle had been at the mercy of the big city boys. Lou Skizas once invited Mickey to a party in Joplin. "When he walked in someone punched him in the nose and broke it," said Ferguson, who saw in Skizas, "a minor league Billy Martin."[175] Skizas was described by Cal Neeman, a teammate with the 1950 Joplin Miners, as a cross between the popular movie actor of the day, Farley Granger, for good looks and crooner Vaughn Monroe for his singing ability.[176]

Jim Kenaga

Jim Kenaga was the son and stepson of osteopaths. His mother, Barbara Cooley, was the adopted daughter of "Judge" Cooley, who reportedly had once served as a judge in the court system of Missouri.

Kenaga's father was a graduate of the Kirksville College of Osteopathic Medicine in Missouri. After his dad finished his residency in Mt. Pleasant, Michigan, he moved the family to Hugo, Oklahoma, and set up his medical practice. Kenaga's mother and father divorced shortly afterward.

Mrs. Kenaga returned to Missouri and later married another graduate of the Kirksville school by the name of Pickrell. Dr. Pickrell moved to Baxter Springs, Kansas, where he established his medical practice. According to Jim Kenaga's wife Judy, Jim's grandfather, "Judge" Cooley, had also moved to Baxter Springs by that time. Other than give Barnett a hard time, Kenaga was assigned the duty of keeping his maternal grandfather out of trouble. Judy said that her husband always told her, "Grandpa liked two things a whole lot —alcohol and women." Thus, even as a young man, Kenaga was regularly assigned the task of getting his grandfather out of places that would get him in a whole lot of trouble, bars and hotel rooms.[177]

In 1948, Kenaga's mother died and he stayed with Dr. Pickrell and

---

[175] Ferguson.
[176] Cal Neeman.
[177] Judy Kenaga.

played a lot of baseball and pulled a number of pranks before graduating from Baxter Springs High. According to Baxter Springs historian, Carolyn Dale, "Dr. 'Pick' remarried, a lady by the name of Mary Ann, who was a dance instructor."

After graduation from high school Kenaga enrolled at the University of Arkansas, where he had both a "real good time" and flunked out. After a stint in the Korean War, during which he had spent the bulk of his time stringing communications lines and not being issued a weapon to defend himself, college now appeared to pose no problem. He graduated from Southeastern State College at Durant, Oklahoma, then began a long career in hospital and nursing home administration.[178] Pretty good for old "Spider Man."

The Heavin Family

The Heavin family settled in the mining area of Southeast Kansas after their father, Clarence, moved to Baxter Springs from Edgar Springs in the Ozark region of Missouri. Mr. Heavin had been a blacksmith by trade but the demand for his skill died out shortly after his arrival in "the land of promise."[179]

So Heavin became the night marshal in Baxter Springs. In that role he did a good enough job to be offered the position of chief of police. Although the pay was better than that of a night marshal, Rex said, his dad wouldn't take it because he was a "Christian man" and loved everybody. He surmised that if he took the chief's position he would make some people mad.[180]

Mickey Mantle's father Mutt was a perfectionist in his teaching of Mickey. Rex Heavin couldn't recall that Mutt invested the same amount time and effort into Mickey's younger brothers. He felt that had Mutt been able to dedicate the same time and effort to Ray and Roy, they too might have gone farther than they did in professional baseball.

One hot afternoon before a Whiz Kids game, Rex had his epiphany, and experience which led eventually to his being called into the ministry.[181] He sat on the streetcar track bridge that spanned Spring River at Baxter Springs,

---

[178] Ibid.

[179] Rex Heavin.

[180] Ibid.

[181] The Rev. Heavin enjoyed recalling an old story about a young farmer being called one day by God to preach. He told his father that while working in the fields, "I saw 'P C' written in the clouds." He went on to explain that meant "preach Christ." His father replied, "That wasn't God calling you to preach but rather to plow corn."

watching an Assembly of God baptismal service. He was moved by what he saw. He recalled after the baptism he and his friend Donald Buckner went down and took a swim in their "Sunday best" overalls where the baptismal service had been conducted. At the conclusion of the swim Rex went over to the Whiz Kids game smelling like the "stinky" waters of Spring River. Had Mantle been out practicing sliding into manure pile bases earlier that day, he and Heavin would have made a "smelly pair" that afternoon.

The Heavins were typical patriotic Americans and God-fearing people, a trait that Rex came to feel much of our society has lost. His brother Clarence had been approached to play professional baseball early in the 1940s but out of sense of duty he enlisted in the Army. He went into the Army and during World War II his club at Shepherd Field, Texas,[182] defeated the Cleveland Indians in an exhibition game. That was as close as Clarence ever got to having a baseball career.

Another of Rex's brothers, Hadley, was killed at Pearl Harbor during the Japanese raid. He was on the U.S.S. West Virginia. The only thing Rex has of his late brother's is his Purple Heart. On one of his scavenges with his brother Frog, around 1948, they came upon an old photo in a Baxter Springs alley. Much to the surprise of both, they discovered it was that of their late brother, Hadley. Both were thrilled to have located it. Later a nephew begged to see the photo, and after he left the house and the photo album was checked, the photo was gone. Rex said, "I could have killed him." I guess he didn't else Rex would never have been ordained a minister in the Christian Church.

The conversation turned to Rex's brother, Charles "Frog" Heavin, and how he came upon that nickname. As a three-year-old, he was going to scare his daddy when he came home from work by leaping out from beneath the dinner table. However, his dad spotted him and said, "Come out from under that table, froggie."

"Froggie" pitched the first game the Whiz Kids ever played as members of the Southeast Kansas Ban Johnson League against Coffeyville, Kansas, in 1949. Mantle homered right-handed off Carl Pevehouse, a hard-throwing lefty, and then later turned to the left side, where he had two singles and a triple off Wayne Fitzgerald and Carl Stewart. Stewart, whom most of the Whiz Kids thought was the toughest pitcher they faced, was in his first sea-

---

[182] At Wichita Falls, Texas.

son. He was a Nowata, Oklahoma, native. Frog said that when Mantle hit the homer and triple to start off the 1949 Ban Johnson League season at Coffeyville, the public address announcer said those were the hardest balls ever hit at Walter Johnson Park. That was also the night Mantle was scouted by Tom Greenwade, and that feat resulted in his signing the following Sunday back in Baxter Springs.

It's not known whether Froggie threw many knuckleballs that night, either to the catcher or to his first baseman. But he may well have. Mishler enjoyed recalling that when Frog was pitching and a ball was hit back to him he liked to throw a knuckler — or perhaps a curve ball to the first baseman. That, of course, infuriated Barney, who would yell from the dugout something to the effect, "Just get the man out!"[183]

In addition to being good at athletics, the Heavin family was musically oriented. Rex said that Chet Atkins didn't have a thing over his late guitar-playing brother, Ernest, who died at age 47 due to a mining-related disease. "Frog" had a country band with Jack Cooper that played for dances at Commerce, Miami, Picher and other nearby towns. Two of the "groupies" were Mickey's parents, Mutt and Lovell Mantle. They appeared about anytime the band performed at either a road house or barn dance.[184] And "Frog" recalled that young Mickey loved country music and would accompany his parents to many of the events on Saturday nights. He said Mickey would sit near the bandstand and said many times that he wished he could play guitar, for he loved country music so much.[185]

Frog Heavin eventually went to work for the Kansas Diagnostic and Reception Center for the Department of Corrections in 1965. His brother Rex said, "He was quite a remarkable person. He took many of the corrections department inhabitants — at some risk to himself — to musical events, such as to hear Charley Pride. One evening I visited with him in Topeka and went along."

And when it came to music, Rex Heavin was no slouch himself. Once while serving as the song leader in a revival at Baxter Springs, the preacher conducting the event, Dr. Billy James Hargis, asked Rex how he would like "to become famous." The renowned anti-communist radio evangelist from Tulsa wanted Rex to go on the road with him. The Rev. Hargis promised

---

[183] Rex Heavin.
[184] Ibid.
[185] Charles "Frog" Heavin.

him that he would become what the noted singer George Beverly Shea was to Billy Graham. Rex turned down the offer. Hargis then went to Rex's dad and asked him to convince Rex to "sign on" with his team. Rex's dad asked Hargis what his son had said. Hargis replied, "He doesn't want to do it." Mr. Heavin said, "I guess that you have your answer."

Heavin and this author discussed the voice and general tonal characteristics, and agreed that Billy James Hargis and Rush Limbaugh were quite similar in those respects.

Heavin stayed in the ministry of the Christian Church for the rest of his working days. He retired after having pastored churches in Davenport and Brahman, Oklahoma; Herington, Kansas; and two congregations in Kansas City, Missouri.

Back in 1961, both Heavin and this author were "struggling" to get out of our respective theology schools. He was attending Phillips College at Enid, Oklahoma, and I was pastoring full-time while attending Bethany Nazarene College, located on the western outskirts of Oklahoma City. It happened that we both wound up in Davenport, Oklahoma, at the same time. The ministers in that small central Oklahoma town were Devine, Heavin, Angel and Sinn. I often remarked to them that if I should change the vowel "A" in my last name, Hall, to "E," I would fit nicely into the group.

Many young men had a impact on Mantle's career from an influence and teammate perspective. They never received recognition for that. The following six individuals were there in the formative years of a future Hall of Famer.

Harry Daniels

There was always one pitcher in the area whose services each team sought. The most highly sought hurler of that era in the Tri-State was Harry Daniels from Columbus, Kansas. The team who could pay the most got his services and they usually won as a result of their investment. Many times the more gifted younger men, such as Mickey Mantle, were allowed to play in those "beer games." (When old Barney Barnett was around, he insisted that they ice down some soda pop for the kids like Mantle.)

Daniels served in World War II and upon his release from service the 1946 baseball season was too far gone for him to join the St. Louis Cardinals organization. In 1947 he headed to Houston, Texas, for spring drills. Upon his arrival, he saw hundreds of guys like himself, in their mid-twenties and pursuing a baseball career. He was offered $150 a month to play Class D baseball at Johnson City, Tennessee, but decided to go back home and resume work for Eagle-Picher as a welder, where he was already making more than the Class D minor league salary.

Daniels worked at the "Big Mine" (so named because it was the largest lead and zinc mine in the world) just north of Commerce and was a friend of Mutt Mantle's. Since Daniels had a reputation as quite a pitcher, Mutt had Mickey come out to the mine so that Daniels could throw him his best pitches after Daniels' day shift concluded. His best pitches were two variations of the fastball. The memories Daniels had of the kid were, "He was a poor hitter. He would miss four out of every five balls you threw him. But when he did manage to hit the ball, he had a lot of power for a fifteen-year-old."

Daniels did a lot of pitching for the Columbus, Kansas, town team and started earning the "beer pitcher" designation after his first outing. That was when he beat a team from Oswego, Kansas, on a no-hitter. Moreover, the opposing pitcher was Dick Brown, who had played for the Kansas City Blues of the American Association, one of the highest-level minor leagues, for two seasons during World War II. In eight games for Columbus, Daniels allowed just two runs and won all eight games. That got Barnett's attention. He made Daniels a member of his "other" team, "the Barney Barnett All-Stars," a group of mostly Whiz Kids with some older guys added who had some professional experience. Barnett would take on some of the "hot" semi-pro teams in the area, such as Sulphur Springs or Bentonville, Arkansas, and usually win.[186] Those teams were mostly populated with players from the University of Arkansas.

Calvin Mishler

Calvin Mishler arrived on the Whiz Kid scene three years before Mickey Mantle joined the club.

Mishler and Baxter Springs baseball figure Barney Barnett went back farther than most anyone interviewed for this book. Mishler recalled that in the early part of the 1941 season he was living in the same block as Barnett, who asked him one day if he who wanted to accompany him to the train

---

[186] Harry Daniels.

station to pick up a ballplayer from Northwest[187] Arkansas who was currently enrolled at Kansas State Teachers College, in nearby Pittsburg. Barnett said the new player was going to do some catching for his men's mining team. When the fellow got off the train, Mishler took one look at him and said to himself, "He sure doesn't look like a catcher to me."

Barnett welcomed the new arrival and told him that he would be staying the rest of the summer in the spare bedroom at home. The boy's greatest claim to fame before that was having been a batboy for Rogers, in the old Arkansas-Missouri Class D League. However, within five years of alighting from that train in Baxter Springs, he was in the big leagues, where he spent the next 18 seasons. The catcher who didn't look like a catcher to Mishler was Sherman Lollar.[188]

Mishler brushed elbows later with another future major leaguer when playing for Barnett's Baxter Springs team in the Cardinal Junior League in 1945. His most vivid memory of that season occurred one day in a game against Webb City, Missouri. Cloyd Boyer of Alba, Missouri, was just back from the service and had been persuaded to pitch for Webb City. He didn't have a uniform, just overalls. So, he pitched in street clothes and beat the Whiz Kids that day. Mishler was written up in the local paper[189] as losing the game. He dropped a fly ball in the ninth inning that allowed Webb City to claim victory. Mishler said the ball was hit so high that he misjudged it and it fell without ever being touched.[190]

Barnett, a ground boss at the Foley Mine for Eagle-Picher, got Mishler a job running cable lines. The cables were attached to eleven ore cans. The empty ore cans were lowered into the shaft, loaded, and then pulled out with the other cable.

Mishler eventually attended Northeastern Oklahoma A & M at Miami and roomed with Barney Barnett, Jr. He said, "You haven't roomed until you have experienced rooming with Barney, Jr."

A few years later, Mishler began working the night shift at B. F. Goodrich in Miami, Oklahoma, many years after his Whiz Kids days and Mantle's ascension to the Major Leagues. A number of the guys who worked the night shift with Mishler would drive down from the north, where

---

[187] Mishler.
[188] Ibid.
[189] Ibid.
[190] Ibid.

Commerce was located. At the south end of Commerce and the north end of Miami was a "Y" in the road. When Mantle was with the Yankees and Billy Martin stayed with him during the winter months, Mishler's fellow employees would report on what "the boys," meaning Mantle and Martin, were doing. One night a shift worker reported that Martin was at the beer joint with his fly unzipped and a fight was going to happen before the evening concluded. Mishler said, "It usually did."

Mishler ran into Mantle a number of times around the country when he was in the Army and his former Whiz Kids teammate was with the Yankees. Those games Mishler saw Mantle play for the Yankees were a far cry from those played at such places as Picher, Oklahoma, where games were played on fields completely barren of grass and the outfield was all rock. Often, a single striking that rock became a triple.

One evening during the Korean War, Mishler encountered Mantle at Columbus, Georgia, when the Yankees stopped over for an exhibition game. Mishler was on duty that day and the game was already in progress when his shift of duty concluded. Thus, he missed a few of the early innings. Mantle was playing the outfield and when he headed back to the dugout everyone yelled, "Mick, Mick, Mick." Mishler then tried a trick similar to Ferguson's calling out "Spavinaw" to Mickey in California; Mishler said he resorted to yelling, "Hey, Whiz Kid." Mantle turned and ran over to where he was seated and asked why he ever came to Columbus. Mishler told him he was in the service. After that game Mantle came to where Mishler and his Army buddy were sitting. They talked until the driver of the Yankee bus honked the horn for him to get on board.

Mishler said the Whiz Kids jacket that hung in his closet when he left to serve in the Korean War had been worn by his mother for awhile. She had decided it would look better if she removed the lettering. When he returned from Korea, he was heartsick to see his old jacket without the identifying markings. He kept it a few more years before throwing it into a yard sale. He said that the stitching outline was still visible and some fellow seeing what it was picked it up immediately.

Every Whiz Kid was given a brown cap with "WK" in gold lettering that signified he was a Whiz Kid. The jacket was maroon with gray sleeves with "Whiz Kids" in white lettering.

Mishler's love of baseball continued through his life. He coached Little League baseball for forty-nine years. He said he saw a lot of "hitters." One who attracted his attention was a little guy who was always at the ballpark hitting golf balls longer and straighter than anyone. He would hit the balls and his father would chase them down. The little guy turned out to be a well-known golfer by the name of Hale Irwin.

Mishler had the fervor of an evangelist when he talked about baseball. He said the Whiz Kids played or practiced at every opportunity. He recalled one time when one of his Little League teams was worried about having new uniforms. He told them of a teammate whose pants didn't match his shirt and who wore an old glove that was barely useable. He informed the kids he thought the guy made it to a New York team and if he wasn't mistaken, he thought it was the Yankees. He even guessed a little further and surmised it might have been Mickey Mantle. In fact, he was sure it was Mantle. The kids got the point.[191]

Wylie Pitts

Pitts' tenure with the Whiz Kids went back to 1945. He was the team's centerfielder when Mantle was its shortstop. Pitts recalled that one day Mantle said he wanted to play centerfield. Pitts said he thought he would like to take a shot at shortstop. One evening the pair talked Barnett into letting them switch positions. Pitts said he nearly killed the first baseman with his throws from shortstop. "It was a disaster. Mickey couldn't play the outfield and I couldn't play shortstop. So, Mantle went back to shortstop and I returned to centerfield after an unsuccessful experiment," Pitts said.

---

[191] Wylie Pitts.

Pitts was signed to a professional contract in 1947 by Tom Greenwade. He was immediately sent to the Yankees' Class D farm club at McAlester, Oklahoma, of the Sooner State League. He played 19 games before returning to Riverton, Kansas, and resuming his career with the Whiz Kids. By 1948 he had become too old to participate in the Cardinal Junior league, and he spent his time playing for the Barney Barnett All-Stars.

That same year he also played for a semi-pro team in Arkansas, the Bentonville Blues. That club played just about anyone available, from the University of Arkansas and House of David clubs to the Kansas City Monarchs of the Negro League. Shortly before Satchel Paige signed with the Cleveland Indians, the Monarchs were in Bentonville and were beaten by the Blues.

Pitts, while playing in Arkansas, was spotted by a Shreveport, Louisiana, "bird dog," Charlie Craig, a Bentonville real estate developer. "Bird dog" was the term used to describe someone who kept an eye on the talent in his area, then passed along reports to a scout for a particular major league organization.

Pitts was assigned to Shreveport, managed by Salty Parker in the AA Texas League. He recalled being "the thirteenth outfielder" on the team. After one episode of batting practice he was told to hit the ball, then round the bases. A left-handed slugger was up next and, as Pitts rounded first, the slugger hit a line-drive which connected with his left temple. Pitts was "out cold" for five hours. Instead of prompt medical attention and a trip to the hospital, he was placed in the clubhouse by Shreveport officials until he was able to make it out under his own power. That was minor league baseball, U.S.A., circa 1950.

During a round of outfield drills, Pitts was thirteenth in line. After all the outfielders but Pitts had taken their chances at snaring fly balls, Parker called off the drills. Pitts, very unhappy, asked Parker about not being able to prove himself. "Don't worry about it," Parker replied. The next day Pitts was on his way to Alexandria, demoted to the Evangeline League, another of those short stays that so many aspiring ballplayers endured in the years just after World War II. It was said in that period that minor league organizations had three teams: one going out, one on the field and another headed in that direction to replace the current team. In the "hey day" of Class D and C teams, it wasn't unusual for a roster of 16-18 players to have a yearly turnover of fifty players.

The highlight of that season was a game Alexandria played against an all-female team called "The Jax Beer Girls."[192] He admitted that the Alexandria club couldn't keep up with the ladies. Wistfully, Pitts said, "If I were starting my career again, I would start in fast-pitch softball. If you can hit that ball, you can hit anywhere."

By the time Mantle had made it to the Major Leagues, Pitts was in the Air Force. On the ascension of Mantle to the Yankees' roster, Pitts sent him a letter of congratulations from a Navy cruiser. While still in the service of his country, someone sent him an autographed baseball of another former Baxter Springs Whiz Kid, Ralph Terry. Pitts recalled, "I threw it once against a wall and it went through the plaster board and I never saw it again."

After returning to the United States, Pitts went to Baxter Springs and coached a kid who could hit a golf ball with the same authority with which Mantle had stroked a baseball a few short years previous. The young man was Hale Irwin, who later became a frequent winner on the Professional Golf Association tour.[193]

The love of the game of baseball ran deep into the very fiber of those Baxter Springs Whiz Kids. When Pitts was asked if he ever thought much about Mantle making it to the big leagues, he replied, "No, we were all too busy worrying about our own careers."[194]

Buddy Ball

Buddy Ball was a native of Riverton, Kansas, and a prime example of the type of guys Barney Barnett sought as he toured the small towns of Southeast Kansas, Northeast Oklahoma and Northwest Arkansas. His philosophy was that since most high schools didn't have baseball programs, he would grab the best athletes to play for the Whiz Kids. He felt that if the talent was there with regard to speed and arm strength, he could teach most boys the fundamentals of hitting and fielding.

Ball said years later he was a terrible player. However, Barnett saw that the young man from Riverton had one outstanding asset, he was fleet of foot. Ball said he could steal bases, bunt and run but couldn't hit the curve. He acknowledged he couldn't have played for many teams but Barnett knew where he could help the Whiz Kids. Ball shared the second base slot with

---

[192] Wylie Pitts.

[193] Ibid.

[194] Ibid.

Ferguson. The infield for the "Kids" in 1948 was Bill Johnson, third base; Mickey Mantle, shortstop; Buddy Ball and Nick Ferguson, second base; and Delbert Lovelace, first base.

After graduating from Riverton High School in 1949, Ball enrolled at Kansas State Teachers College in Pittsburg, Kansas. He coached at Joplin, Missouri, Junior College, then succeeded Jack Hartman as head basketball coach at Coffeyville, Kansas, Junior College, when Hartman left to coach Southern Illinois University at Carbondale. Ball coached in "Javatown" for seven years, then five years at Eastern New Mexico University.

Lon Farrell, a friend of Ball's at the University of Arkansas, ran[195] the athletic department for Frank Broyles, the athletic director. Lon encouraged Buddy to come over and meet the football coach, Lou Holtz. Ferrell assured Ball that he would really like the man. When Ball visited the Razorback campus, he and Holtz began to develop a mutual admiration. Buddy became Holtz's recruiting coordinator. That job lasted five years until Broyles fired Holtz.

After Holtz was fired at Arkansas, he had the Minnesota Golden Gopher job in 10 days. He asked Ball and two others to make the move to the "Land of 10,000 Lakes" with him. Buddy said, "They had a lot of money up there, so I went for two years, saved my money then headed to Duncan, Oklahoma, where my daughter lived."

With his life's savings from coaching he set up Bud's Easy Shop Car Wash and Quick Lube in Duncan.[196] Bud ran the business for 17 years, made a lot of money and retired in 1997.

Bill Mosley

The contact between Mickey Mantle and Bill Mosley was rather special, and remained so even after Commerce school days when they were teammates in football and basketball. They double-dated. Mickey went to see Bill play college football in Kansas at Fort Scott and Pittsburg. Mosley went to see Mantle perform in both the minor and major leagues.

One such visit to a minor league game was after Mantle had been sent down in 1951 during his first season with the New York Yankees to their top minor league team, the Kansas City Blues. He had asked Mosley and his wife Neva to join him in Kansas City for a series while Mosley was attending Fort

---

[195] Buddy Ball.
[196] Ibid.

Scott Junior College. Mosley recalled, "Mickey said he would leave tickets. Before the game I got to sit in the Blues dugout. After the game I saw more food than I had ever seen."

Harold Youngman, who had sponsored the Southwest Chat Company amateur basketball team, on which Mantle and Mosley had played during their school years, "took Merlyn and Mickey and Neva and I out to the Riverside Club. They threw food and drink at us, the likes we had never seen before. I estimated that outing must have cost Youngman a thousand dollars when a thousand was a lot of money," recalled Mosley. Harold Youngman sponsored the Southwest Chat Company amateur team that Mickey coached after joining the Yankees. Mosley played a number of times on that basketball team but was more in awe of how Mantle could have performed the next day following that huge meal. But he did, and for "toppers" it was a double-header.[197]

PHOTO COURTESY OF CASS BARNETT

Harold Youngman, on left, and Mantle, on right, during one of their many hunting trips. Youngman was Mantle's financial advisor, even though much of the advice was rejected. According to those who knew Mantle, it was understood that wise investments weren't his strong suit.

[197] Mosley.

After the Korean War, Mantle and Mosley's paths didn't cross as often. In the early part of the 1980s, Mantle was invited to be the special guest of the opening of a Dillon's Super Market in Topeka, Kansas. By that time Mosley had established himself as a winning football coach at Seaman High School in Topeka. Before going to the store to sign his autograph for the "adoring" fans, Mosley said, Mantle stopped by his school and spent about three hours. As Mosley recalled, "Everybody wanted an autograph and Mickey told me to take down all their names." After much urging, Mosley told Mantle that he had better hurry or he would be late for the super market's grand opening. Mantle replied, "Aw, I'll just work a couple of hours overtime."

PHOTO COURTESY OF LEE DODSON

Mantle signs photos for the throng at a Topeka grocery store grand opening. The lady on the right is the late Kathleen Dodson, whose husband was a minor league hurler in the Yankee organization. He once struck out Joe DiMaggio on three consecutive pitches in an exhibition game in 1947.

Mosley recalled that when he accompanied Mantle to his car that day, his former teammate took the time to sign a personal note to everyone who had requested his autograph at Seaman High. Mosley said that Mantle seemed to love the time spent at the school and especially enjoyed one student who asked, "Did you play with Babe Ruth?"

During that visit to Topeka, Mantle invited Mosley to play in his golf tourney at Loma Linda[198] the following spring. Mosley explained that he had to be in Topeka late that Sunday, so Mantle arranged the pairing so that Mosley could play early both Saturday and Sunday and get home in time to go about his regular duties on Monday at the school. He felt that Mantle went out of his way to accommodate him, and appreciated that coming from an old friend who had hit the big time. What remained as Mosley's fondest memory of Mantle was that he was well-liked by everybody and he never cut a teammate with an unkind word.[199]

Bill Pace

One Whiz Kid came out of Treece, Kansas, the same place where Mickey Mantle's future wife, Merlyn, lived for a number of years. Bill Pace was a 1948-49 teammate of Mantle's on the Whiz Kids. After part of one season of professional baseball with Miami, Oklahoma, of the KOM League, he entered college, then went on to a coaching career at the University of Georgia under Wally Butts, before getting the head coaching position with Vanderbilt University.

Delbert Lovelace recalled that Pace was a "handsome dude" and that attribute helped him immensely in his recruiting duties when he was hired at Georgia. Someone else also thought Bill was a good-looking guy. Merlyn said that when she was a young girl in the Treece school system, Pace was the "big athlete" and that she had a crush on him long before she ever met Mickey.

While at Vanderbilt, Pace did what that few men have accomplished lately with that football program—he won;[200] at least, he won more than Commodore fans had experienced for awhile or since. His most notable accomplishment as head football coach there from 1967 until 1972 was guiding the Commodores to a 5-4-1 record in 1968 — one of the few winning seasons for the school in the last half-century — and he'll always be remembered by Vanderbilt faithful for one game in particular: a stunning 14-10 victory over Bear Bryant's Alabama Crimson Tide in 1969.

While attempting to rejuvenate the football fortunes at Vanderbilt, Pace

---

[198] Loma Linda is a small elite community centered around a golf course. Developers thought that if Mickey and Merlyn Mantle lived there, it would turn out to be a mecca for golf and other social events.

[199] Mosley.

[200] In the 15 years before Pace, Vanderbilt had five winning seasons. In the first 30 years after his departure, there were three winning years.

as athletic director also pushed for the re-establishment of baseball as a part of the school's sports program. Vanderbilt became very successful, winning the Southeast Conference championship on one occasion. Unfortunately, Pace died of a heart attack in a Nashville restaurant while having his morning coffee in 1992.

13

1949: A Contract Is Signed

Following the sequence of events when Mickey Mantle signed his first baseball contract was one of the more difficult tasks of writing this book. The account that Mantle gives in an early book[201] about his life doesn't match up according to day and date. Referring to Tom Greenwade, the New York Yankee scout, this is a quote from Mantle's 1953 book, appropriately titled

Mantle wore this suit for his 1949 graduation photo. However, the night of his graduation he was wearing his Baxter Springs Whiz Kids uniform in a game at Coffeyville, Kansas.

The Mickey Mantle Story: "Greenwade told Dad he had time to size me up on Friday night, May 16, 1949. Baxter Springs was scheduled to play at Coffeyville. That was fine

PHOTO COURTESY OF BOBBIE CRAMPTON

---

[201] Mickey Mantle, as told to Ben Epstein, *The Mickey Mantle Story* (New York: Henry Holt and Company Inc., 1953), 29.

except for one thing — I was scheduled to graduate from high school that night and already had scratched myself from the line-up."

The biggest problem with that date as it appeared in Mantle's book is that it contradicts the Gregorian calendar. May 16 was on Monday in 1949. Regrettably, many of the early books written about Mantle, as well as his own recollections in later life don't match what has been documented through the various news sources of that era. Researching the best information available today revealed that, most likely, this was the sequence of events that led to Mantle signing his first professional baseball contract, which was dated June 13, 1949.[202]

It was on Friday, May 27 — not May 16— when Greenwade watched Mantle play for Baxter Springs and get four hits in five at-bats during a 13-7 win at Coffeyville, Kansas. Greenwade decided that weekend to offer Mantle a professional contract and, two days later, Mickey and his father Mutt signed a provisional contract with the Yankees in Baxter Springs, where the Whiz Kids beat Alba, Missouri, 6-4, that day. After playing in two more games with the Whiz Kids, on June 3 and 5 and a practice game on June 6, Mantle reported sometime before June 11 to a training camp the New York Yankees operated at Branson, Missouri.[203] On June 13 Mantle reported to the Yankees' Independence, Kansas minor league club, which was playing a series at Chanute, Kansas. The next day he played his first professional game.

Let's look more closely at that spring of 1949, when Mickey Mantle closed out his amateur baseball career and entered the ranks of the professionals. While Tom Greenwade, who achieved and deserved a reputation as an uncommonly successful baseball scout, is given the credit for Mantle's discovery by professional baseball historians, there well may be an unsung hero in the tale who played at least as significant a role.

What put Greenwade in the stands at Coffeyville that night to watch Mickey Mantle evidently was the work of a former Yankee ballplayer-turned-scout, Johnny Sturm. In the summer of 1946, Sturm recalled, he was just beginning his work as a scout and went to Joplin, Missouri, where he had begun his baseball career as a player in 1936. When he got there he started asking around as to the best young ballplayers in the area. By 1948

---

[202] *The Independence Daily Reporter*, Aug. 15, 1995, a reproduction of the contract. On Aug. 14, 1995, *The Reporter* printed a copy of Mantle's $1,150 bonus check.

[203] *The Joplin Globe*, June 11, 1949.

the word that started coming to him was Mickey Mantle of Commerce, Oklahoma. That name was not wasted on Sturm and he kept it in mind. Sturm helped Greenwade with tryout camps the rest of 1946 and in 1947, then became manager of the Joplin Miners in 1948. He recalled picking up *The Joplin Globe* during the remainder of Mickey's high school years; often, the paper carried stories about the home runs Mantle was hitting for the Baxter Springs Whiz Kids during the summer.

Among Sturm's friends was a fireman from Joplin who was umpiring in the Southeast Kansas Ban Johnson League, in which the Whiz Kids played. Early in the 1949 season, Sturm asked the umpire to let Mantle know that he wanted him to come to Joplin and try out with the Miners. There was some risk involved, for Mickey had not as yet graduated from high school and thus couldn't be signed to a contract, under the laws of organized baseball.

As Sturm recalled, "Mickey shows up the next day with his glove and shoes. I said, 'C'mon, kid, put on the uniform.'"[204] Mickey and his father Mutt had driven to Joplin with Mickey's friend Delbert Lovelace. Lovelace had been asked if he would like to go along with the Mantles, was delighted at the invitation and accepted. He said he positioned himself next to Mutt as they watched Mickey take some swings. He recalled that Mutt sat there for awhile and then "with great pride said, to me, 'I have waited for this for 17 years. It is a dream come true.'" Then, as if to emphasize that his memory was clear on that moment, Lovelace declared, "That is the gospel truth that Mutt uttered those words."[205]

Sturm, still recalling that day, said, "When Mantle got dressed and out on the field Paul Tretiak was at bat and I told him to let this kid hit. I told Mantle to hit five balls to right field, and five to left field. When those ten hits were finished I told him to bunt and run until he reached third base."

Sturm said Mantle "hit liners to left and right and he opened a lot of eyes. He ran from first to third and he did it as fast as anyone on the team. I had Al Pilarcik in the outfield, who was a track star back home, and Mantle was every bit as fast as Al." It was his speed and his arm that got all the attention.[206] Mantle's cousin, Jimmy Richardson, attributed the speed to running to the outhouse and back. "You froze to death in the winter and the flies ate you alive in the summer, so you had to get out

[204] Johnny Sturm.

[205] Delbert Lovelace.

[206] Sturm.

there and back in a hurry," Richardson said.[207]

The next test Sturm gave the young Mantle was a fielding trial. "I got a fungo [bat] and sent him to shortstop," Sturm said. "He fielded grounders for four or five minutes and then I called him in and talked about his fielding. I told him that he went into the hole and behind second for balls but he did so with a decided limp."

Mantle replied, "That is because of the osteomyelitis I got from a shin injury in football."

Sturm then told Mantle, "You can't play shortstop or second base in pro ball because the runners would always be going for the shins and you couldn't do the job. With your speed you'd better be in center field, where you can run down everything that is hit out there."

Sturm said he recalled vividly what happened after that encounter. "I went into a little office behind home plate and called Lee McPhail at the Yankees' home office in New York. I told him I had just seen the best damn prospect of my life. He can run like hell, he has a great arm, he can hit from both sides and he can hit with power," Sturm said.

The message Sturm had for McPhail was to get Greenwade down there and sign the kid. As Sturm recalled, the tryout was on a Tuesday and Mantle didn't graduate until that Thursday. However, his memory probably failed him here; as best as could be determined, Mantle's high school class graduated on a Friday, May 27.[208] Sturm's Joplin Miners were about to make a road trip to St. Joseph, Missouri, so he urged Mantle to "Hide out until I get my team back to Joplin." Sturm assured Mantle that Greenwade would be there to sign him upon the Miners' return.

Sturm was greatly worried about signing Mantle promptly and knew that Whiz Kids patriarch Barney Barnett Sr. and Joe Becker, a scout for the Boston Red Sox, were close friends. In the 1948 team photo of the Whiz Kids Becker is standing next to Mantle. Sturm told McPhail of the Yankee front office was "If you don't sign Mantle, Joe Becker is going to sign him to a Red Sox contract."

When the Miners returned to Joplin, Greenwade was there. He was in a surly mood, according to Sturm. His first comment to him, Sturm said, was,

---

[207] Jimmy Richardson.

[208] LaFalier, who married the sister of Mickey Mantle's wife, and Ivan Shouse of Commerce, Okla., interviews. Both men graduated from Commerce High School that night and agree as to the date, which was printed on their diplomas, which they still had when interviewed.

"What the hell, you want me to get fired?" Sturm countered with, "I called McPhail so the Yankees could sign him before someone else did." Greenwade retorted, "I've seen that kid and he ain't worth a shit."[209] Of course, that was a case of jurisdictional bureaucratic defensiveness at its zenith. Greenwade knew Mantle had talent, but was not sure where it could best be utilized. He also knew the rules, that he couldn't sign Mantle until his high school class had graduated.

For a couple of days after Sturm and the Miners returned from St. Joseph, Mantle was nowhere to be found. Obviously, he had heeded Sturm's plea to "hide out." However, Sturm was a little worried that his "find" might have gone to some other organization for a tryout. But a couple of days later, Mantle contacted him. When Sturm asked him where he had been Mantle replied, "Me and a buddy went to see a Browns game." Sturm asked how he got there, fearing the Browns had contacted him and invited him to St. Louis. Mantle replied, "We hitchhiked."

According to Sturm's account, Mantle was playing a game in the Southeast Kansas Ban Johnson League for the Baxter Springs Whiz Kids against the Coffeyville club a couple of days after his return from the Browns game. Sturm told Greenwade, "Go over and sign him, and I don't care what you think."[210] As Sturm mused, "Tom goes over there to sign Mickey and it rained the game out and he didn't sign him that day."[211]

When Mantle was finally signed, Sturm said that Greenwade also had to throw in a "little extra" for a used car for Mickey's dad Mutt.

In his heart Sturm said he knew he was the one person who had carried the ball in getting the Yankees to give Mantle a shot at the game. He was the one who harassed, and in Greenwade's mind, even went over his head, to get Mantle signed to a Yankee contract. After many years of reading and hearing how Greenwade had discovered Mantle, Sturm could take it no longer. He wrote Mantle a letter that contained these words, "I think you forgot me and my part in getting you signed." Sturm said he never got a reply to that letter. However, at the 25th anniversary of Sturm's becoming a Yankee he

---

[209] Johnny Sturm.

[210] Ibid.

[211] If so, then Greenwade must have gone to see Mantle play before May 27. It was a particularly wet spring in the Tri-State that year. It is known, however, from all accounts, that Greenwade was at both the May 27 and May 29 games when Mantle played for the Whiz Kids. As noted a bit further on, it rained hard at the end of the May 29 game, which may be what Sturm was recalling. However, no Whiz Kid games were rained out that weekend of May 27-29.

was at Yankee Stadium. He recalled that Mantle was there and came up to him and said, "John, I owe you a hell of a lot." At that moment Sturm felt a measure of vindication for the recognition that he felt had been so long denied him.[212]

An unbiased observer of the entire situation was longtime minor and major league teammate of Mantle's, Bob Wiesler. "I know Tom Greenwade got all the credit" for signing Mantle, "but Johnny Sturm, the 1949 Joplin manager, was the guy always telling Greenwade to sign him."[213]

Checking the pages of local newspapers published that spring of 1949 was particularly revealing as to Mickey Mantle's activities during this important point of his life and career. *The Joplin* (Mo.) *Globe* in particular followed closely the activities of amateur baseball in its trade territory — Southwest Missouri, Northeast Oklahoma, Southeast Kansas and Northwest Arkansas. That paper and others in the area documented that Mickey Mantle played with Baxter Springs in several non-league games against the semi-pro team of Joplin candy maker Sunny Jim's, two semi-pro teams, the Commerce Merchants (the renamed Eagle-Picher mining company team) and the Coffeyville Boosters, and Miami Junior College (Northeastern Oklahoma) before beginning regular season play in their new league, the Southeast Kansas Ban Johnson League.

The Whiz Kids lost each of the several practice games they played that spring against Joplin's, Sunny Jim's semi-pro team. The Joplin lineup consisted of a few young men who already had experience in professional baseball at the Class D level, the most prominent being Travis Kunce, who had spent two seasons with Miami, Oklahoma, in the KOM League.

On April 25 they played a practice game with Alba, a team from the league the Whiz Kids were joining that year, and lost. On May 5 they whipped Miami Junior College, 14-5, in the game in which Mantle hit home runs from different sides of home plate in two successive at-bats against an older pitcher, Max Buzzard, who had a couple of years of minor league experience.

Three other practice games are recorded before the Whiz Kids began regular-season play in the Ban Johnson league. The games were victories against the Commerce Merchants on May 18[214] and two games against the Coffeyville Boosters, a semi-pro team of older men, which the Kids beat

---

[212] Sturm.

[213] Bob Wiesler.

[214] *The Baxter Springs Citizen*, May 19, 1949.

13-6 on May 22 in Baxter Springs and 8-2 on May 25 at Coffeyville.

By 1949 the Eagle-Picher mining company team that had produced a number of fine baseball players moved to Mantle's hometown of Commerce and been renamed the Commerce Merchants. The team, which at one time had featured Guy Froman, who played many years at a high level in the minors, had a number of older players including a battery of Elmer Peacock and Roy Buffalo. Later that year, both of these Native Americans signed professional contracts and joined the nearby Miami Owls of the KOM League.

"Baxter boys defeat Coffeyville Boosters, a Negro team 13-6," *The Joplin Globe* reported, after the May 22 contest.[215] Three days later, *The Coffeyville Journal* reported, "Just to prove their 13-6 victory over the veteran Coffeyville semi-pro club at Baxter last Sunday was no fluke, Hans Wagner-like Barney Barnett brought his hustling young Whiz Kids squad to Forest Park last night where they turned in a business-like 8-2 triumph on a nifty 3-hitter by 20-year-old, Frog Heavin."[216]

By this second game against the Boosters, Mantle was becoming the focus of attention. The Coffeyville paper said "Mantle, the slickest looking kid ball player seen on the local pond in the postwar era, slashed a line drive home run down the right field line in the seventh."[217]

The sweep of two games against the older Boosters team got the notice of the Coffeyville Refiners, the reigning Ban Johnson champions. In fact, the two wins came as a shock to all baseball experts in Southeast Kansas, who hadn't thought the Whiz Kids were that good.

These practice games against good local teams, some of them loaded with older players, including some who had some professional experience, set the table for an interesting 1949 regular season as the Kids began play in their new league. And Mickey Mantle's widening reputation was making the Kids even more of a conversation piece in the region than usual.

That Friday evening, May 27, was when things began to fall into place for Mantle to begin his professional baseball career. First, it was the night that Mantle's high school class of 1949 was holding graduation exercises.[218] Graduation meant he now was eligible, under the rules of professional base-

---

[215] *The Joplin* (Mo.) *Globe*, May 23, 1949.

[216] *The Coffeyville Daily Journal*, May 26, 1949.

[217] Ibid.

[218] LaFalier and Shouse.

ball, to sign a contract. Second, as was almost certainly known to Mickey and his parents, the New York Yankees' famed scout, Tom Greenwade, was going to be at the game in Coffeyville to see Mickey play. But what to do about the conflict? Probably, the Mantles didn't give the matter a second thought; Mickey skipped his high school graduation exercises.[219]

The game at Coffeyville meant more to the Mantles than anyone else that evening with the possible exception of Greenwade. Delbert Lovelace recalled, "Regarding the game played in Coffeyville, I really cannot recall the specifics. I do think we were all aware of a scout being in the crowd and I can remember how hard Mick hit the ball. At this time, it seems everything he hit was hard. Balls, hit on the ground, even, were intimidating for most of the infielders at that level of play. I don't recall if the game went the full route, but I do know it started raining hard as we were getting ready to pack and go home."[220]

The Coffeyville Journal was well aware that Greenwade was on the "trail" of Mantle that night. The *Journal* sportswriter interviewed Greenwade after the game and there was evidence that he had his eye on more than the young Commerce prospect. The Journal reported, "Tom Greenwade, who is watching Baxter shortstop Mickey Mantle, still can't understand how centerfielder Wylie Pitts had failed to stick with Independence[221] in the KOM League in 1947. After watching Pitts get on base six times via a pair of triples, two singles, a hit batsman and a base on balls, Coffeyville fans can't either. He hit 4 for 4, totaling eight bases, scored four runs and stole five bases."[222]

Years later, Pitts recalled, the *Journal* sportswriter wasn't the only one who was aware of Greenwade's presence in the stands that night. All the Whiz Kids knew of it, he said. And Pitts, in particular, was aware of the scout's presence because of having been signed to that Yankee contract two years before.[223]

Five of the eleven Baxter boys who played that evening wound up in professional baseball: Mantle, Pitts, Bennie Lee, Bill Pace and Jim Kenaga. And

---

[219] Mosley.

[220] Delbert Lovelace.

[221] *The Coffeyville Daily Journal*, May 28, 1949. Either Greenwade or the *Journal* sportswriter had his wires crossed; Pitts didn't play at Independence in 1947 but rather at McAlester, Oklahoma, in the Sooner State League.

[222] *The Coffeyville Daily Journal*, May 28, 1949.

[223] Pitts.

Coffeyville's pitcher Carl Pevehouse wound up in the Class D KOM League before ending his baseball career.

"Both teams started with left-handed pitchers." *The Joplin Globe* reported. [Bob] Kenaga for the Whiz Kids allowed only three hits in six innings. Mantle and Lee both got home runs in the eighth [inning] for Baxter."[224] Overall, besides hitting a home run in his first game in the tougher Ban Johnson league, Mantle also hit a double and two singles in five at-bats. The homer was while batting right-handed against the Coffeyville starter, Pevehouse; a hard-throwing left-hander, while Mantle's other hits were while batting left-handed against right-handers, Tom Fitzgerald and Carl Stewart.[225] Charles "Frog" Heavin, who played third base in the game for the Whiz Kids, said that when Mantle hit the homer and the double the public address announcer said those were the hardest balls ever hit at Walter Johnson Park.[226]

Here's how *The Coffeyville Journal* reported the game the next day:

Baxter Batters Bash Bans 13-7
In SEK Ban Johnson Loop Bow

When SEK Ban Johnson League fathers dragged Barney Barnett's Whiz Kids into the tottering Beejay circuit there were numerous eyebrows raised in loop strongholds. If the Whiz Kids perform in other SEK centers like they performed here Friday night, there will be more than eyebrows raised. Combining the effective 7-hit pitching of southpaw Jim Kenaga and righthander Bob Steele with a sustained 16-hit attack that was good for 27 bases, Barney's Baxter boys pounded out a decisive 13 to 7 victory over the defending champion Coffeyville Refiners.

The [Coffeyville] Bans who showed little infield skill and puny power were no surprise to co-pilots Bill Brant and Wes Temple who winced after starter, Carl Pevehouse, who had worked neatly for seven frames, was shelled from the ridge by a seven run barrage in the eighth. Scheduled to open the Beejay campaign at Parsons tonight Cliff Clay's Blues, Brant and Temple learned things Friday night that their three hastily pulled-off practices had failed to reveal.

With only three players back from last year's SEK and Kansas pennant squad, the Refiners could hardly have been expected to display championship form—which they didn't. The pitching was adequate seven-ninths of the way, the hitting and fielding not below opening par.

---

[224] *The Joplin Globe*, May 28, 1949.

[225] *The Coffeyville Daily Journal* and *The Joplin Globe*, both May 28, 1949.

[226] Charles Heavin.

11 Straight Strikouts

Pevehouse, who personally accounted for the first eleven putouts via the strikeout route, didn't get the same defensive and offensive backing that Baxter supplied for southpaw Jim Kenaga. In fact, Peve and the backstop Jerry Page had to go it alone for 3 2/3 innings.

A hit batsman, a base on balls and three straight strikeouts constituted the Whiz Kids first inning batting stint. Peve walked the leadoff man in the second then sent three more batsmen down on strikes. Successive singles by Wylie Pitts, Mickey Mantle and Frog Heavin broke the scoring ice in the third before the strong-armed lefthander whiffed three straight batters. The first two hits would have been handled by an alert defense.

An infield boot inserted between a pair of strikeouts, Pitts' triple and a single by Mantle accounted for two unearned runs in the fourth. Successive singles by [Delbert] Lovelace, [Bill] Pace and Joe Daniel with two down in the fifth added Baxter's fourth tally. Baxter scored two more in the sixth, went down in the seventh and sent Pevehouse to the showers with two homers, a triple and single with one away in the eighth. [Author's note: The box score shows those runs being scored in the seventh inning.]

An error, two safeties and a pair of walks off reliever Tom Fitzgerald didn't help any and Carl Stewart, a yearling righthander from Nowata [Oklahoma] went the rest of the way.

Passes by Dub Berry and Bill Goodson, Page's bunt and a 2-run single by Pete Edwards in the fourth had put the Refiners with striking distance—2 to 3. They added a single tally in the seventh on two passes, some base thefts and battery miscues; used singles by Page and Stewart with some more bobbles and walks for a run in the eighth; and finished off with three scores on a walk, an error, Bill Goodson's double and another single by Stewart in the ninth.

BAXTER	AB	R	H	PO	A	E
Pitts cf	4	4	4	2	0	0
Mantle ss	5	2	4	3	0	2
Heavin 3b	6	1	2	2	1	1
Lee lf	5	1	1	2	1	0
Harbaugh 2b	5	1	0	1	2	0
Lovelace 1b	4	2	1	4	1	0
Pace rf	3	0	1	2	0	1
Myers rf	2	0	0	0	0	0
Daniel c	6	2	2	11	1	0
Kenaga p	4	0	0	0	1	0
Steele p	2	0	1	0	0	0
TOTALS	46	13	16	27	7	4

REFINERS	AB	R	H	PO	A	E
Burton 1b	2	0	0	0	0	2
Bilby 2b	1	0	0	1	0	0
Gamble 1b	1	1	0	0	0	1
Berry lf ss	3	2	1	3	2	0
Goodson 3b	3	2	1	1	1	0
Page c	3	1	1	16	0	1
Pevehouse p	3	0	0	0	0	0
Fitzgerald p	0	0	0	0	0	0
Stewart p	2	0	2	0	0	0
Edwards ss	3	0	1	0	2	2
Bartlett lf	2	0	0	0	0	0
Long rf cf	4	0	0	0	1	0
Patterson rf	1	1	0	0	0	0
Kauffman 1b	4	0	1	6	1	0
TOTALS	32	7	7	27	7	6

Scores by innings:

Baxter.........................001 212 700 – 13

Refiners....................000 200 113 – 7

[NOTE: It is believed the seven runs were scored in the eighth inning.]

The Coffeyville club that the Whiz Kids faced in 1949 had been the National Ban Johnson League champions in 1947. Many of those fellows, including Carl Pevehouse, seen in the second row, far right, were on that club. Pete New, front row, second from left, eventually pitched against Mantle during the 1949 KOM League season and held him pretty much in check.

Summary:

RBI—Heavin, Pitts, Edwards 2, Daniel 2, Mantle 2, Lee 2, Steele, Bartlett 2, Goodson 2. **2B**—Mantle, Goodson. **3B**—Pitts 2. **HR**—Mantle, Lee. **SAC**—Page. **SB**—Pitts 5, Berry, Lovelace, Edwards, Heavin, Goodson, Long, Harbaugh. **DP**—Lee, Daniels, Heavin. **LOB**—Baxter 14. Refiners 7. **ER**—Baxter 9. Refiners 3. **SO**—by Kenaga 7, Pevehouse 14, Stewart 1, Steele 4. **BB**—off Kenaga 4, Pevehouse 1. Fitzgerald 2, Stewart 3, Steele 4. **Hits off**—Kenaga 3 for 2 runs in 6 Innings. Pevehouse 14 for 10 runs in 7 innings. Fitzgerald 2 for 3 runs In 1/3 innings. Steele 0 for 0 runs in 1 2/3 innings. Steele 4 for 5 runs in 3 innings. **HBP**—by Pevehouse (Pitts). **WP**—Pevehouse, Steele, Fitzgerald, Stewart 3. **PB**—Daniel 2. Winner Kenaga. **Loser**—Pevehouse. **Umpires**: Crawford-Crowell. **Time**—2:40.[227]

---

[227] *The Coffeyville Daily Journal*, May 28, 1949.

Earlier in the day that Friday when Tom Greenwade was checking out Mantle (and others) for the Yankees in Coffeyville, another shortstop in the Johnson league, Ken Boyer of Alba, signed with the St. Louis Cardinals.[228] Boyer's older brother Cloyd was at the time playing with the Cardinals' Triple-A minor league team at Rochester, New York. Cloyd also pitched a few innings in the major leagues that year, his first year with the Cardinals, before winning a spot with the St. Louis team the next season. A younger brother Clete later also played in the major leagues. But the weekend was to become even more memorable for the Ban Johnson League, just two days later.

On Sunday, May 29, at Baxter Springs, the Yankees' Greenwade told Mickey and his father Mutt that Mickey would be given a contract to play in the Yankee organization. This occurred just after the Whiz Kids had played their home opener in their new league, beating Alba, 6-4. Wylie Pitts recalled vividly, more than a half-century later, the night the Yankees signed Mantle. In his memory it was a surreal scene similar to that of the movie *The Natural*, when Robert Redford was running the bases after hitting the movie's climactic home run. Redford's homer had sailed high into the lights, which were exploding as if they were fireworks. Pitts said that as the Whiz Kids' game against Alba was concluding, it began to rain very hard. This caused some of the lights at Baxter Springs to burst and more would have done the same shortly, had the power not been shut off to save them. Meantime, seated in Tom Greenwade's car, Mutt and Mickey Mantle received the good news: the Yankees would sign Mickey to a professional baseball contract. Boom, pow, crash went the lights. More than a half-century later, Pitts swore it happened just that way.[229]

The next weekend, the Kids played at Alba, Missouri, that Friday, June 3 (results unknown), then hosted and lost to Parsons, Kansas, 5-3, that Sunday, June 5. Mantle played in both games, and he may have played one additional game for the Kids the next day, Monday, June 6, a practice game against Alba, who may have decided while on the way home from a game the day before at Parsons, to play in Baxter Springs.

On June 11 the Joplin paper reported that Mickey Mantle had reported to a Yankees' minor league training camp at Branson. Globe sportswriter, Porter Wittich wrote: "Mickey Mantle, popular shortstop with the Baxter Springs Whiz Kids the last two seasons, has been signed by the New York

---

[228] *The Joplin Globe*, May 29, 1949.
[229] Pitts.

Yankees and at present is at Branson for training. He is a graduate of Commerce High School this spring and will probably be assigned to Independence, Kansas, of the KOM League."[230]

Also going to Branson with Mantle was Carl Pevehouse, the Coffeyville pitcher. Greenwade has made a similar deal with Pevehouse and after a week of training he was offered a $500 contract for the rest of the 1949 season with the Yankees' organization. Pevehouse, an orphan, believed then that he would need a college education to make it in life. Rather than accept the risks of trying to make baseball pay off meaningfully for him, he went back to Coffeyville and discussed his situation with the sports editor of *The Coffeyville Journal*, Jack Miller. Miller phoned the Oklahoma A&M baseball coach, Toby Green and told him there was this good pitcher in town by the name of Carl Pevehouse. On that recommendation Oklahoma A&M gave him a baseball scholarship. Pevehouse majored in history and coaching and returned to Coffeyville to make a career with Page Milk Company.[231]

---

[230] *The Joplin Globe*, June 11, 1949.
[231] Phyllis Pevehouse.

14

1949: The First Innings of Professional Baseball

On June 13 Mantle went to Chanute, Kansas, where the Yankees' Class D team, the Independence Yankees, was playing a series. The following day, June 14, Mantle played his first professional baseball game.[232] Mantle had had both the Yankee and Cardinal scouts looking at him for some time, more so than any of the other major league organizations. Greenwade of the Yankees and Clifton A. "Runt" Marr of the St. Louis Cardinals had developed a rivalry between themselves, covering the same territory for two opposing teams. Both men had seen Mantle play a few times and both had come to the same conclusion: He cannot play shortstop in the major leagues. According to Mickey's brother, Ray Mantle, "after my brother became a star with the Yankees, Marr told his wife Sadie to go and look at the scouting notes he had made on Mantle. Marr said, 'If I made a single bad comment about the kid I will kill myself.'"[233]

Nonetheless, many and probably most of Mantle's coaches, teammates

---

[232] *The Independence Daily Reporter*, June 15, 1949.

[233] Ray Mantle.

as well as the area baseball fans seemed also to doubt that the young man was a future major leaguer. With the exception of a loyal father, Mutt Mantle, the Whiz Kids' perceptive coach Barney Barnett, Sr., and scout Johnny Sturm, most baseball people of the Tri-State acknowledged that Mantle was a good local athlete but saw nothing particular in his future. Many probably thought Mickey would end up in the mines, as so many others before. But that perception probably began to change in a few minds, at least, after Mantle's breakout season at Baxter Springs in 1948.

During 1948 at least one major league team, the Pittsburgh Pirates, had a scout take a look at Mantle. The scout actually was a minor league manager doubling as a scout one evening for the Pirates. But at least Mantle, then age 16, had caused some notice in one of organized baseball's front offices. Pittsburgh had a Class D club at Bartlesville, Oklahoma, that was managed by former Texas League pitcher Ed Marleau. Al Solenberger, a member of the Bartlesville organization for four seasons who retired as the KOM League's all-time hits leader, said one of his most vivid memories of those days occurred on a road trip to Carthage, Missouri.

Once the Bartlesville bus got to Miami, Oklahoma, the trip further along Route 66 led east by northeast through the towns of Commerce, Oklahoma, and Baxter Springs, Kansas. Solenberger recalled, "The mention today of the Whiz Kids brings back memories for most of the Bartlesville team. We lounged around for quite a while in front of what I recall being a rooming house in Baxter Springs that summer evening as Marleau scouted Mantle for the Pirates. I don't remember Marleau making privy to the team what he saw or how he rated the young player for the Whiz Kids."[234]

An interesting possibility developed in early 1949 when an old friend took an interest in Mantle, one that would have put Mantle out of the reach of the Yankees, at least for awhile. Mantle, while in high school, had befriended one of the former Miami Owls players in the KOM League, Joe Pollock. Pollock had attended most of Commerce High School's baseball games when Mantle played there until the end of the 1949 spring semester. Pollock saw something special in the lad and was determined to do something about it.

In early May 1949 Pollock had a plan. He went to the offices of R. O.

---

[234] Al Solenberger.

"Hoot" Gibson, president of the Miami Owls[235] and proposed that Mr. Gibson sign Mantle because he had great potential and, being from nearby Commerce would draw fans to the Owls games. Gibson was adamant. He maintained that while Mantle may have been a good high school performer, there was no way he would ever succeed at the professional level.

Pollock, who had seen what Mantle could do from the time he first saw him as a 14-year-old kid, disagreed with Gibson, to the extent he made this proposition to the Miami boss: "I will go down to the bank and borrow $500. With that money I will place a wager with you that within three years Mickey will be playing at the Triple A level or higher."[236]

Gibson shunned the bet, and probably was glad later that he had. Pollock went about his business and never went back to the Miami boss to say, "I told you so." Add three years to 1949 and, as every Mantle fan knows, Triple A was one step below where the kid from Commerce was by then blazing his path to the Hall of Fame.

On the evening of June 11, 1949, W. B. "Cap" Tole, the president of the Independence, Kansas, baseball team, telephoned New York for Lee McPhail, head of the Yankees' minor league operations. It was late in Independence and two hours[237] later in New York when McPhail got the call. It was even later when Yankee scout Tom Greenwade was awakened in his room at the Boothe Hotel room in Independence and given his marching orders for the following day by McPhail: Do what Tole wanted — get Mantle up to Independence. McPhail had decided that Independence seemed to want Mantle more than any other club, and it was also Mickey and Mutt's desire to have Mickey play as close to home as possible.[238]

What was actually going on in this situation was a chess game among Greenwade, McPhail and the McAlester (Oklahoma) and Independence clubs. A report in *The Independence Daily Reporter* clarifies the matter: "Yankee Business Manager John Vallina announced this morning that

---

[235] If Miami had signed Mantle, he would have been the property of the Topeka, Kansas, Owls of the Western Association, which then would have had the rights to sell his services to whomever made the best offer.

[236] Joe Pollock.

[237] Usually, there's a one-hour time difference between Independence and New York, which are in the Central and Eastern time zones, respectively. However, in 1949, Independence was not on daylight savings time, so when it was noon in Independence it was 1 p.m. in St. Louis and Kansas City and 2 p.m. in New York.

[238] *The Independence Daily Reporter*, sports column by Les Davis, shortly after Mantle appeared in Independence, June 1949.

Mickey Mantle, the 17-year-old Commerce, Oklahoma, athlete who came into prominence as a member of the Baxter Springs Whiz Kids, had been assigned to Independence as a shortstop. Tom Greenwade signed Mantle after seeing the slugger pound out a pair of doubles and a homerun off a Coffeyville [Ban Johnson League] twirler recently. Mantle was sent to Branson, Missouri, camp and will join the Yankees at Chanute, probably today, Vallina said. Although when Mantle was signed there was some talk of his coming to this club, particularly since he had requested it, …members of the Independence Baseball Association [had] predicted, and it followed logically with Yankee policy, that the prospect might be sent elsewhere. The [Independence] Yanks have had considerable success this year and McAlester having had comparatively little, the thought was that Mantle would go to the Yankee member of the Sooner State League. Darrell Waska, who has been with the club for the past couple of weeks, joining from Twin Falls, Ida., will be sent to McAlester probably today, to make room for Mantle, a shortstop also."[239]

There was an undercurrent running regarding jurisdictional rights to Mantle. It was always known that New York had given Tom Greenwade that part of the world where Mantle lived as his protected scouting territory for the Yankees. Greenwade was becoming aware of fellow Yankees scout Johnny Sturm's interest in Mantle and was touchy about it, as we have seen. Also, Vallina recalled that Tole had watched Mantle play for Baxter Springs and was smitten by the young man's apparent talent. One day, quite unexpectedly, Dutch Zwilling, another Yankees scout, who had the Kansas City area as part of his territory, showed up at Independence before Mantle was signed and seemed anxious for Independence to sign him. He even intimated to Tole that he would be willing to go down with him to Baxter Springs to look at Mantle. It didn't take long for Greenwade to get wind of Zwilling's "meddling." Greenwade found Zwilling's presence unwarranted and took immediate action. According to Vallina, "Greenwade spoke with Lee McPhail by telephone and after the conversation Zwilling was very close to losing his scouting job with the Yankees." In fact, for a very long time Vallina was convinced that Zwilling later had been given the axe due to the bad blood he had caused by trying to meddle in the Mantle signing.[240]

---

[239] *The Independence Reporter*, June 13, 1949.
[240] John Vallina.

On the morning of June 12, 1949, Tom Greenwade, Cap Tole and business manager John Vallina met for breakfast in Independence at the Boothe Hotel. It was at this time that Greenwade informed the Independence executives that Mantle was being assigned to their KOM League team.[241]

In one of the great strokes of genius, Tole kept the Independence club's copy of the first professional baseball contract that Mickey Mantle ever signed. It was stored in an Independence safe deposit box until Mantle's death in 1995. At that time a collector on the East Coast purchased it. Tole kept this author apprised of that transaction, which was somewhat protracted.

A copy of the contract that Tole retained after he sold the Independence club's copy is dated June 13, 1949, and bears the signature of Mickey Charles Mantle and, because Mickey was not of legal age, the signature also of his father, E. C. (Elven Charles) Mantle, signed as parent guardian. After being signed in Tole's office in Independence, Mickey went off to join his team, scheduled to play that night at Chanute. The document was then forwarded to George Trautman, president of minor league baseball, who signed it on July 22, 1949. The contract was then sent back to E. L. Dale at Carthage who, as KOM League president, signed it on August 2, 1949, at his office at *The Carthage Evening Press.*

The terms of the contract were not adhered to in the strictest terms. The Mantles were given a bonus for signing — a check dated July 11, 1949 for $1,150, of which $750 would be forfeited if Mickey didn't last with the Independence club until June 30. He did become eligible for the $750 at the end of the month, but the remaining $400 should not have been paid until Trautman's approval, which was not granted until July 22, 1949.

Tole also promised to pay Mickey $140 a month for June, July and August.[242] Fortunately for the Yankee organization, there wasn't much negotiating at any juncture of the process. According to Tole, "Mutt was anxious for Mickey to sign and get along with a baseball career."[243] So, for a grand total of bonus and salary, the Independence Yankees got the "Mantle package" for all of $1,570.

Thus stands the story today of Mickey Mantle's signing his first professional contract, as best it could be pieced together a half-century later. Some aspects of his signing have died with many who were very closely affiliated

---

[241] Ibid.

[242] Copy of contract belonging to W.B. "Cap" Tole, as seen by the author.

[243] Tole.

with it. The road to that signing was not always straight or narrow. There were many twists and turns. But when, at last, pen struck paper, the stage was set for one of the more memorable careers in U.S. sports.

As for the player whom Mantle replaced at shortstop for Independence, Darrell Waska recalled years later that he wasn't playing badly at all when the team officially announced the signing of another shortstop. That is why this author believes Independence pushed the panic button as far back as June 6 to bring in another shortstop long before they knew whether Waska could make the grade as a Class D player.

While the negotiations regarding Mantle were going on, Waska was traveling with the Independence Yankees on a road trip, first to Pittsburg, Kansas, on June 8-11 and then to Chanute, Kansas, for games on June 12-15. In the June 12 game, Waska got two hits in five at-bats. The next morning, instead of preparing for the second game of the series, he was heading west to pick up his belongings at Independence and then on to McAlester, Oklahoma in the Sooner State League. Waska remembered that Monday, June 13, in this manner. "Yes, I was the shortstop for the '49 club and doing well when replaced by a young player out of high school. I never got to meet Mantle. I remember the trip back to Independence that night to pick up my equipment."[244]

The baseball career of Waska, a Chicago native, was turned upside down with the arrival of Mantle. While Mantle began his rapid ascent in the ranks of organized baseball, Waska spent 1949 being shuttled among five teams — Independence, McAlester, Ventura in the California League, Twin Falls in the Pioneer League and Quincy of the Three-I League.[245]

Waska made about the same number of errors in the field as Mantle did at Independence in 1949 and each had the same number of home runs, seven.[246] At McAlester, Waska was a teammate with future major leaguers Whitey Herzog and Don Leppert that season. Even with players like that, McAlester managed to finish 30 games out of first.[247]

Mantle was one of the fortunate to have decided to play for the Yankee organization. The young men signed by New York quickly realized they were with a special group. Opponents of the Yankee farm teams knew it,

---

[244] Darrell Waska.
[245] Ibid.
[246] Ibid.
[247] Ibid.

also. The "baby Yanks" were treated differently by their bosses than they would have been while playing for minor league teams affiliated with other major league teams or unaffiliated clubs. Most other minor league teams' players had to scrape to make ends meet. Tommy Gott, who roomed with Mantle in 1950 and managed in the Yankee chain after his playing days, called it "The mystique of the New York Yankees." He described it as something that was unspoken, yet pervasive. He recalled, "Young signers were given the best of everything from the buses they rode through the 'bush' leagues to the hotels where they slept." It was the Yankees' way of telling young hopefuls that rainbows did exist and that the pot of gold was at the opposite end of where they were currently.

Gott said that although the rule was never on paper or put in a contract, "an outfielder in the Yankees' system had better hit 30 homers a season at the D and/or C levels or they wouldn't play in the 'house that Ruth built.' Anyway not as a member of the Yankees."

Also, according to Gott, "The Yankees had an unwritten rule but it was pretty much cast in stone. That being, if a player was on a minor league team that won a pennant he would get a promotion to a higher classification the next season. A better player but on a lesser team would be overlooked for a promotion based on that system. There were exceptions to that rule, but not that often."[248]

Although the young Yankee farmhands had the best buses, stayed in the finer hotels and dressed better it didn't mean they ate "higher on the hog." An average Class D and C player in the era Mantle was doing his duty as a minor league shortstop received between $2 and $2.25 per day, for meals, while on the road and during home games they received no meal allowance and lived on the base salary of $150 for the Class D leaguers and $225 for Class C performers.[249] Those per diem rates and salary caps were placed on all teams in each minor league in order to make some things equitable. Of course, there always were ways of passing money under the table or even passing the hat among fans in the stands when a player accomplished a great feat. Sometimes when the hat was passed a player could make as much money by that single action as he could in an entire month playing ball.

Tole was 95 years old when Mantle died. When the bidding for Mantle's

---

[248] Tommy Gott.

[249] These salary levels were based on guidelines set by the commissioner of minor league baseball, as verified through the reading of many scrapbooks of many former Class D and C players.

contract started, it commenced at $1,500, then went to $5,000, $10,000 and $25,000 before $50,000 was accepted. With the contract also went the three check stubs that Mantle received in salary ($140 each), along with the $1,150 bonus check given to Mickey on July 11, 1949. When Tole was asked why he turned down those low bids for Mantle's contract, he replied, "I'm old, not stupid."[250] Three months after selling off the most prized contract ever signed by a KOM League ballplayer, Tole died at his Independence, Kansas, home.

There were numerous former players, teammates and baseball officials who had tremendous influences on the young Mantle. These brief biographies depict how people went to bat for the youngster from Commerce.

Joe Pollock

When he tried to get the Miami baseball club to sign Mickey Mantle to his first professional contract, Joe Pollock had known Mantle for three years, since 1946, when the KOM League was organized and placed one of its teams at Miami. The Miami ballpark was just four miles from Mantle's home in Commerce. Games in which Pollock played were among the earliest professional baseball games that Mantle ever saw. Before World War II, Mantle had made a few trips with his dad some 300 miles up old Route 66 to St. Louis to see the Cardinals or Browns, or to Joplin to see the Miners play. But 1942 would have been his last opportunity to see minor league baseball until the KOM League set up shop almost in his backyard in 1946.

Mantle not only attended the Miami games but hung out around the park before the games while the players warmed up. In this way, Mantle got to know some of the players; many and probably most regarded Mantle and the other local kids as pests, especially when they interfered with preparations for a game. But Pollock somehow liked Mantle, and Mantle liked and admired Pollock and his speed on the playing field, a trait the young Mantle had come to value. The Miami fans liked Pollock, too. He was a crowd favorite. A speedster out of Cleveland, Ohio, Pollock had been in the same high school football backfield with a man who later won the Heisman Trophy in 1944, Les Horvath, and had played minor league baseball in the Canadian American and Kitty leagues before the outbreak of World War II.

A while after Mantle was well-established with the Yankees, Pollock

---

[250] Tole.

returned to Cleveland for five years. When the Indians hosted the New York Yankees, Pollock would be at Municipal Stadium and Mantle would take him and his young son Kenneth into the Yankee dressing room after the game. Mantle enjoyed taking young Kenneth around to meet all the guys. This only made Pollock that much more proud of Mantle.[251]

Johnny Sturm

Yankees scout Johnny Sturm's professional baseball career began when he broke in as a player with the Joplin Miners in 1936 under manager Benny Bengough. Joplin was in the Western Association, a league located in the heart of the great drought belt of the mid-1930s. He remembered a game that season at Bartlesville, Oklahoma, "when the temperature was 124 degrees in the shade and there were splits in the dry ground six feet wide and they were so deep no one could see the bottom."[252]

The mining towns of Southwest Missouri, Southeast Kansas and Northeast Oklahoma were pretty rough and tumble in those days. Sturm said that women usually chose not to attend most of the games, for there would be so much cussing they would be offended. Many of the players would wind up in jail for various offenses and management spent a great deal of time and money getting them out and ready for the next game.

In 1939 Sturm became involved in an interesting situation when it had become apparent the Yankees were looking for someone to fill the shoes of Lou Gehrig before too many more seasons passed. The New York World Telegram ran an article replete with photos of all the players in their Yankee system who were being considered for the position. The most notable mentioned were Tommy Henrich, Babe Dahlgren, Fred Collins, Mike Chartak, Ed Levy, Leonard Gabrielson and Johnny Sturm.[253]

Not quite two months later Gehrig ended his streak of consecutive games at 2,130 when he took himself out of a game on May 2, 1939, at Briggs Stadium in Detroit. Babe Dahlgren became the first Yankee other than Gehrig to play first base for the Bronx Bombers since 1925 when Gehrig replaced Wally Pipp.

Sturm, a six-foot, 175-pound left-handed first baseman born in St. Louis, was playing first base for the minor league Kansas City Blues in 1939. Two

---

[251] Pollock.

[252] Sturm.

[253] *New York World Telegram*, March 25, 1939.

years later he played the bulk of the season at first base for the Yankees, hit .239 for the season and got into the World Series. Sturm had a respectable record but the world was at war and he was called into the service, serving 1942-45 as the athletic director at Jefferson Barracks in St. Louis.

In 1946, the war over, Sturm was again assigned to the Kansas City team by the Yankees. Less than a month into the season, batting against Emery Rudd of Louisville, Sturm was struck in the head by a pitch and did not play for a week. Four weeks later he broke his wrist in two places in a mishap at second base. The Yankees offered him a chance to stay in baseball. He was told that he could run tryout camps with a fellow out of Willard, Missouri by the name of Tom Greenwade.

After two years of helping Greenwade scout, Sturm became manager of the Yankees' team at Joplin in 1948. The next year, not long after he had given Mantle a tryout at Joplin, one of Sturm's former players showed up with a tall kid with him. The former player introduced his friend as Kenny Boyer. As Sturm recounted the story, "I told Boyer that I had seen him play. In fact, I had seen the whole family. I remember seeing a whole team of Boyers play. They had their own field and they lived just a few doors down from that ballfield at Alba, Missouri."

Sturm very much wanted Boyer to play for his team at Joplin in 1949. By that point in the season, the Joplin third baseman, Olin Martin, was leading the Class C Western Association in hitting and Binghamton, New York, of the Class A Eastern League was pressuring Sturm and others in the Yankee organization to promote Martin to their club. Sturm had in mind signing Boyer in case Martin was taken away from Joplin. However, as Sturm recalled, Boyer told him, "I don't want to be a Yankee." Sturm, able to laugh about it a half-century later, remarked, "I couldn't get Kenny to put on that uniform for anything. I told him that Mantle was going to make money by signing with the Yankees and 'you aren't going to make any money with the St. Louis Cardinals.'"

But Kenny's big brother, Cloyd, was with the Cardinals' International League team at Rochester, New York, that year and Sturm said, "All he could think about was following in his brother's footsteps." So, Martin remained at Joplin that year and won the Western Association batting title. Boyer signed with the Cardinals and joined their minor league team at Hamilton, Ontario, in the Pennsylvania, Ontario, New York (PONY) League.

Sturm was the type of manager who had confidence in his ballplayers and went the extra mile for them. When the 1949 Joplin season concluded, he recommended that each of his players be promoted to Binghamton, New York, for at least a tryout in 1950. That infuriated the Yankee top brass. Lee McPhail retorted, "We thought you were our man to put the finger on talent and recommend players for the class in which they should be the next year." Sturm, not too upset with the displeasure of his boss, replied, "Give them a shot at Class A; you can always send them back to Class B."[254]

Lee McPhail

According to several men who managed in the Yankees' minor league chain, Lee McPhail was an amazing man. He always came to the minor league spring training sites to discuss every individual player the Yankees had in camp. Tommy Gott, a teammate of Mickey Mantle at Joplin in 1950, had been assigned to manage the Greenville, Texas, club of the Sooner State League in 1957. Gott recalled an incident revealing of McPhail's encyclopedic grasp of all things relating to the minor league domain he ruled.

Gott's Greenville team and four other Yankee farm clubs were training that spring in Hattiesburg, Mississippi. McPhail came in the night before each team was to trim its roster. He carried a briefcase, which he never opened, and according to Gott, he knew something about every player in the camp. McPhail started with each manager by asking his opinion of each player being considered for "rejection." His policy was that if there was just one manager who thought a boy shouldn't be cut, then he wasn't.

Gott recalled this process went on for a very long time each spring. Being the manager of a Class D ball club, the lowest on the totem pole, he was last to make his recommendations known to McPhail. Gott placed a name before the group and stated that he didn't think the boy could ever make it to the major leagues and that he should be cut. "At that point," Gott recalled, "Mr. McPhail asked me if I knew the boy's father had died the past winter. Of course, I didn't know that. So, Mr. McPhail talked about how the boy could still be grieving over the loss of his father. After he finished his spiel he then asked me if I was sure the boy ought to be let go and all I could say was, 'No.'"

Gott said he always marveled at how much McPhail knew about all those players. He doesn't find it difficult at all to believe Sturm when Sturm said

---

[254] Sturm.

he had recommended Mantle to the Yankees. According to Gott, "McPhail had people reporting to him that no one knew about."[255]

Tom Greenwade

Tom Greenwade was a former minor league pitcher and manager. His scouting career included stints with the St. Louis Browns and Brooklyn Dodgers before he joined the New York Yankees. By the time he arrived on the Yankee payroll he had signed such future major leaguers as George Kell, Bob Swift and Rex Barney.

In addition to being able to recognize and sign significant major league talent, Greenwade also was a most personable man, and had become on good terms with Lee McPhail, his boss in the Yankee system. Greenwade had talked McPhail out of some black angus cattle that McPhail had imported to this country. One of the inducements for Greenwade to leave the Brooklyn Dodger organization was McPhail giving some of the cattle to Greenwade. So, Greenwade fed his new breed of beef cattle on the green grasses of Southwest Missouri and spent the rest of the time looking for "green" ballplayers in the area for McPhail's Yankees.

Willard "Billy" Johnson

Whiz Kids player Willard "Billy" Johnson merited Tom Greenwade making the trip down from Willard, Missouri, to check him out before word got around that Mickey Mantle was the player in the area who should be attracting the most attention among organized baseball people. Johnson never got too much attention after the signing of Mantle, with the exception of the recognition he received from things Mantle said in some of the books written about him. Johnson's sentiments were summed up in a sub-headline atop an interview with a newspaper in Ohio one day a half-century later: "Former baseball player says Mickey Mantle may not have been discovered were it not for him."[256]

Johnson was a fine player. When asked if he was as good as Mantle he chuckled and said, "I think I was better." Over the years he has told his friends the only reason Mantle made it and he didn't was due to the organizations for which each of them signed. Johnson was signed by the Philadelphia Athletics.

---

[255]   Gott.
[256]   Chad Klimack, *The Advocate,* Pataskala, Ohio, Nov. 5, 2001.

Johnson, whose given name was Willard Adrian, has heard all the stories over the years that Greenwade was really interested in him rather than Mantle at the start. Johnson didn't hold the young Mantle in too high a regard at the time he joined the Whiz Kids. "He was only on the team because his dad worked with Barney Barnett," Johnson swore. He didn't remember ever seeing or even speaking to the Yankees' Greenwade until 1955. At that time Johnson was pitching a game at Forbes Air Force Base in Topeka, Kansas. Greenwade recognized him and came up to ask him what he was doing as a pitcher. Johnson said he replied, "Well, somebody has to do it."[257]

Johnson was never signed by Greenwade. The Philadelphia organization signed him in 1950 and sent him to Welch, West Virginia, in the Appalachian League. Through most of that season he was reported in the local media as hitting around .350. However, he leveled off and finished the season with a .318 average.[258] While that wasn't so high compared to Mantle's .383 mark that same season at Joplin,[259] Johnson's .318 was seven points higher than Mantle's average for his first professional season the year before at Independence, Kansas.[260]

Johnson went into the Air Force for three years in 1952. He played on a world championship Air Force team for Cheyenne, Wyoming, in 1953. After his discharge from the service, the Kansas City Athletics signed him to a minor league contract. In 1956 the A's sent him to Columbia, South Carolina, in the South Atlantic League. He promptly hurt his arm and then was sent to Abilene, Texas, in the Big State League. Abilene could afford to carry him on their roster without him counting against the club's total players because he was a returning military veteran.[261]

---

[257] Willard "Billy" Johnson.

[258] *The Official Baseball Guide for 1951.*

[259] Ibid.

[260] *The Official Baseball Guide for 1950.*

[261] Johnson.

15

1949: The Independence Yankees

There were no signs on the horizon that the 1949 Independence Yankees would come even close to being equal to the team that was put on the field the previous seaons. None of the names on the roster were going to strike fear into either the hitters or batters of the KOM League, which had a tradition of being a pitchers circuit.

One writer said, "I saw young Mickey star in football, basketball and baseball, play for the Baxter Springs (Kan.) Whiz Kids, then for another semipro team in Independence, Kan., before breaking through with the New York Yankees."[262]

Calling the Independence, Kansas, Yankees a semi-pro team was akin to calling that town Independence, Missouri, once the fame of Mantle had spread nationwide. Prior to that time only the Missouri town of Independence received much attention and that was due to President Harry Truman. Truman made the Missouri town a household word but not until William Inge wrote *Picnic* did Independence, Kansas, receive wider acclaim. Mantle had attempted to put the town on the map, but it

---

[262] Copyright © 1995 Hastings Tribune. This page created and hosted in cooperation with Computer Consultants of Hastings, Inc.

kept getting confused with its border state counterpart.

Many scribes of the eight newspapers of the KOM League 1949 didn't see how Independence could replace such players as Al Pilarcik, Denis Jent, Harland Coffman, Bill Bagwell and Jimmy Finigan from the 1948 KOM League Championship club.

The 1949 Independence club lived a little "higher on the hog" than did the 1948 club since the KOM League owners voted to raise the per diem rate from $2.00 to $2.25 during their winter meeting. That amounted to the "gastronomical" sum of $1,215 year in the operational budget for each team in the league. That was a significant outlay of funds. Independence was just a "rung or two" above the rest of the teams in the KOM League in that they had a real bus and it also had air-conditioning.[263] Most of the other teams rode in dilapidated old school buses that sometimes started out well on a road trip but usually broke down somewhere around 2:00 A. M. in some desolate area of Southeast Kansas, Northeast Oklahoma or Southwest Missouri. Once, the Ponca City Dodger bus broke down and the players climbed on the top of the vehicle to sleep for the rest of the night. It was about the only place they could stretch out and it was also cooler outside the bus. When the sun arose the next morning they were awakened by the sounds of horns honking. The driver had placed the bus at the entrance of an industrial plant. The horns were honking — not due to the entrance being blocked, but because many of the Ponca City players had sought refuge on top of the bus without benefit of wearing any type of clothing.

The managerial career of Harry Craft began on April 11, 1949 when the Independence Yankees reported for spring training at McAlester, Oklahoma. The former Cincinnati Redleg centerfielder was sent down by the Yankees from their minor league roster of the Kansas City Blues to be the player/manager of the Class D Independence club. Many of the young men he had in camp that spring didn't see many playing dates once the season commenced. Independence started out as so many lower classification minor league teams of that era did, with three teams. There was one that was on the field, another that would be leaving shortly and a third one coming in to fill the void.

When Craft and the Independence Yankees arrived home on April 27 in

---

[263] Independence chartered their bus service from Kansas Trails Bus System of Coffeyville, Kansas. Trails placed an advertisement in the Independence scorebook that said "The Independence Yanks travel by Kansas Trails Chartered Bus! It is a grand idea for your group too!"

preparation for the opening season, this was the roster:

Pitchers: Jim Callahan, Kenneth Kleasner, Keith Speck, Richard Martinez; Steve Kraly, Burl Moffitt, Bob Wiesler, Kenny Bennett, Carroll Hughes and Joe Crowder.

Catchers: Dick Duda and Rex Boehm.

Infielders: Jack Hasten, John Cimino, Lynne Stemme, Jack Rose, Ralph Karr, Charlie Weber and George McMaster.

Outfielders: Bob Casey, Scotty Marlew, John Norman, Dick La Carra and Bill Chambers.

Within a couple days Jim Bello (Belotti) and Don Matthews showed up and some of those who arrived on the 27th were never heard of again.

Those who showed up on April 27 and never appeared in a box score were: Carroll Hughes, Rex Boehm, Jack Hasten, George McMaster, Bob Casey, Scotty Marlew and John Norman. Richard Martinez wasn't around long before being signed by the Miami, Oklahoma, Owls.

From that original roster names such as Nick Ananias, Bob Newbill, Lou Skizas, Jack Whitaker, Darrell Waska, Mickey Mantle, Rex Wehunt, Bill Holderness, Jim Cobb, Bob Mallon, Al Long, Len Wiesner and Sammy Joyce were added during the season. A 20-year old utility infielder by the name of Danny Meyers showed up on August 1 but due to injuries was never inserted into a game. Within a week he was gone.

Jim Cobb didn't get to spend the entire season with the Independence Yankees but was able to get out of town with three team baseballs and the only known cap from that team still in existence.

There were forty-one young men who may have claimed they played with Mantle for the 1949

Independence Yankees. At least eight of those players never put a toe on the field in a regular season game unless the official scorer missed it or the Independence newspaper failed to print it. And, a dozen or more young men were released by June 13, which was the day Mickey joined the club.

Independence opened the 1949 season with a win over the Iola Indians. Bob Wiesler walked seven and struck out nine on his road to victory. The starting lineup that evening for the Yanks included:

Jack Rose-2b	Don Matthews-ss	Ralph Karr-lf
Dick La Carra-1b	Jim Bello-rf	Lynne Stemme-cf
John Cimino-3b	Dick Duda-c	Bob Wiesler-p

Able-bodied managers were sent to Class D teams in order to fill roster spots as well as to lead their respective teams. Harry Craft had been counted on to fill in as needed. However, he told his team early on that he wasn't about to take a chance with his life by facing some of the hard throwers of the KOM League. He admitted he didn't see guys with any more speed on the pitching staffs at the Triple A level, but at least they had an idea where the ball was going after they let go of it. Craft had a hard thrower or two on his 1949 Independence roster that included future big leaguer Bob Wiesler who could strikeout 16 every time out and walk the same number if he set his mind to it.

The most ominous sign of trouble for the new Independence manager occurred mid-way through the second game of the season against the Iola Indians. Benny Leonard, the Iola, Kansas, second baseman from Henryetta, Oklahoma, attempted to break up a double-play and Independence shortstop, Donald Matthews received a leg injury, covering second, when Leonard slid into him.

Matthews was able to resume playing after one game on the bench. He started three more games and pinch hit twice before obtaining his release from the club. That injury may have led to the hastening of the signing of Mantle more than any other item. It obviously had an impact as to where he would be assigned within the Yankee organization.

The total number of games played by Matthews—all or part of seven. Then Jack Rose was shifted from second base to shortstop and played 16 games in that slot. Darrell Waska was summoned from Twin Falls, Idaho of the Pioneer League and arrived on June 3. He had played in 13 games when he got the news he was being replaced on the roster by a young man the Yankees had officially promised a $1,500 contract that was eventually signed on June 13, 1949. A stipulation to the Mantle contract contained this disclaimer. "Player is to receive a bonus of $1,150 to be paid by the Independence club as follows. $400 upon approval of contract by the National Assn. And the remainder $750 payable on June 30th, 1949 if player retained by Independence or any assignee club."

Mantle's debut in professional baseball was delayed one day due to a rainout. The first game he played was June 14, 1949 at Chanute, Kansas. The *Independence Daily Reporter* carried this story the following day.[264] The headline read "Yankees Tie for KOM Lead With Victory Over Chanute." Sub-headline read:

Speck Holds Hosts To Four Hits
As Locals Capitalize on Errors

Blasting out eight hits and capitalizing on six Chanute errors, the Independence Yankees moved into a tie for first place with the Iola Indians by downing the Chanute Athletics last night, 13-2.

Keith Speck, the big right-hander for the Yanks, limited the A's to only four hits over the nine frames and struck out an even dozen while issuing seven passes.

In the meantime, the Iola Indians, who arrive here this evening for a four game series with the Yankees, split a twin-bill with the Pittsburg Browns, losing the first by 5 to 1 and winning the second by 4 to 2.

Jack Whitaker proved to be the biggest gun for the Yankees last night. The chunky backstop smacked out a pair of hits right where they would do the most good and was credited with

four runs batted in. Billy Holderness hit two for five including a triple and Mickey Mantle, newest addition to the Yank roster, hit two for four and fielded his position effortlessly.

The Yanks scored twice in the second inning with two down. Bill Chambers walked and Mantle singled. Both scored on Whitaker's safe blow.

In the sixth the Yanks broke out with six runs. Lou Skizas, who went hitless last night walked. Jim Bello strolled and the bases became filled after John Cimino struck out and Chambers was hit by a pitch.

Mantle walked, forcing in Skizas, and Whitaker singled into center scoring Bello and Chambers. Keith Speck doubled into center and then Holderness blasted his triple down the right field line.

Four more runs were scored in the

---

[264] *The Independence Daily Reporter*, June 15, 1949.

eighth on a single by Mantle, walk to Speck, single by Holderness and one by Charlie Weber. Bello was safe on an error and a couple of runs came in on that.

Chanute scored once in the seventh and once in the eighth. With two away in the seventh Marks doubled and was sent to third by successive walks to Tripod and Fadell. Marks came in on a wild pitch.

A walk, single and a long fly by long Bernie Tye accounted for the other Athletic rally.

Ken Bennett is the likely mound choice for the Yankees tonight as they square away for the bitter fight for pos-session of first place.

Elsewhere in the league, Carthage whipped Bartlesville by 12 to 5 with outfielder Phil Costa blasting a triple for the Cubs with the bases loaded. Tedd Gullic, Pirate boss, protested the game at Carthage.

Miami split a double with Ponca City, taking the first 9 to 7 and losing the last by 16 to 6. Duane Melvin of Miami also tripled with the bases loaded last night.

At Iola, the Indians were held to only two hits in the seven innings curtain raiser by Bill (Jim) Waugh, Pittsburg hurler.

Yankees (12)	AB	R	H	PO	A	E
Holderness, 2b	5	1	2	2	3	0
Weber, rf	5	1	1	0	0	0
Skizas, 3b	4	1	0	0	2	1
Bello, 1b	4	1	0	8	2	1
Cimino, cf	5	0	0	2	0	0
Chambers, lf	3	2	0	2	0	0
Mantle, ss	4	3	2	2	2	0
Whitaker, c	4	1	2	11	0	1
Speck, p	3	2	1	0	1	0
TOTALS	37	13	8	27	8	2

Chanute (2)	AB	R	H	PO	A	E
Tarascio, 2b	4	0	0	2	3	1
Ware, lf	4	1	1	1	0	1
Pflasterer ss,	4	0	3	2	3	2
Morganthaler, cf	4	0	0	2	0	1
Tye, rf	4	0	0	0	0	1
Norbut, 1b	3	0	0	13	0	0
Marks, 3b	3	1	1	0	1	0
Tripod, c	2	0	0	7	0	0

Fadell, p	3	0	0	0	3	0
(x) Hansen	0	0	0	0	0	0
TOTALS	31	2	4	27	11	0

(x) Grounded out for Fadell in the 9th

Innings:

	R	H	E
Yankees...........030 006 040	13	8	2
Chanute...........000 000 110	2	4	0

Summary:
RBI, Holderness 2, Weber 2, Mantle 2, Whitaker 4, Speck, Tye. **2b,** Speck, Pflasterer, Marks; **3b,** Holderness; **SB,** Marks 2; **3b,** Holderness **DP,** Holderness-Bello; **LOB** Yankees 6, Chanute 9; **ER** Yankees 8, Chanute 1; **SO** Speck 13, Fadell 6; **BB,** Speck 7, Fadell 5; **HBP,** Chambers and Whitaker by Fadell; **WP,** Speck 3, Fadell 3; **PB** Tripod; **umpires** Mohs and H. Duncan: attendance 584; time 2:20.

The major baseball news of the day that Mantle played his first game at home in the KOM League was of the off-field variety and quite shocking. The Associated Press ran this article:

Philadelphia Phillie first baseman, Eddie Waitkus was shot by "loonie" Ruth Steinhagen, age 19, in a Chicago hotel. She said she idolized Waitkus and shot him because "I wanted the thrill of murdering him." Later she said, "I admire him now more than ever before. He showed me so much courage as he lay there on the floor, the way he looked up at me and kept smiling."

On June 22 the papers around the country carried a photo of Ms. Steinhagen playing baseball on the grounds of the Cook County jail in Chicago. The caption read, "Here, Ruth plays her favorite position—first base."[265] Well, what else?

Mantle's first home game was against stiffer competition. The Iola Indians were managed by a long-time semi-pro and minor hurler, Winlow "Windy" Johnson. Johnson won many games at the National Baseball Congress Tournament at Wichita, Kansas in the early 1940s. He sent Bill Upton to the mound at Independence that evening. Upton later had a "cup of coffee" in the big leagues. Upton was getting the best of Independence

---

[265] *The Independence Daily Reporter,* June 15, 1949.

and lefty Bob Wiesler until the 8th inning. That is when the Yanks scored six runs and that ensured the league lead. Wiesler who started for Independence in that game was another member of the talent-laden Independence club who was in the Major Leagues within two years.

After the first home appearance of Mantle, Les Davis offered this analysis. "The game last night marked the initial appearance of Mickey Mantle, new Yankee shortstop, on this field. The newcomer, a switch hitter, fielded his position flawlessly and banged out a base hit where it would count…Games such as the one last night are really not recommended for those who can't take it—but it always adds a thrill when the home team comes from behind." [266]

Mantle's KOM League career started off with a three game hitting streak and he played errorless ball in two of those three contests. By the time game four had concluded he had made three errors and the hitting streak was over. The hoopla over Mantle's appearance in Independence was not any greater than any other young rookie joining a Class D ball club. Les Davis wrote a brief sketch on each player joining the club that year. These were his remarks about Mantle:

> "Meet a Yank—Mickey Mantle, latest addition to the squad moves into the position of youngest member. Mantle was born on October 3, (sic) 1931, and his home is Commerce, Okla. A star high school football, basketball and baseball player, Mantle likes to hunt and fish, is extremely fast and played ball with the Baxter Whiz Kids for two years. He is a switch hitter. Mickey stands five ten and weighs 175." [267]

By the time Mantle was into his sixth game the "veterans" of Brooklyn's minor league Ponca City Dodgers were trying to psyche out the young rookie. Don Keeter was catching for Ponca City and as he crouched to give his signals, he would spit tobacco juice on Mantle's shoes. Keeter freely admits that he wasn't a frequent chewer. However, it served its purpose. Mantle would turn to ask what was going on and, of course, Keeter would act as though nothing had happened. However, something had happened, the spitting on the shoes had served as a distraction for the young hitter.

From the middle of June to July 17 Mantle was just another young play-

[266] *The Independence Daily Reporter*, June 16, 1949.
[267] *The Independence Daily Reporter*, June 18, 1949.

er wondering if he had bitten off more than he could chew. After July the 21st contest, and into the 1949 KOM League championship series the Ponca City manager, Boyd Bartley had developed a great deal of respect for the young shortstop. Keeter recalled Mantle hitting a lot of long ball outs against the Ponca City club. It got to the place where Bartley gave Keeter orders to have Mantle brushed back or knocked down almost every time he made a plate appearance. The only time that backfired was when Keeter didn't call for the brush back pitch and Mantle homered off ace-reliever Chuck Lamberti in the third game of the first round of the playoffs. As it turned out that was Mantle's last Class D home run.

There are many twists of fate and the inevitable question of "what if?" Harry Craft was living in Waterloo, Iowa and was familiar with a young prospect from West High School in his hometown, by the name of Harold Neighbors. The young man had taken West Waterloo to three state basketball tournaments and was refuted to be one of the best baseball players in the state.

Thus, Craft had been in touch with the Yankee scouts and advised them that Neighbors should be signed. However, other teams were on the prowl and both the Chicago Cubs and Pittsburgh Pirates had an interest in the young man. The Yankees messed up on the date of Neighbors' graduation and the Pirates signed him the day before the Yankees arrived. Neighbors would have waited to sign the next day had he known the Yankees had that much interest according to his widow, Patricia.

As fate would have it the Pittsburgh Pirates assigned their new prospect to Bartlesville, Oklahoma of the KOM League. His widow Patricia said, "Bartlesville was playing Harry Craft's Independence team when the public address announcer at Bartlesville made the announcement a new player had joined the team. Upon hearing who that 'new' player was Craft exploded and shouted, 'He's supposed to be playing for me, not against me.'"

Neighbors entered the KOM League with a 'bang' at the time Mantle came into it with a 'whimper.' After many years of researching that era, this author often asked the question to himself and others, "If the Yankees had signed Neighbors what would have been Mantle's fate?" It wouldn't have been a stretch to conclude that Mantle's first month of pro baseball could have been his last. Two decades after Neighbors death that question was posed to his widow, Pat. She chuckled and said, "You know, Harry used to raise that same question."[268]

The teams Mantle faced in the KOM League either had a seasoned player or two or a manager who had been in the game for many years. For example, Tedd Gullic the Bartlesville skipper, Charlie Bates the head man at Chanute and Boyd Bartley with Ponca City, had all been in the Major Leagues prior to their arrival in the KOM League. Don Anderson at Carthage, Omar "Hoss" Lane at Miami, Olin Smith at Pittsburg and Windy Johnson at Iola were all long-term pros.

In many ways Mantle was fortunate in being managed by Craft. There wasn't much of anything the other managers could pull off that Craft hadn't seen before and thus was able protect the young Mantle from it. Thus, he was as Mutt Mantle said when he dropped his eldest son off to play in Independence, "You are in Harry's hands now, do what he tells you."[269]

Prior to Craft's death on August 3, 1995 there had been frequent contact with Craft and his wife Nell by this author. Craft had suffered a stroke and was unable to communicate verbally with anything more than a "grunting" sound during his last days. He lived five years after suffering his stroke and one of his most frequent callers was Mantle. The Craft family didn't talk about the fact that Mantle and Harry were in frequent contact. Even though Mantle was very sick toward the end of Craft's life he held the friendship with his mentor in high regard. Just ten days following Craft's death, Mantle joined him.

Even without outstanding statistics Mantle, during his early days in the KOM League, had caught the eye of those who knew the finer points of the game and could judge talent. There was always a friendly feud between Bob Dellinger, the sports editor of *The Ponca City News*, and Les Davis, sports editor of *The Independence Daily Reporter*. In a "Strictly Sporting" column, Les had this quote: "Bob Dellinger of *The Ponca City News* says one can name the best infield in the loop as fast as he can say 'Castiglione, Frazer and Skizas'—he informs us, however, that he wrote that quaint little chant prior to seeing Mickey perform against the Dodgers there."[270]

The early days in the KOM League were not easy for Mantle. There were players on that club getting far more raves than he. Lou Skizas was the hitting sensation through most of June. One sportswriter in the KOM League

---

[268] Mrs. Pat Neighbors.
[269] Ray Mantle.
[270] *The Independence Daily Reporter*, June 18, 1949.

observed that, "Skizas is as hard to get out as a sparrow in an attic."[271] His average was a lofty .478 after 13 games and Mantle was languishing at the .220 level and confiding in his roommate, Bob Mallon that he wasn't sure he would be around long enough to collect the remainder of his signing bonus.

By the time the KOM League All-Star game rolled around the Independence Yankees had Lou Skizas—3rd baseman; Bob Wiesler— pitcher and Jim Bello— outfielder as the first team representatives. Those who made the second team were pitchers Keith Speck and Steve Kraly as well as outfielder-second baseman, Charlie Weber.

Independence newspaper promotion for the 1949 KOM League All-Star game. This game saw Mickey Mantle as a participant only because he was playing for the first place team. At that juncture in his career he was the fourth or fifth best shortstop in the league.

SEE THE K.O.M.
ALL-STAR GAME!
RIGHT HERE IN INDEPENDENCE
MONDAY, JULY 11, RIVERSIDE STADIUM, 8:15 P. M.
INDEPENDENCE
YANKEES
vs.
ALL-STARS
Bring The Family, The Neighbors . . . .
Everybody! Root For The YANKS!
No Increase In Prices.

Mantle played in the All-Star game by virtue of being on the Independence club who was in first place at the break. He had two hits, one run batted in, had six chances in the field and made two errors. His roommate, Mallon wound up taking the loss.

Other members of the 1949 Independence club have retained their memories of Mantle. Bob Newbill who had a couple of years under his belt in professional baseball by 1949 was a catcher. However, in the minor league scheme of things a player had to be versatile enough to play many roles. During one difficult time the club was short of roster players and Craft put Newbill at first base. When asked to recall his most vivid memory of playing on the same infield with Mantle, Newbill responded, "We were quite a pair, he couldn't throw and I couldn't catch."[272] Weber had one of the more tougher and dangerous positions on the club since he played second base. Weber recalled, "Mick was the worst shortstop I ever played alongside. He would almost kill you. He would field a grounder and if I was covering second base in an

---

[271] *The KOM League Remembered*, newsletter, Volume 2 Issue 7 (December 1995).

[272] Bob Newbill.

Mantle's first action shot was in a photo taken of Charlie Weber's first and only KOM League home run. As Weber nears home plate, Mantle is the fellow third from the far right "hustling" out to greet him.

attempt to turn the double play, he would throw the ball as hard as he could at me, no matter how far or close he was to second base."

While Mallon roomed with Mantle, his letters home to his father and mother lauded the hitting skill of Skizas. This is the letter he sent after a couple of weeks with Independence:[273]

Dear Mom & Pop:

Say, Dad, you ought to be down here—it is really delightfully cool. They say they are having the funniest weather they have ever had here in Kansas. But it has been real nice and cool.

We won our fifth straight game last nite, 4-2. We end the series with Iola the second place team, at Independence, Wed. Nite. It will be my turn to pitch again Thur. Nite. It is a very crucial series. I guess I have eight more games to start, we have about 40 more games left, and there are five starting pitchers. I am going to bear down and try to make myself a good record here. I have made

---

[273] Hall, *Majoring in The Minors.*

a good start, and if nothing happens I should win a few more games. I feel OK but my feet are a little sore, but they are getting better. I am sending you a box score of my game. This fellow Skizas, the third baseman can really hit. He is only 17. I room with Mantle, the shortstop. He was hitting .230 a week and a half ago, he went on a hitting streak and jumped up to .300 in that time. He's as fast as lightning, beat out a lot of infield hits and bunts. There isn't much more news around her so I'll close for now. Love, Bob

P. S. The mosquitoes chew you to death down here. I never saw so many.

The Independence club always welcomed the visiting Miami Owls, and for good reason.

ONE WAY
TO KEEP
COOL . . .

**BUT· HERE'S
A BETTER WAY!**

BASEBALL TONITE!

Independence
YANKEES   VS.   Miami
OWLS

Riverside Stadium — 8:15

The big turnaround for Mantle came on the evening of Monday, July 18, in a home double header against the Miami, Okla. Owls. In the first game of the twin-bill, which was scheduled for seven innings, Mantle went 3 for 3 as the Yankees won, 6-5. In the second game Miami got off to a fast 4-0 start and then vaporized. The press was not kind in the assessment of the Miami performance. Les Davis's account stated:

"The second game, a highly hoped for baseball game, turned into a burlesque about midway that saw some of the paying customers get up and leave before the, excuse the expression, 'contest' was finished.

Miami used five men on the pitchers mound in the second fray. They started with Larry Belrose who just joined the club. He gave way to Ray Stockton in the third and Stockton turned over the hurling chores to outfielder Casey Wonka in the sixth.

Wonka was sent to second base soon thereafter and shortstop Duane Melvin tried to assume the pitching duties. Melvin was finally moved to first and Omar B. Lane (manager and first baseman), became the fifth to serve them up. Not only did every Yankee get a hit in the second game, but all got at least two hits. Every man scored at least once and all drove in at least one run...An outstanding feature of the Yankees during the past four games has been the hitting of Mickey Mantle. The speedy little Sooner has racked up the excellent total of 12 hits in the last 17 trips.

Many have been in ideal spots, too."[274]

The next day, KOM League President, E. L. Dale, reviewed the situation of that second game at Independence and ruled Miami's performance was detrimental to baseball and levied fines against the club. However, that evening was not detrimental to Mickey's statistics. In the second game he went 4-6 making his total evenings work a productive 7 for 9. That game "jump started" him toward the .300 plateau that he attained within that same week.

Somehow Joltin' Joe DiMaggio must have known that there was a youngster in the Yankee system starting to make some noise. On the same night Mantle went 7 for 9 DiMaggio hit a triple, two singles, drove in two runs and cut down the potential winning run in the 9th by throwing out a White Sox runner at the plate. The Yanks lost the game in the 10th inning.

On July 20th Mantle picked up another couple of hits and got this review. "Mantle continued his hitting spree by collecting two in three trips, running his streak to 14 in 20 trips. Charlie Weber also is hitting well and now has eight in his last twelve trips."[275]

There was no way of stopping Mickey as evidenced by another news story the following day. "The Yankee loss was not due to lack of hitting by Mickey Mantle. That young man who is on a terrific hitting spree, continued his merry way up the batting average ladder by pounding out two hits in four trips to stretch his streak to 16 hits in 24 trips."[276]

Ironically, the day that Mantle finally reached the .300 plateau the KOM League released the batting averages of all players for the games played through July 17. Mantle was listed at .229 and only Johnny Cimino at .227 and Bill Chambers at .220 had worse batting average among the starters for the Independence Yankees. The 71 point rise in batting average came in six days.

From that point of the season until the end it was a race among Casey Wonka, Bernie Tye, Dick Drury and Mantle as to who would lead the league in hitting. At the conclusion of the season it was announced, unofficially, that Mantle had won the batting title. However, the race turned out just a bit differently:

[274] *The Independence Daily Reporter*, July 19, 1949.
[275] *The Independence Daily Reporter*, July 21, 1949.
[276] *The Independence Daily Reporter*, July 22, 1949.

Dick Drury	Bartlesville	.317
Kent Pflasterer	Chanute	.314
Casey Wonka	Miami	.31347
Udo Jansen	Bartlesville	.31343
Mickey Mantle	Independence	.31269
Bernie Tye	Chanute	.31210
Harry Neighbors	Bartlesville	.311

Mantle and roommate Bob Mallon were starting to bloom about the same time. On July 24th Mantle hit his second home run of the season in a victory over Chanute and Mallon picked up his second win.

Many baseball fans not familiar with the conditions of ball parks, the ineffective lighting and assuming players of the late 1940s had baseball gloves the size of the ones worn by this generation have long thought Mantle was the worst shortstop in minor league history. He was far from that. The following chart[277] compares him to his peers in the KOM League for the 1949 season:

NAME	TEAM	GAMES PLAYED	NO. ERRORS	FIELDING PCT.
Dick Faught	Iola	111	47	.907
Cal Frazer	Bartlesville	123	67	.899
Hank Paskiewicz	Carthage	88	45	.895
Bill Hodges	Ponca City	99	48	.893
Sal Nardello	Pittsburg	118	75	.886
Mickey Mantle	Independence	89	47	.886
Kent Pflasterer	Chanute	123	73	.874
Duane Melvin	Miami	95	71	.863

The KOM League was not unlike the other 24 Class D leagues in operation during 1949. Most of the players filling those positions were youngsters in their first year of professional baseball. With each league fielding between six and eight teams then nearly 200 fellows played the majority of the games

[277] *1950 Official Baseball Guide*, published by The Sporting News.

for their particular team at the shortstop position.

The following is a list[278] of the other Class D Leagues in 1949 and indicates the person making the greatest number of errors in that league at the shortstop position:

LEAGUE	TEAM	PLAYER'S NAME	NO. OF ERRORS
Alabama State	Enterprise	Joseph Popely	65
Appalachian	Bristol	Alfred Majewski	61
Blue Ridge	Wytheville	Donald Lavigne	69
Costal Plain	Greenville	Donald Lavigne	69
Eastern Shore	Federalsburg	Robert Westfall	50
Far West	Klamath Falls	Maurice Nordell	78
Florida State	St. Augustine	Willard Ehrhardt	65
Georgia-Alabama	Opelika	Paul Flores	74
Georgia-Florida	Cordele	William Broukal	86
Georgia State	Eastman	Russell Gagnon	55
Kitty	Cairo	Marion Rossi	73
Longhorn	Midland	Stanley Hughes	88
Mississippi Ohio Valley	West Frankford	William Asel	63
Mountain States	Pennington	Robert Grose	76
North Atlantic	Hazelton	Joseph Cadden	65
North Carolina State	Lexington	Hoyle Talbert	51
Ohio-Indiana	Springfield	Milton Kress	94
Pony	Hamilton, Ont.	George Kremer	66
Rio Grande Valley	McAllen	Emilio Mozo	73
Sooner State	Lawton	Arnold Fritz	60
Tobacco State	Fayetteville	Herman Mason	61
Virginia	Emporia	D. Charouhas	71
Western Carolina	Shelby	Phillip Fago	54
Wisconsin State	Wausau	Robert Boddy	82

---

[278] Ibid.

Also, many people who have a minimal understanding of Mantle's season at Joplin in 1950 assume he was also the worst shortstop the Western Association ever produced. Mantle did make 55 errors that season. However, a young man at Hutchinson, Kansas made 19 more than Mickey and within seven seasons Milt Graff was playing shortstop for the Kansas City A's.

Mantle had a penchant for doing the unexpected. By 1950 many of the routine grounders that he fielded flawlessly wound up as errors when he attempted to make his throw to first base. Being a frustrated knuckleball pitcher, he would many times throw knucklers from his position to Cromer Smotherman at first base. Smotherman once yelled out in desperation, "Throw the ball right, Mick; I'm a married man." Not only did Mantle hear the remark, but it resonated so that everyone in the grandstand that evening also got the flavor of baseball's colorful jargon.

Aside from the common misconception that Mantle was the worst shortstop in minor league history is the counter belief that he was one of the most powerful hitters in the annals of Class D baseball. Stories abound in the town of Independence, Kansas, about the mammoth home runs he hit while there for 89 games. If he hit those towering tape measure jobs he did it in batting practice, not in a sanctioned game. Mantle hit only one home run in Independence and his remaining six were on the road. This a rundown[279] of his home runs:

DATE	PITCHER	RIGHT/LEFT	TEAM	HOME/AWAY
June 30	Jim Waugh	Left	Pittsburg	Away
July 24	Al Fadell	Right	Chanute	Away
August 2	Ed Wolfe	Right	Bartlesville	Away
August 6	George Erath	Right	Carthage	Home
August 12	Jeptha McCormick	Left	Pittsburg	Away
August 28	George Erath	Right	Carthage	Away
September 2	Emil Jurcic	Left	Pittsburg	Away

[279] Ibid.

On September 10, 1949, the Ponca City Dodgers and Independence Yankees were in the first round of the KOM League playoffs. The game was played at Conoco Park in Ponca City. In the eighth inning both Mickey Mantle and Nick Ananias homered in a losing cause. Both round trippers came off ace Ponca City reliever Chuck Lamberti. The account of that pair of homers reported by Les Davis was eye catching. "In the eighth, the Yanks went ahead on the strength of a pair of home runs by Ananias and Mantle. Both blows traveled some 850 feet."[280]

The KOM League season always closed on Labor Day. By virtue of Ponca City finishing fourth and the Independence Yankees winning the pennant, the Shaughnessy series started at the Yankees' home park.

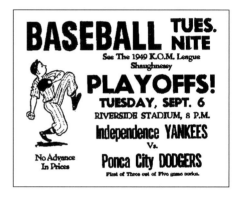

The home run that Mantle remembered most fondly was during the Yankees' last visit to Carthage, Missouri. Carthage had some excellent talent and the league's leading home run hitter. Bob Speake, a native of Springfield, Missouri joined the team June 14, the same day Mickey played his first professional game at Chanute, Kansas. Speake wound up hitting seven more homers than Mantle. However, Mantle's last home run, in Carthage, is one that both he and Mantle long remembered.[281]

Bill Hornsby, the son of Hall of Famer Rogers Hornsby, joined Carthage August 3, after playing most of the season with Centralia, Ill., in the Mississippi-Ohio Valley League. He had infuriated manager Lou Bekeza a week earlier, when Bekeza thought Hornsby was loafing in pursuit of fly balls. After benching him for a week, Centralia finally found a club willing to take him. Upon arrival in Carthage he had adapted well, and was playing center field on a regular basis. His career at Carthage was going just fine until the night of August 28. It was the second game of a doubleheader, in the second inning, after a 4-3 Carthage win in the first game. The following is a direct quote from *The Carthage Evening Press*: "Near-disaster struck the Cubs in the second inning of the nightcap. George Erath, heading for his 20th con-

[280] *The Independence Daily Reporter*, September 10, 1949.
[281] Hall, *Majoring in The Minors*.

secutive scoreless inning, had two men out when (John) Cimino grounded into right past (Don) Anderson, and (Mickey) Mantle followed with a line drive into right-center. Hornsby was off with the crack of the bat and just as he was about to haul the ball down, he glanced over his shoulder and the ball struck him in the head, bouncing about 30 feet away. Mantle easily circled the bases behind Cimino before the ball could be retrieved, and Hornsby crumpled to the ground next to the wall. A doctor (Thomas McNew) was summoned and Hornsby was able to leave the field under his own power a few minutes later. Hornsby was not seriously hurt."[282]

That story had real impact (pun intended). To verify the newspaper account, this incident was brought to Speake's attention since he was playing first base for Carthage at the time. Forty-seven years after the fact, Speake remembered it well. According to Speake, Mantle hit the ball so high that it rose above the light standards. Hornsby couldn't locate the ball in the night sky, and he continued to search for it without success. Speake claims that Hornsby circled under the ball for "about 15 minutes" and then the moment of reckoning happened. Rather than Hornsby finding the ball, the ball found him and immediately dimmed his lights. Both Speake and Mantle claimed that was one of the funniest things they ever witnessed in a baseball game. Wonder how Hornsby ranked it?

Don Schmitt was playing alongside Hornsby that evening, and declares that Hornsby was never knocked out. As he lay on the ground, he yelled to Schmitt, "Go get the ball!"[283]

Erath, whose scoreless inning streak was halted by the ball that hit Hornsby in the head, believes Hornsby lost the ball in the lights. Erath recalled that incident as just another great memory for a minor league career that lasted through the 1954 season. He gave up his dream of the major leagues after an exhibition game he played in 1951 for Greensboro, N.C. He faced some major league hitters that day and realized that he didn't have what it took to make it "all the way." In 1955-56 he was the general manager of High Point-Thomasville of the Carolina League. The club was affiliated with the Cincinnati Reds and one of the first players to come under Erath's charge was Curt Flood. Erath claims that every major league ballplayer today should send Flood part of his paycheck for what he did for the free agency issue.

Upon first arriving at Independence, Mantle didn't have a roommate.

---

[282] *The Carthage Evening Press*, August 29, 1949.

[283] Don Schmitt.

When Bob Mallon joined the team fresh out of McKinley High School in St. Louis, Mantle asked the Yankees to let the pair room together. Mallon was a big 6' 4" pitcher and was in every way as bashful as Mantle. Neither were "tearing up" the opposition and they expressed their fears as they lay in bed at night thinking about what baseball did or didn't hold for them.

Mantle fretted that he would be "long gone" before he ever saw the remaining part of his signing bonus. Mallon was the first of the pair to have success. Upon winning his first game he managed to get hold of the game ball. He took it back to his 10th Street rooming house. As he lay in bed that night he was tossing it into the air over and over. Mantle observed the ritual for a few minutes and said, "Give me the ball, Bob." Mallon asked why and Mantle replied, "I want to autograph it." Mallon had the perfect comeback, "Why would I want your autograph?" The only writing implement in the room was a green ink pen and with that Mantle signed probably his first autograph.

Mallon cherished the ball for it was his first victory. However, over the years it became even more special. Not many young men, if any, other than Mallon, can claim that the game ball of their first victory as a pitcher was signed by a teammate who became a Hall of Famer.

There were a couple of other balls that Mantle should have got around to signing. As fate would have it, the first of that roommate duo to hit two homers in one game was Mallon. He tagged Bob Wheeler of Bartlesville for the two four baggers as Mantle went hitless. The hitting performance was witnessed by the last of the legal spitball pitchers, Burliegh Grimes. Manager Craft had been summoned to his native Iowa where his seven year old son, Tommy, was a patient in an Iowa City hospital. Tommy was diagnosed as having polio in the early stages.

Grimes received a great ovation when he was introduced to the 886 fans at Bartlesville the evening of August 3, 1949. Behind Mallon's slugging and seven-hit pitching it gave Grimes a perfect record, 1-0.

The fans at Bartlesville may have appreciated the old spitballer but the fans at Carthage, Missouri were not as kind. They knew of his "Boiling Boilie" reputation. Back in 1946 Grimes was managing the St. Louis Cardinal farm club at Rochester, New York, in the International League. According to the syndicated Sports Roundup, an Associated Press daily feature, Grimes earned the "Boiling Boilie" nickname.[284] Grimes' penchant for getting chased by the umpires made it necessary for the Cardinals to replace him with Eddie Joost. Joost managed one game and won. His second game as manager was rained out and by that time the St. Louis brass had arrived. When they spoke with Joost about being the permanent skipper of the Red Wings, he indicated he still had aspirations of returning to the major leagues. Thus, the Cardinals relieved him of his managerial duties.

Grimes had a previous stint with Independence in 1948. He was the interim manager after the firing of Frank "Goldie" Howard and prior to the hiring of Malone Battle "Bones" Sanders. It was not an amicable situation when Grimes showed up, for Howard had been hired by the Yankees in 1947 on the recommendation of Tom Greenwade. Greenwade once stated, "I have no higher regard for anyone than I have for Goldie Howard."[285] It hurt Greenwade greatly when he had to inform Howard he was out as manager. His words to his respected friend were, "As far as the Yankees are concerned, whatever Burleigh wants, Burleigh gets."

The "Boiling Boilie" nickname must have been the east coast version for the sportswriters of the Midwest used the term "Boilin' Burly."[286]

Well, what Burleigh got at Carthage on his first visit there was robbed. Some fan grabbed his baseball cap, and minor league baseball teams running on small budgets didn't have the funds to provide extras of anything. So, Burleigh spent the evening in the Independence dugout with the Carthage fans singing a one-line ditty, over and over, "Who stole Burleigh's hat?"

Grimes first game managing the Independence Yankees at home in 1949 was quite an exciting evening. When he approached the third base coaching box, in the bottom of the first inning, he was greeted by a chorus of 933 Independence fans yelling, "Hello, Burleigh."[287] The young Independence players were as intrigued with the new Carthage centerfielder as they were "Old Stubblebeard" another of Grimes' nicknames. The Carthage player was Bill Hornsby, the son of Hall of Famer, Rogers Hornsby. Bob Mallon recalled watching every move of the young outfielder and by the time the game concluded Hornsby had matched Mantle with two hits and had driven in three runs to Mantle's one. It did appear that the young Hornsby might be the better player on the field that evening. Another "best" was the

---

[284] Associated Press, "Sports Roundup" column, July 30, 1940. No author cited.

[285] Bunch Greenwade, Tom Greenwade's son.

[286] Les Davis, *The Independence Daily Reporter,* "Strictly Sporting" column, August 5, 1949.

[287] *The Independence Daily Reporter,* August 6, 1949.

observation Mallon had of Grimes. He felt the interim manager was a dead-ringer for the folk-singing star of that era, Burl Ives.

What Hornsby showed on his first night in Independence was not repeated in the remainder of the series as he went 0-10. That prompted the scribe in Independence to remark. "The Carthage centerfielder, Bill Hornsby, has a couple of strikes on him at all times. Wherever he goes people hear his name and immediately think of his illustrious father, Rogers 'Rajah' Hornsby, one of baseball's all-time greats. People can't help but expect much of the youthful ball hawk. He didn't appear particularly impressive at the plate but proved to be very effective in the middle garden."[288]

The New York Yankees had scheduled a try-out camp August 5 at Riverside Park, the home of the Independence Yankees and Craft was to be in charge. With his departure to be at the bedside of his son, the tryout camp was turned over to Grimes. He utilized the services of the Independence Yankee players in conducting that session. It must have brought some memories for the young Mantle who was only a few weeks removed from having been evaluated himself.

The account of the try-out camp process was reported in the Independence media: "Some of the boys who show up well are expected to be given an opportunity to further display their diamond ability at the Branson, Mo., try-out camp to be held later this summer. On the roster of the present Independence team are many boys who got their start through a Yankee try-out camp. Most notable of the recent ones is Mickey Mantle, the hard-hitting shortstop from Commerce, Okla. Mantle was invited to a camp at Branson, this spring and, signed to a contract prior to coming here to join Craft's KOM League leaders."[289]

The process the Yankees used demonstrates that Mantle didn't go directly from the Baxter Springs sandlot to the KOM League. There was a period of training he underwent at Branson prior to his being assigned to Independence.

The day before Mantle hit the home run at Carthage that struck Hornsby on the head the Independence Baseball Association broke from tradition and decided to publish a souvenir book about their team. "For the first time, the Independence Baseball Association will offer for sale tonight, a souvenir book of the Yankees and the KOM baseball league. The book compiled and published through the *Reporter's* facilities, contains a short

[288] *The Independence Daily Reporter*, August 9, 1949.
[289] *The Independence Daily Reporter*, August 2, 1949.

history of the league, a history of Independence's return to organized base-ball, individual pictures of Harry Craft's baseball career, the standings of the teams and the close of all the season's since the KOM was formed. They list the league officials and the officials of the IBA (Independence Baseball Association). With a cover of traditional baseball green the 16-page book will be offered for sale to anyone wishing to remember the current baseball season. A suitable place has been left on the back of the book for the auto-graphs of the team members. No other team in the league has as much rea-son to issue such a book as the Yankees. Their rise from a dismal last place finish in the first year of competition in the KOM to first place at this time is deserving of the unqualified support of the fans. The Baseball Association is offering the book for sale at twenty-five cents per copy." [290]

Cap Tole, the President of the Independence baseball club, was as pre-scient on the publication of the souvenir yearbook as he was in retaining the original contract and cancelled paychecks of Mantle. Those four items eventually brought $50,000 to Cappy some 46 years afterward. By that time Cap was 96 years of age and he sold the items in November of 1995 and died the following January.

Front cover of the 1949 Independence Yearbook.

SOUVENIR BOOK

The
INDEPENDENCE YANKEES
and
K-O-M LEAGUE

◇ ◇

1949

The photo of Mantle in that yearbook was nothing spectacular. It showed him in the ground ball fielding position with his head up. That little booklet didn't make either the Independence Baseball Association or the *Independence Daily Reporter* rich. The booklets were kept by the officials until the final game of the 1949 playoffs against the Iola Indians. After the game there was a celebra-tion and each player was given one of those yearbooks. They were passed among their teammates to have each to make a comment and sign their name.

Mantle signed each as either Mickey Mantle, Mick Mantle or printed his name, Mick Mantle. He always dotted the "I" in his first name with a round circle. He wrote a message in only one of those yearbooks and it was for the fellow who played second base, Charlie Weber. Mickey printed this message: "To my double play combination partner. Mick Mantle."

---

[290] *The Independence Daily Reporter*, July 27, 1949.

Those yearbooks lay in various places around this country until Mantle's death and then became a hot item in the collectibles market. Dealers went on buying sprees to get hold of them, offering upwards of $2,500. Shortly afterward they showed up for sale for $5,000 and advertised as "one of a kind." Well, there were hundreds of those things sold at Independence home games for a quarter, for six weeks, and very few were ever autographed by anyone. There were 18 of those items signed by team members and none of them had every player's signature on it for an obvious reason — no individual signed his personal copy. One of those yearbooks became the "proud" possesson of a memorabilia collector who stole this author's copy at the 1998 KOM League reunion. Some sins are unpardonable and the theft of that yearbook falls into that category.

Mantle's respect and admiration for his 1949 Independence Yankee teammates was manifested in a hand-written letter he sent to one of his teammates after joining the Joplin Miners. Many members of the 1949 Independence squad had gone on to Grand Forks, North Dakota, a Class C club in the Northern League. The following unedited letter was written on the stationery of the Hotel Warren in Salina, Kansas and dated May 5, 1950:

> *Hello Boys, I don't know if they can get this letter through all that ice and snow to you guys or not but if they don't write and tell us. How is every body doing up there? Pretty good I hope. I guess "Virgie" (Speck) will win 20 games this year and Bob M. (Mallon) will win 18 or 19. If Ken's (Bennett) luck holds out he might win 3. I know old Sam (Joyce) will burn up that Northern League. Tell Nick (Ananias), Jack (Whitaker) & John (Cimino) if their ave. [average] ever drops below .350 to come down to Joplin & I will give them a few pointers.*
>
> *We beat Salina last night behind Bob Wiesler. That's two straight for Bob. They have only scored 4 runs against him in 2 games boy his control is really a lot better.*
>
> *After "Virgie" left down here I started making my errors behind Steve (Kraly). I made two errs. the other night that caused him to get took out of the game. We are in second place now. Tell Ted Atkinson hello for me will you. We are going to the show so I will close for now. Be sure and write real soon. Mick Chas.[291]*

---

[291] Keith Speck collection.

HOTEL WARREN

EUROPEAN   FIRE PROOF
MRS. WARREN E. SMITHER, General Manager
GEORGE CURTIS, Resident Mgr.
Salina, Kansas
May 5, 1950

Hello Boys,

   I don't know if they can get this letter through all that ice + snow to you guys or not but if they don't write and tell us.

   How is every body doing up there? Pretty good I hope. I guess "Virgie" will win 20 this year + Bob M. will win about 18 or 19. If Ken's luck holds out he might win 3. I know old Sam will burn up that Northern League. Tell Nick, Jack, + John if their ave. ever drops down below 350 to come down to Joplin + I will give them a few pointers.

(over)

   We beat Salina last night behind Bob Wiesler. That's two straights for Bob. They have only scored 4 runs against him in 2 games boy his control is really a lot better.

   After "Virgie" left down here I started making my errors behind Steve. I make two errs. the other night that caused him to get took out of the game. We are in second place now. Tell Ted Atkinson hello for me will you. We are going to the show so I will close for now. Be sure + write real soon.

Mick Chas.

A reproduction of the letter quoted on previous page, penned by Mantle's own hand.

The foregoing letter was Mantle's account of the ball game played at Salina, Kansas, on May 4, 1950. The following is the Associated press write-up in *The Joplin Globe* for that game with the Salina Blue Jays:

Bob Wiesler Turns in Good 5-Hit Job

Joplin broke Salina's six game winning streak here tonight with a 6-3 win in a Western Association game played in a terrific windstorm.

While winds estimated at from 40-50 miles-per-hour blew, Joplin scored four runs in the first four innings for an easy margin. Two more tallies in the ninth put the game on ice.

The only score directly attributed to the wind was a triple by Maurice Nordell, Salina player. The wind caught Nordell's smash fly in the seventh and carried it away from outfielder, Tom Gott.

It took three singles for Joplin to score in the second with Lou Skizas hitting to center with two out. Cal Neeman lined a single to center and Bob Wiesler singled Skizas home.

In the third, Cromer Smotherman walked with one out, went to second on a fielder's choice and scored on Tom Gott's single.

Neeman singled with one away in the fourth. Wiesler walked and Al Billingsly singled Neeman across with two gone. Wiesler scored on an infield error.

Billingsly singled to open the ninth and took second on a fielder's choice.

Smotherman and Mickey Mantle walked filling the bases. Gott singled in Billingsly. Smotherman scored from third on Waters' long fly to center.

Two of Joplin's errors came in the ninth and Wiesler had all sorts of trouble, giving up two walks, but he finally escaped with one run against him as he struck out the side to run his total to 12 for the game.[292]

With punctuation and grammar aside, Mantle truly cared for his former Independence Yankee teammates and was interested in staying in touch. His comments on the game the previous evening never mentioned the harshness of the climate. That letter indicated that there was a closeness that Mantle felt with many of the guys and it also displayed his evaluation of his shortcomings—the errors, and his strength—the hitting. He was complimentary of his current teammates and wanted to share their success with his former teammates. The May 5, 1950 letter was read at the dedication of the Mickey Mantle baseball facility in 1999. Merlyn Mantle commented later to this author, "I find the letters most interesting, since Mickey was not one to write."

Merlyn's reference to letters was due to the fact that another letter, written to the same group of former Independence Yankees, was penned in 1951 from New York. On New York Yankee letterhead the following letter was sent in early 1951. The only designation on the letterhead to pinpoint the exact date was "Tuesday, 11 A. M." However, that isn't a lot of assistance in determining the year it was composed. In the letter Mantle mentioned Lou Skizas being at Norfolk, Virginia, and his reference on Tuesday to a Collier's magazine coming out on Friday places the date of that letter as May 29, 1951. This is the content of the letter:

> *Hi Keith, I just got your letter. And was really glad to hear from you again. You know the last letter you wrote, well I lost it on the way back to N. Y. & I didn't have your address. I saw your brother while we were*

---

[292] *The Joplin Globe*, May 5, 1950.

in Texas. He looks a lot like you but a little better looking—Ha! Ha! How is everything in the Army! That was pretty good your brother getting out maybe he can start in playing pro ball now. Lou Skizas is at Norfolk doing real good. When you go to K. C. tell Bob (Wiesler) hello for me. Steve Kraly is in the Army.

Boy I wish you could come up here we could really have a hell of a time. We really had some good times at Indy didn't we? A lot of time(s) when I'm laying around I remember some of the stuff we did. How about the time in Ponca (Ponca City, Oklahoma) when Hastings thought the hotel was on fire—about four in the morning. I don't have near as good a time up here as I did the last two years. You know all of these guys are married. I wish you and Lou (Skizas) & Bob (Mallon) could come up here. We would ripe [rip] this town wide open-huh?

Write me again. I have to go to take hitting. Oh yea look in Friday Colliers if you want to see a good looking bastard-A Pal—Mickey.[293]

The incident that stuck in Mantle's mind about Ponca City was their stay at the Jens-Marie Hotel. It happened to be his first trip to Ponca City with the club. The accommodations were the "top of the line" since Ponca City was an oil boom town. The visiting teams were able to get those rooms for $2.50 a night with two to a room. If there was just one to a room the price was $1.50 and thus out of the question as far as teams paying that exorbitant price. A real stir occurred shortly afterward when the Jens-Marie hiked room rates for KOM League teams to $1.75 per man.

The room rate issue got the attention of all the top officials of each team in the league and they contacted the president of the Ponca City Dodgers, Ted Parkinson. They implored him to do something about the rates since he had "pull" in that town. Parkinson responded to that request with this message: "Mr. Lee Newman. In regards to rooms for the boys at the Jens-Marie; the owner is as stubborn as the South end of a Missouri Mule headed North. There would be no chance of getting him to change his mind."[294]

During the June 18-20 series in Ponca City things got a little exciting after most of the players had turned in the for the night. It could be said that the "ladies of the night" had done likewise, in a wry sense. However, the

[293] From the Keith Speck collection.
[294] Letter from Ted Parkinson to Lee Newman, written April 30, 1951. Taken from the John Hall collection.

silence of the night was broken by the clanging of a fire alarm. Everyone ran into the hallways. The Independence ball club was on the second floor and most of the "ladies of the night" had set up shop on the third floor. There was a stampede for the staircase not unlike cattle being spooked by a late evening thunderstorm on the prairie. The Independence Yankees saw the "ladies of the night" mostly wearing their working "uniforms." It was a scene a young man from Commerce, Oklahoma, had never witnessed and it made an impression that stayed with him at least a couple of years, probably longer.

Ponca City games against Independence were big attractions for fans of both clubs. Ponca City was a Dodger farm club and they liked nothing better than beating a Yankee team since the Brooklyn version of the Dodgers couldn't do it at the Major league level.

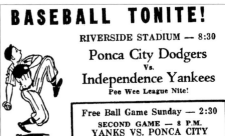

BASEBALL TONITE!

RIVERSIDE STADIUM — 8:30

Ponca City Dodgers
Vs.
Independence Yankees
Pee Wee League Nite!

Free Ball Game Sunday — 2:30
SECOND GAME — 8 P.M.
YANKS VS. PONCA CITY

Roommate Mallon recalled Mantle as being a good kid who never smoked, drank or hit on the women. He mostly talked about a girlfriend he had back home and the only other woman he ever mentioned was Doris

Doris Day may have been Mantle's favorite movie star while in the KOM League. However, a year later he is standing behind one of the glamour girls of the World War II era. Left to right: Phil Rizzuto, Jerry Coleman, Yogi Berra, Mickey, Betty Grable, John Mize, Johnny Hopp, Joe Collins, Gus Mauch and Bob Wiesler.[295]

Day. Miss Day was his favorite movie star and he made an attempt to see all of the movies she made.

---

[295] Photo courtesy of Bob Wiesler.

Mallon's least favorite thing to do was warm up Mantle. Mallon, being a pitcher, would have to warm up some of the other players when he wasn't going to be in a game. He recalled, "I sure do remember that knuckle ball. I got to where I would not warm up with Mantle, it was bad. I would rather warm up Crowder, Wiesler, or Speck than to try and catch that knuckle ball."

As most former baseball players who worked their way up to the top from the low minors to the Major Leagues, an overwhelming majority recall their first year in organized baseball as the most memorable along with being the most satisfying. It was a time in their lives when they were out on their own for the first time and they all had aspirations of making it big. They also believed everything the scouts and their first managers and team owners told and promised them. By the start of their second season's they found out the world could be very cruel and that not everyone in life who gave their word lived up to it.

Baseball was not the only thing the 1949 Independence Yankees enjoyed. Mantle and teammate Joe Crowder hailed from the same part of the Midwest and hunting, fishing and "frogging" were things they both relished and excelled in doing. The pair especially enjoyed going frogging after a night game with the latest addition to the ball club. It was even better when the latest arrival was from a big city and didn't have a clue of what the sport entailed. Lou Skizas joined the Independence Yankees from Fond du Lac of the Wisconsin State League. He had never seen any of his teammates in that league go frogging and he never experienced such a foray as a kid growing up on the streets of Chicago.

Frogging is basically simple. The frogger takes a bright light, shines it into the frogs eyes, thus blinding it. Then, the "frogger" reaches down and grabs the frog barehanded, throws it into a bag and the next day has a great dinner. For those who have never seen frog legs in a frying pan they get their next surprise as they observe the legs jumping around as the tendons retract, and expand. Mallon recalled that Mantle and Crowder once had enough frog legs to feed the entire ball club toward the end of the season.

Sammy Joyce joined the Independence club late in the 1949 campaign from Greenville, Mississippi of the Cotton States League. Joyce had attended both Georgia Tech and the University of Chattanooga before signing a professional contract in 1948. After he had been on the scene at Independence for a short time he gained enough of the young Mantle's confidence to do something no one else had succeeded in doing. Joyce, a devout

Presbyterian, recalled that Mantle attended a celebrity golf tournament in Chattanooga many years later and he introduced him as the first person ever to succeed in getting him to attend church.

With Mantle consenting to attend religious services with Joyce, Mantle asked his friend to attend one of his "religious rituals." Yep, Mantle took Joyce on his first frogging trip. He recalled doing what Mantle had told him in order to render the frog motionless. Moving his flashlight along the bank of the river Joyce spied two bright eyes. When he reached for the frog he got more than expected, he had grabbed hold of a snake. Joyce laughed about it 45 years after the fact but said, "If there was a record for snake throwing, I would hold it."[296]

Sammy Joyce arrived in Independence too late to make it into the 1949 team photo. Six years later he got his photo taken with a couple of his former teammates. The New York Yankees were headed north from spring training and stopped in Chattanooga, Tennesse for lunch.   Joyce is on the far right. The first three fellows to his right are Mickey Mantle, Bob Wiesler and Enos Slaughter. Tom Sturdivant is second from the far left.[297]

Thus, Mantle and Crowder spent most of their frogging trips in the company of each other since the turnover on the ball club was minimal and few guys ever went with them on a second trip.

Mantle was not one to shun a stunt just because he had never attempted it in the past. Following a game in 1949 at Riverside Park in Iola, Kansas,

[296] Sammy Joyce.
[297] Photo courtesy of Bob Wiesler.

the Independence Yankees boarded the best bus in the KOM League and headed for the only open eatery at night in town, Dave Hart's Café. The Independence club drove around in air-conditioned comfort while the remainder of the clubs made do with antiquated church and school buses. After the meal that night Mantle, Al Long and a couple of the other fellows got back to the bus before the rest of the ball club had finished their meal.

Never shunning a challenge Mantle sat down in the drivers seat of the Greyhound and decided he would take it for a spin. He had never driven anything of that magnitude in his life. However, Long recalled, "He turned the key, the big bus started and Mantle drove the bus around the Iola square

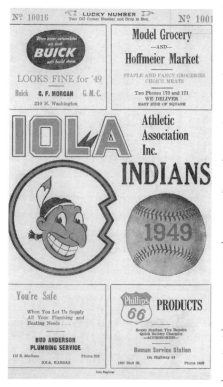

This (left) is the cover of a very rare scorecard. It is one of three that have been discovered that includes Mantle in a minor league game.

This (above) depicts the starting lineups for the visiting Independence Yankees and the home club, the Iola Indians.

a couple of times. That bus banged every curb on that city square; he had that bus all over the road but didn't wreck it. The most amazing thing was that he didn't get in trouble from Craft for driving it."[298]

Iola was the scene of Mantle's first championship in professional baseball. He was not a factor in the outcome of any of the games. The Yankees

---

[298] Al Long.

whipped the Indians in the first game of the championship series as Mantle went 0-5. In the second game the Yankees pulled off another one run victory, 1-0 as he went 0-2. Then, in the final game the Yankees won a close game by the score of 8-1. Mantle went 1-4 in that game. That game was tied 1-1 through 10 innings and Independence broke the game open in the 11th when Iola committed wild pitches, throwing errors, dropped balls by infielders covering a base and Iola infielders throwing to bases and hitting runners in the process. It was a sad time indeed for the scrappy Iola ball club.

However, that night had its own form of melancholy for the seventeen-year-old Mantle. That last game with his Independence teammates was a very emotional time for him. This was the completion of his first professional season and he was moved by the significance of it. He had formed some close friendships and knew that episode in his life could never be repeated. Keith Speck, a pitcher on that team recalled that Mantle cried like a baby for he correctly reasoned, "We will never be together like this again."

Mantle's greatest fondness for the game of baseball and his teammates was with the team one level below where he was currently performing. It may have been that he felt the closeness of that group or looked upon that group as his "extended family." Toward the end of his life Mantle drove up to Baxter Springs with a friend. Wayne Metcalf, who oversaw the Little League Park and small museum attached to the baseball facility, noticed a car parked there early one morning and went over to see what the person wanted. Wayne recognized Mantle but didn't make a big "to do" about it. Mantle wanted to know if he could go inside the museum and see what was on display. As he roamed through the display he was excited when he saw the photos and items from his Baxter Springs Whiz Kid days. As Wayne recalled, "That didn't impress his friend who was only interested in the things from Mickey's life that pertained to his days with the New York Yankees."[299]

By the end of the 1949 season Mantle was another "prospect" and although there were signs of brilliance, it was by no means assured that he would go too much higher on the baseball ladder. Trained baseball men could see the raw talent in Mantle, for he could run, throw — although not always accurately — and above all he had an almost inherent knowledge of the finer points of the game learned long ago from his dad, Jess "Redneck" Lovelace and Barney Barnett.

---

[299] Wayne Metcalf.

The 1949 Independence Yankees. Over time some of the autographs faded from this photo but the faces and memories remain vivid. <u>Front row</u>, left to right: Jim Bello (Belotti), Steve Kraly, Charlie Weber, Ken Bennett, Bill Chambers, Jack Whitaker, Lou Skizas and Mickey Mantle. <u>Back row,</u> left to right: John Cimino, Bob Mallon, Joe Crowder, Keith Speck, Harry Craft, Bob Wiesler, Bob Newbill, Nick Ananias and Al Long.

Members of the Independence Yankees (1949):

Burl Moffitt, Kenneth "Jack" Rose, Darrell Waska, Len Wiesner, Jack Whitaker, Alvin Long, Robert Mallon, Bob Newbill, Keith Speck, Ken Bennett, Charles Weber, Bob Wiesler, Jim Belotti (Bello), James Cobb, Harold Groves, Dick Duda, Lou Skizas, Jack Hasten, Arnold Joyce, Nick Ananias, Joe Crowder, Mickey Mantle, Bill Holderness, Bill Chambers, John Cimino and Steve Kraly.

16

1950: The Joplin Miners —
Spring Training

Tucked into the Missouri Ozarks was the sleepy little town of Branson that hosted spring training for a bunch of young men who considered themselves the future Bronx Bombers. They were the lads from the Grand Forks, North Dakota, Chiefs; Independence, Kansas, Yankees; Quincy, Illinois, Gems, Joplin, Missouri, Miners; and Fond du Lac, Wisconsin, Panthers all branches of the far flung network of New York Yankee minor league system.

Mickey Mantle made the trip to Branson that spring with his dad at the wheel and his twin brothers Ray and Roy in the back seat. According to Mantle's first cousin, Jimmy Richardson, the trip to Branson that day in 1950 was the longest trip the family ever took. Mutt was notorious for his driving. Whenever he went on a trip his top automobile speed was 30 miles an hour. Ray, Roy and Jimmy always spoke of that journey. As it turned out it took from sun up to sun down to make the round trip to Branson and home again. That trip on the old winding highways was about 150 miles one-way. The first car Mutt ever owned was a Buick La Salle. Over the intervening years he purchased Chevrolet Fleetwoods.

When Mantle stayed on with the Western Association club that season he commuted between Commerce and Joplin each day. That too, took about an hour to make a 30-mile trip with Mutt at the wheel. Occasionally, Mutt would let Mickey drive and when the speed got up around 50 miles per hour Mutt would yell out a couple of times in a quick bursts, "You're going to airplane it, boy."

The boys at Branson in 1950 were the Class D and C hopefuls who were corralled in that southern Missouri village to have them in a place where there was nothing to do but play baseball, sleep and play baseball and thus avoid the very appearance of temptation. The only amusement in Branson in those days was the Owen Theater and if any of the ballplayers had 45 cents it would gain them admittance to a double feature, serial, cartoon, newsreel and previews of coming attractions. The nearest "real" attraction to Branson was the resort site of Rockaway Beach.

Mantle's first professional photo, shown in the *Joplin Globe,* was one taken of him during the spring of 1950.

Al Long, who had signed a Yankee contract in 1949, was in camp in 1950 when he decided the boredom of Branson had taken its toll. Being from nearby Springfield he was the guy "in the know" about places like Rockaway Beach. So, early in the month of April a group jumped in the old 1935 Ford owned by soon to be Joplin second baseman, Al Billingsly, and set off for a great time at Rockaway. What Billingsly didn't realize at the time that 1935 Ford was to become the "team car" and celebration vehicle at the end of that same season.

What Long and the rest didn't

understand was that recreation cities in that part of the country didn't open until after Memorial Day. So, back to Branson they headed. On the trip they encountered a couple of "slight" problems. First the headlights went out on the old car and secondly, darkness had overtaken the landscape of the Ozarks.

Anyone knowledgeable of that part of God's green earth understands that those old winding two lane highways of the mid part of the 20th century were difficult enough to traverse during daylight let alone trying to pick your way through hairpin curves in the dead of night.

Lee McPhail, and the rest of the Yankee brass, would have had a fit had they known that a great part of their future was been endangered by a bunch of "kids" riding around the hills of Missouri in a car without headlights and ultimately what a loss it would have been to the game of baseball. In that car were guys like Bob Wiesler, Steve Kraly and Mickey Mantle. Not that their lives were more precious than the boys who never got out of the "bushes," but the 1950 Joplin Miners were a special team in the annals of minor league baseball. Regarding Mantle's reaction to that harrowing ride he recalled the "Commerce Comet" sitting there chuckling "he! he!" in his usual manner of expressing himself when having a good time.

Mantle was known for his knack of bugging his teammates with "boogers." Keith Speck recalled going to spring drills at Branson in 1950 and Mickey liked to hang them on the top of Billingsly's 1935 Ford. Tommy Gott recalled that when Mantle would get a "good one" he would stop whatever he was doing, show all the guys, leave the playing field and run to the locker room to place it in a conspicuous place for all to see at a later time.

Gott recalled that Mantle's "pranks" were without peer on the Miners club during the 1950 season. He recalled that he and Mantle were staying in a hotel room on the road and had arrived late in the afternoon. When they checked in and got to their room they noticed some activity across the hall. Gott and Mantle made a pledge not to tell any of their teammates that a "lady of the evening" had set up shop right next to their room.

Following the night game Gott recalled, "We didn't go out after the game but headed back to the hotel. When we arrived back the lady across the hall was doing a brisk business. There was customer #1, then customer #2 and Mantle was taking in the 'sights' through the keyhole most of the time." Gott recalled, "As Mickey and I were arguing over whose turn it was for keyhole duty, a scuffle ensued. The 'lady of the evening' heard the commotion outside her door and called the bell captain."

Gott and Mantle scurried back to their room and closed the door. A discussion arose as to who would answer the inevitable knock on the door. As usual, Mantle won the argument. As Gott recalled, when the bell captain knocked on their door Mantle acted as if he was asleep. After a few minutes of the discussion Mantle arose from his feigned sleep wearing only his boxer shorts and displaying a body that appeared to have been sculpted by the gods. He asked the bell captain, "Are you calling me a peeping Tom?" Not wishing to confront a man of Mantle's stature the bell captain replied, "Oh, no, no, no."

Having the minor league training camp of the New York Yankees in a small town would seem to be a great boost for the morale of the citizenry and a boon to the economy. However, business in Branson went along at its usual laid back pace. A local drugstore placed this sign in their window in order to welcome the Yankee farmhands: "Yankees weuns' air dern glad to have youen's. Please make our stores your sittin,' 'spittin,' and whittlin' place."

In an era when a Coke was a nickel and townsfolk of Branson would pick up the ballplayers at the cabins where they resided while in spring training and give them a ride downtown, there wasn't much to spend their money on and not much time to do it either. Each Yankee farm club at Branson had their own set of rules. The Yankees' general rules were: No drinking of liquor, no gambling and a curfew. Each club got to set their own curfew and Harry Craft imposed 11:00 p.m. on his Joplin boys.

The newspapers basically ignored the fact that spring training was being held in their city. It may have stemmed from the fact that the only other team to have trained in that city prior to that time was the 1947 Leavenworth Braves. The Braves were the doormats of the Western Association and set records for futility unchallenged for the rest of the history of that league. The most extensive news coverage ever given to spring training in Branson was printed in 1951 and that due to a tragic drowning.

Another guy with the first name of Mickey and last initial of "M" was on the spring roster of the Fond du Lac, Wisconsin, Panthers of the Wisconsin State League. He lost his life in a boating accident. Seventeen-year-old Mickey Mahon, graduate of Beaumont High in St. Louis, along with Ed Wheatley went boating in an aluminum canoe on Lake Taneycomo early on April 14. Mahon's boat overturned and he couldn't swim. Wheatley swam to shore, but before the second canoe in the boating party could get to

Mahon, he went under. Mahon couldn't float, being dressed in heavy clothing that included a leather jacket. The depth of the water where he went under was 25 feet. After a coroner's inquest it was ruled the drowning was accidental. The coroner heard from all parties in the boating trip and ruled that with high waves and a strong undercurrent it was an unavoidable, yet tragic loss of life.

Herb Heiserer a young Yankee hopeful that spring, recalled the drowning and its aftermath in this manner: "I remember that terrible day in April 1950 very well. I, too, was in Branson with Bob Mallon that day. I also played against Mahon and Wheatley in St. Louis I was there for a couple of weeks doing a tryout with the Yankee organization, several weeks before my high school graduation. As you probably know I went back to St. Louis unsigned. About a month later, I signed with the Philadelphia A's and reported to Buffalo in the International League. Sure was a shock, high school to AAA in 24 hours. I'll never forget that very sad day in Branson. When Mr. Mahon first got to Branson, I can still hear him saying, 'somebody tell me that they made a mistake about Mickey.' "[300]

That memory causes Bob Mallon, Mickey's roommate with Independence, to shudder to this day. Mallon and Mahon had competed against each other many times in their native St. Louis high schools. Mallon recalled that it was a stupid thing to go boating in days when life jackets were not all that common. Like Mahon, Mallon couldn't swim, yet he recalled going boating on that lake before Mahon died. Following that death Mallon had learned his lesson and avoided the water thereafter, except for a post-game shower.

Tom Hesketh, a young pitching prospect in the Yankee organization, recalled the drowning. It was a scene that marred that entire spring and Hesketh, now a Cincinnati businessman, said the event is as vivid as watching Mantle hit a home run and kissing home plate in joy over that wallop. After the death of Mahon, Lou Magoula, Yankee scout, who had signed the St. Louis athlete, had to identify the body and then inform the parents of their son's tragic demise.

It seems ironic in retrospect that the drowning of Mahon is about the only mention that can be found in *The White River Leader*, the Branson newspaper, regarding the fact that the New York Yankees had five minor league clubs in their city in the late 1940s and early 1950s. Most local citi-

---

[300] Herb Heiserer.

zens would have never dreamed that from that group of young men would contain some of the greatest names in the game of major league baseball in a few short years.

Bob Childs had this to say about his only association with Mickey: "At spring training in Branson, Missouri, in the spring of 1950, Mantle was with Joplin and I was with Grand Forks and both teams took spring training there. At that time it was just a cheap resort area and we all stayed in cabins in the area. We played games against each other as well as other spring training activities. In a game we had with Joplin, I was pitching the first four innings and the first time Mantle came up I was lucky enough to get him on strikes. The next time up he hit a towering fly ball to dead center field (no fences at that park). It would have cleared any fence in any ball park, but our center fielder had a lot of running room and caught the ball. However, I was amazed, as Mantle was almost to third base by the time the ball was caught. He could fly around those bases. So thanks to no fences, Mantle was 0 for 2 against me. He had great talent at that time and can not imagine the records he would have if not for injury or meeting up with Billy Martin."[301]

Great Expectations

Gathered at Branson in early April 1950 were raw rookies, a few guys who had played a year or two previously in the Yankee system and the men who were to make the selection as to where each would serve his "sentence" during that summer which saw the face of baseball changed forever. The previous spring training camps held in that sleepy Ozark town were conducted on the YMCA ball field and at City Park in the downtown area. In 1950 there was a new facility on the other side of Lake Taneycomo.

The ominous clouds of Korea were lurking on the horizon during the early spring drills of the young Yankee hopefuls. By mid-season many of those boys were of draft age and confident Uncle Sam would furnish the uniforms they would be wearing by the time the 1951 season rolled around.

Bunny Mick Remembers[302]

In January of 1950, before Mantle reported to the Branson camp, the New York Yankees conducted a camp for the best prospects in the organi-

---

[301] Robert Childs.

[302] Bunny Mick's recollections shared with this author through conversations and letters for an eight-year span.

zation. It was held near the end of that month at Lake Wales, Florida. This was the spring training site of the Kansas City Blues. Malcolm "Bunny" Mick recalled, "I was the young Yankee farm manager there to assist Casey Stengel and all the big shots. Bill Dickey, Frank Crosetti, Jim Turner, Burleigh Grimes, Johnny Nuen and others. The truth is you could say I was Casey's 'lackey.' He had me follow and assist him with base running, bunting and foul fungo flies."

David Waters (left) and Mantle (right) bask in the sun at Lake Wales, Florida. They were both so sun-burned they were unable to bear the weight of the their baseball uniforms for three days. Of course, neither had bothered to wear sun tanning oil.[303]

"This was Mickey's first spring camp ever," Mick said. "No baseball injuries yet and he could fly! That's where we clocked him at 3.1 seconds, crack of the bat to first base—still the record. Furthermore, he did it more than once." Mick said one of his "lackey" duties was making sure the groundskeeper had the field in good shape every day. About the fifth day, during batting practice, Mick had about eight catchers taking foul fungoes in foul territory down the left field line. Johnny Nuen whistled to him to come to the batting cage. Mick recalled that he left leaving about eight guys sitting with nothing to do. Among them were Gus Triandos, Hank Foiles, Clint Courtney and Elston Howard. When Mick arrived at the batting cage

---

[303] Photo courtesy of David Waters.

Nuen showed him the first base line which was all torn up. He said, "Get Charlie, the groundskeeper, to roll and pack it better." Mick retorted, "It was good this morning but I'll tell him again."

The next day, same thing. Nuen whistles, and Mick leaves the catchers, goes to the cage and Nuen says, "I found out what is wrong with the base line." Mick said, "What?" He said, "Stay here with me." Mick replied, " I can't do that, have to look after Casey's catchers." Nuen said, "Leave 'em there." Mick admitted being nervous, "But Nuen's had the rank, after all he made an unassisted triple play at first base in 1928," he chuckled.

Mick recalled, "Well, Mantle comes to bat next. Back then you bunted two, got about five or six swings and then ran hard and made your turn at first like it was a two base hit. Well! Mantle hit that last one and we're on the third base side of the cage looking straight to first base. When he took off I thought we were following the horses down the home stretch on a rainy day at Churchill Downs. Dirt was flying back at us and there were about 12 or 13 craters down that line. He destroyed the whole line. He ran a lot like Rickey Henderson, with respect that his head didn't move, he would just reach out and snatched the dirt back with each foot. It was amazing! I've still never seen anyone else run like that."

After that early camp of two to three weeks, the Kansas City Blues opened their spring camp in Lake Wales, Florida and the Yankees sent Mick there to help Joe Kuhel, the manager, for a month before he reported to Branson to pick up the Independence team. They also sent Mantle to the Kansas City camp, so Mick (Bunny) and Mick (Mantle) both went through three spring training camps together that year. Wonder how many people have done that?

During that camp Kansas City played the Philadelphia Phillies in an exhibition game. So Mantle, with less than 100 pro games behind him, was facing a big league team that would win the National League pennant that year.

Mick recalled, "In the first or second inning he came up against Jim Konstanty, I'm pretty sure. He hit a lofty line drive about 360 feet to left center and Richie Ashburn made a nice backhanded play on it. I'm sitting by Kuhel on the bench as Mickey jogs by shaking his hands. I said 'Hurt yourself?' He said, 'No, hit it on the handle.' I looked at Joe and said, 'You hear that?' Joe replied, 'Yeah.' 'Kind of a smart-ass answer,' I said."

Mick had never seen Mantle act like that so he and Kuhel forgot about it. Then about the seventh inning Mantle came up again against another right-handed pitcher. Mick recalled, "I don't remember that pitcher's name. You need to visualize the contour of the Lake Wales Park to appreciate what happened. Centerfield is the shortest of the three fields, about 405 feet. Left, right and centerfields are a straight line of Austrian Pines about 80 feet tall. So, the leftfield line to the pines is about 500 feet and right field is about 525. The next ball that Mick hit, batting left, goes straight over the leftfielder's head and a mile high. Wrong direction for a lefty, but I saw that leftfielder's number for an awfully long time. I saw it until he vanished into the trees. I would estimate it was 450-460 feet where the fielder and the trees met. However, the ball was over half-way up into the trees."

As soon as Mantle hit that blast Kuhel turned to Mick and said, "I believe he did hit the first one on the fists." According to Mick, that night the Yankees moved Mantle to the Branson training site because they knew Kuhel would want to keep him in Triple A.

Mick recalled, "The next morning at practice, Kuhel said, 'Where's that kid? Where's that kid?'" The Yankees told General Manager, Parke Carroll to tell Kuhel what had happened. As Damon Runyon would say, 'Kuhel was upset quite some, and no little.'"

"That home run and the one Mantle hit in Branson a month later that went into Lake Taneycomo ranks right up there in the 550 foot plus category with the one he hit out of Griffith Stadium and the one he hit against the facade in right field at Yankee Stadium," according to Bunny Mick

Lee McPhail convened a group of men that April and the half-way point of the 20th century who had been designated managers for those Yankee minor league clubs. Jim Adlam was the Quincy, Illinois, Gems manager of the Three-I League, Malcolm "Bunny" Mick went to the KOM League affiliate, Independence, Kansas, Jack Farmer got the Grand Forks, North Dakota, assignment in the Northern League, Wayne Tucker drew the Fond du Lac, Wisconsin, post in the Wisconsin State League and Harry Craft got "saddled" with the Joplin, Missouri, Miners of the Class C Western Association.

Most of the managers the Yankees assigned experienced a full season with their respective clubs. Mick, however, was one of two exceptions and wound up replacing Johnny Mize in August with the Kansas City Blues when "Big John" got recalled to New York. Receiving a far worse fate was Jack Farmer. Bob Childs was a pitcher who broke camp with the Grand Forks ball club that spring. He recalled the events of the last day in the life of his manager: "When we arrived in Grand Forks after spring training the town was under water from a flood of the Red River and there were snow piles in the outfield at the ball park. Jack had called a meeting at a downtown hotel for that morning as we were to work out at the University of North Dakota's field house. He did not show and Bob Wiltse and one other fellow went to the house he had rented. There they found he had passed away."[304]

According to Childs, "The sad part of it was Jack's wife and twins were to arrive in Grand Forks that day, which they did to find this sad situation. If I recall they were from Georgia or another southern state, in any event it shook up the entire club for a bit. The Yankees sent Cedric Durst, who played outfield with Babe Ruth for a while with the Yankees, to replace Farmer. Durst was quite an old fellow by this time, but did a decent job managing for the rest of the year. Those twin children of Jack's were only 1 or 2 years old at that time, so it had to be a tough row to hoe for Mrs. Farmer."[305]

Craft had managed the previous year at Independence of the KOM League and had fashioned a ball club that "dominated" that league in both the regular season and playoffs. Domination in this case was winning the pennant by one game and finishing a game and a half ahead of the third place club. The playoffs went the limit and then some. The deciding game against Iola, Kansas went into extra innings.

With Craft's success as manager in his first season he was not the first selection for the Joplin managerial assignment in 1950. Greenwade, the New York Yankee scout, had been impressed by the way the 1949 Carthage, Missouri team performed under some adverse conditions. Potentially, one of the finest pitchers in the league took a line shot off his pitching hand in the season opener and the Carthage ball club could not keep pace without the services of Matthew Leroy Robert Saban.

Saban later toiled for many years in the Sally League and was always on the verge of making the roster of the Washington Senators, but never quite got the break that he and many others thought he deserved. Saban later had the chance to be the pitching coach for the New York Yankees when George Steinbrenner hired his first cousin, Lou Saban in the front office of the Yankees.

Greenwade was convinced that Don Anderson was the man to lead the

---

[304] Robert Childs.
[305] Ibid.

Joplin Miners in 1950. On the last road trip to Independence in 1949 Greenwade contacted him. He told the Carthage skipper that he had discussed it with the Yankee brass and they were amenable to him taking the Joplin job for the 1950 season.

Greenwade knew as early as August of 1949 the players who were slated to make the jump from the Class D Independence Yankees to the Class C Western Association Joplin Miners. Greenwade explained that Mantle, Skizas, Wiesler and Steve Kraly would be at Joplin and that it would be a great job for Anderson. Greenwade also threw in the caveat that the Yankees wanted a manager who could also play full-time.

In 1949 Johnny Sturm had been the playing manager at Joplin handling the bulk of the games as the first baseman. Craft had also been slated to be a playing manager at Independence in 1949 and shied away from that duty when he witnessed the speed and some of the "inaccuracy" of the hurlers of the KOM League.

With Anderson, the Yankees would have a manager who could play either first or second base and was a gifted base stealer with his specialty being the theft of home. Anderson made the trip from Independence back to Carthage that August evening mulling over the possibilities of managing a kid named Mantle the following season. Anderson had great admiration for young Mantle's talents and in his report to the Chicago Cub front office at the season's end said, "Get the kid if you have to kidnap him."

Anderson took a few days to review his options for 1950 and discussed it with his wife, Edith, and then decided to spend the 1950 season back in the KOM League. Anderson's primary reason for staying put was not that he didn't like Greenwade or relish the chance of managing in the Yankee organization. His main reason for declining the chance to go to Joplin, was his loyalty to Chicago Cub farm director, Jack Sheehan.

Anderson has never harbored any regrets for that decision. Forty-nine ball seasons later he remarked, "I guess the Yankees couldn't find a playing manager for Joplin so they promoted Harry Craft. I am happy Harry got that opportunity for he was a good and decent guy."[306]

The Independence Connection

Harry Craft, very shortly after arriving in Branson for the 1950 spring workouts, had a pretty good idea on who would form the nucleus of his

---

[306] Don Anderson.

club for his sophomore year in managing. The native of Ellisville, Mississippi realized the necessity of good pitchers and he surrounded himself with three of his top aces from the 1949 Independence Yankees, which he had led to the KOM League pennant and playoff championship. Steve Kraly an 18-6 performer, "Bullet Bob" Wiesler the KOM League's strikeout king in 1949 and right-hander Joe Crowder were the nucleus of the spring hurlers. With the addition of Frank Simanovsky Joplin had an invincible trio of lefties. Simanovsky, posted a 21-3 record and wound up as not only as the MVP of the Miners, but also the Western Association.

Simanovsky was the "forgotten" man of the 1950 Joplin Miners since he went into the Korean War and following his release was unable to regain the form that had made him such a standout with the Miners. Simanovsky's scrapbook contains a 1951 clipping from *The Cedar Rapids Gazette*, in which Gus Schrader penned a prophetic column:

Odd How Things Work Out, Isn't It?

What a difference a break can make in a career. Did you read the papers last week? Well, even if you did, maybe you didn't connect two widely separated stories.

In Cedar Rapids, a local news story carried the names of the latest group of lads to join the Marine Corps. Among them was "Frank Simanovsky, son of Mr. and Mrs. L. R. Simanovsky, 195 Twenty-first Avenue SW."

From New York, the Associated Press sent a sports story concerning the 1951 prospects of some of New York Yankee baseball hopefuls. The Yanks had announced the calling up of 20 recruits for inspection. The story continued, "The player likely to get most attention at the Yanks' Phoenix spring camp is a 19-year-oldster who is not even listed on the roster. He is Mickey Mantle, the Joplin (Mo.) jolter and the apple of Manager Casey Stengel's eye. Mantle was a shortstop sensation at Joplin last year. He hit .383 to lead the Western Association."

Well, that's the words; now here's the music. Simanovsky and Mantle were teammates at pennant-winning Joplin last year. While Mantle was winning the league batting title, Simanovsky was achieving the circuit's top pitching record—21 wins against only three losses, one of the best in any league last season.

Like Mantle, Simanovsky was advanced to Binghamton in the Class A Eastern League—a jump of two classifications. Things looked rosy for both, with the Yankee stadium only a couple of hops away.

Then Simanovsky, the tall Czech southpaw from Cedar Rapids enlisted and thereby suffered a setback of one, two, three, four or maybe more years. Maybe it'll be just long enough so that he'll never catch up and never get his big-league shot.

Mantle will, and here's why. He has been classified as 4-F by his Miami, Okla., draft board. The kid has a bone disease in his left ankle and is regarded as too much of a physical risk by the army.

Odd how things work out sometimes, isn't it? And it's even more odd because things never stop working out.

Who knows? Maybe Mantle would be glad to trade his chance with the Yanks for a sound left ankle and Simanovsky's bunk in the marine boot camp. Maybe Frank will thank his lucky stars some day that things worked out the way they did.

Mantle is certainly entitled to a chance in 1951, and it's not his fault that

he's 4-F with the draft. Last season was his first in organized baseball, but he hit 26 homers, 11 triples, 30 doubles and drove in 134 runs. In spite of his ankle ailment, he is regarded as a speedster on the bases. (Ed Note: Mr. Schrader was incorrect in one aspect of his story. It was Mantle's second year of professional baseball.)

Simanovsky, of course, neither sought or was given any special consideration by the armed services because he had a baseball career budding. Frank is undoubtedly hoping that Mantle makes the big time and gets his praises warbled in the newspapers.

But if that happens, you can bet that every time Simanovsky picks up a sports page, his happiness for an old teammate will be accompanied by a cruel pang of regret about his own baseball career.[307]

Simanovsky's baseball career included stops with the San Diego Devil Dogs while in the service. After Korea he hoped to resume his climb to the top. He was slated for the Birmingham Barons in the Southern Association but the season and his career ended later that same year at Iola, Kansas in the Western Association. A league that he had led in pitching just four short years and one long war earlier.

But Gus Schrader's prediction that Frank would always root for his Joplin teammate, Mantle, was right on.

In 1996, Simanovsky was living in California and his grandson, Ryan Jamison, had been recruited to play baseball for the University of Missouri. He proudly brought the young man to the university campus and took photos of Jamison in his new surroundings. Not wishing to leave the university town without the photos being developed, Simanovsky went to a local "fast photo" shop.

---

[307] Gus Schrader, *The Cedar Rapids Gazette*, ca. February 1951.

Arriving at that shop was a total shock to him. Hanging on the wall were photos of a very young Mantle and a team photo of the 1950 Joplin Miners. Simanovsky was nearly speechless. He informed the cashier that he was in the team photo and was curious as to how the shop came to possess it. The cashier informed him that someone who wrote about old minor league baseball had permitted them to display a set of rare photos.

The Joplin Miner management was prescient during the summer of 1950: They had a promotional team photo signed by all the players. <u>Front row,</u> left to right: Len Wiesner, Steve Kraly, Cromer Smotherman, Dave Waters, Al Billingsly, Mickey Mantle, Tom Gott, Lyle Westrum, Lou Skizas and Carl Lombardi. <u>Back row,</u> left to right: W.R. Satterlee (club president), Harry Craft, Frank Simanovsky, Jerry Buchanan, Bob Wiesler, Dick Fiedler, Dan Ferber, David Benedict, Cal Neeman, Joe Crowder, William Wolfe (groundskeeper) and Roy Beavers (secretary/treasurer).[308]

Simanovsky quickly asked for the telephone number of the owner of the photos and shortly he was conversing with this author at a local coffee shop in Columbia, Missouri. He invited me to the training facility of the University of Missouri baseball where we watched his young grandson display from the right side what Frank had done from the left—throw hard and accurately. Time passed quickly, the talent developed, and in three short years young Ryan had signed a professional contract with the San Diego Padres.

One spring afternoon Yours Truly watched Jamison out of one eye and trained my gaze on Simanovsky with the other, as he sat cuddled up in a windbreaker fending off the harsh winds of an early season game. I wondered then, as I do now, what he saw as he looked on that field. Did he have any regrets of what might have been? He never expressed any bitterness that fate had dealt him a cruel hand, for it had treated so many others in a similar fashion. But

---

[308] Photo courtesy of Frank Simanovsky.

one thing was obvious in all my dealing with Simanovsky: he was proud to have been a Joplin Miner and to have played with a legend, Mickey Mantle.

Frank Simanovsky and wife, Pat, enjoyed the time watching their grandson, Ryan Jamison, pitch for the Missouri Tigers. Frank also enjoyed reliving some of the stories of his days with the Joplin club.[309]

Joe Crowder was ahead of his time. Crowder was a relief pitcher from the day he entered professional baseball. He was another of the scores of young men Greenwade signed out of the four-state area of Kansas, Oklahoma, Arkansas and Missouri.

Crowder was a fire-balling right-hander who threw what is called a "heavy" or "dead" ball. He was raised in the Southwest Missouri town of Seneca and his father's occupation was that of a cemetery worker. Crowder's dad wanted him to be a ballplayer so the younger man would go to the graveyard and play catch with his dad during working hours. It was not much of a stretch to say that he learned to throw the "dead" ball due to the place he practiced so often.

During the spring of 1950 Crowder was skipping some rocks across the smooth surface of Lake Taneycomo where the minor league Yankees held spring training. One of his teammates told him that he better save his arm. He retorted, "Aw, I want to keep in shape. If this club ships me out I might have to make a living knocking opossums out of trees." That club was not about to ship him out. In his first 24 appearances he was used strictly in relief roles, coming in each time to save a game for the Joplin starter. Only when he had a lot of rest and the other members of the Joplin staff were tired did Crowder get his first start. Of course, he won it.

Crowder eventually worked his way up to the staff of the Birmingham Barons of the Southern Association. He had been impressive enough in relief roles for the Barons that he was earmarked for bigger things in 1954. Tom Greenwade advised the Crowder family of that fact at the funeral serv-

---

[309] Ibid.

ice for Joe that was held following the 1953 World Series.

During the World Series of 1953 what should have been a jubilant Mantle was a fellow sitting alone in the clubhouse at Ebbets Field in Brooklyn in a very sad frame of mind. Mantle and Crowder were kindred spirits. Raised a short distance from one another, they found they had common interests when they joined the Independence Yankees in 1949.

One of the favorite pastimes of Crowder and Mantle was going frogging after night ball games. Many a "city slicker" went on one of those trips, but in most cases they didn't go again.

On the afternoon of October 2, 1953, Crowder headed off from his Seneca, Missouri, residence for Grand Lake of the Cherokees in Oklahoma to do some fishing. He stopped by to invite a friend and former member of the 1947 Independence Yankees, Max Buzzard, to join him on a weekend fishing outing. Buzzard declined since he was coaching the local high school team at Seneca that Friday evening and promised his young football team that he would take them to Fayetteville, Arkansas the following day to see the Arkansas Razorbacks play a Southwest Conference game. How he wished later he been able to go along with Crowder. Buzzard felt that his presence might have changed what happened.

During the evening hours Crowder's hat, replete with his fishing lures, fell into Grand Lake and he advised his friend on the boat that he was jumping into the water to get it. He told his fishing partner to come and pick him up when he retrieved the hat. Some distance from the boat Crowder waved to be plucked from the water. The outboard engine would not start and by the time it did Crowder had disappeared beneath the surface.

After a night of searching in vain for Crowder, his body was not located until the middle of the day on October 3, 1953. That day was a "black day" in Mickey's life. The ritual of the Yankee/Dodger World Series was in progress. The Yankees had Whitey Ford on the mound against Clem Labine and the Bronx Bombers lost 7-3 to the Dodgers. Mickey had gone 1-5 with the bat but was to soon learn he had lost something more— his pal and fishing buddy, Joe Crowder.

Mantle had a loyalty to his friends that grew out of his Northeast Oklahoma upbringing. He was an "aw shucks, gee whiz" kind of guy. When the World Series concluded, Mantle went back to Commerce and convened all the ballplayers in that part of the Midwest and they had a charity game for the Crowder family at Miners Park in Joplin. The amount raised was nearly $2,000, which defrayed the cost of the funeral expenses, and other items that Mrs. Crowder needed in raising her now-fatherless children.

During that exhibition game Mantle hit a long home run out of Miners Park. When the game was over he was conversing with Jack Hasten who had been on the early season roster at Independence in 1949. Hasten mentioned that Mantle really got good wood on the ball. Hasten recalled, Mantle replied, "Yea, I guess I got better wood on that pitch than any ball I hit all season."[310]

That was quite a statement, since during the regular season Mantle hit a ball that measured 565 in old Griffith Stadium. He hit it off Chuck Stobbs, but few people alive today could tell you who Mantle hit the home run off of in the exhibition tilt during that fundraiser for the Crowder family.

The treachery of inland lakes of the Midwest with the sudden squalls that they produce can be life threatening. Max Mantle recalled one incident that could have altered the history of Major League baseball and the lives of four young men: "The fear of an early death nearly happened to the Mantle boys on the same body of water that took the life of Crowder. Max said the scare that befell him, Ray, Roy and Mickey happened on a duck hunting trip when their outboard motor malfunctioned. They sought refuge on a small island in the lake. Max remembered the day as being cold and blustery and there was no material on the island with which to build a fire. "For about four to five hours we nearly froze to death," Max said.[311]

Mantle's love for the outdoors was infectious. He convinced one of his former teammates to settle in the Northeast Oklahoma lake region after his baseball career concluded. Cliff Mapes moved to Oklahoma but still had to work to make ends meet. He wound up getting a job in Eagle-Picher's Blue Goose Mine at Cardin, Oklahoma due to Mick's dad, Mutt's, influence in getting him hired. Mapes had become a Yankee after a big season at Kansas City in 1947. When Mapes joined the Yankees in 1948, Gus Mauch was in charge of the distribution of uniforms. Mapes recalled what happened, "Gus went into the uniform room where he found jersey #3. Then he remarked, 'I think you will be the next Babe Ruth.'"[312]

Well, a quick check of the records show that Cliff only hit 4% as many homers as did Ruth.

When the Yankees got around to retiring Ruth's #3, Mauch went to the

---

[310] Jack Hasten.

[311] *The KOM League Remembered*, newsletter, Volume 2, Issue 8 (January 1996).

[312] *The KOM League Remembered*, newsletter, Volume 2, Issue 6 (November 1995).

uniform room and dusted off #7 and that became Mapes number even after Mantle joined the Yankees in 1951. Mantle started off wearing #6. Later Mapes gave up his #7 to Mantle because he respected his speed. Mapes claimed that he never resented having to give up either numbers three or seven. Once personalized license plates came along, Mapes had his Oklahoma plate changed to read "#3 #7." It remained his license plate number until his death.

What Kind of Spring — 1950

Joplin entered their spring training camp in 1950 without an assigned first baseman, but they had the nucleus of the team Craft managed at Independence in 1949.

Mantle may have been one of the few switch-hitters during the 1950 campaign in all of baseball. It prompted a Joplin fan later to inquire, "If Mantle is a switch hitter, who turns on the switch?"[313]

While there was a dearth of switch-hitters in baseball there was a fellow in the White House named Harry Truman who could toss them with either hand. An Associated Press story said, "President Truman reported his throwing arm in good shape today as he received his annual season passes for the American and National League games. He promised to throw out the first ball at the American League opener between the Washington Senators and Philadelphia Athletics. Harry threw with right arm last year. Clark Griffith, president of the Washington club, presented the American League pass, Ford Frick, president of the National League, gave Mr. Truman the complimentary ticket for the National circuit. It was Griffith's thirty-seventh visit to the White House for this purpose. He is now 80."[314]

Truman and Griffith were born and raised in the same geographic area. Griffith was born in the small village of Stringtown, Missouri in 1869 and Truman was born just east of there at Lamar some 15 years later. There was obviously a kinship between the Washington Senators president and the Nation's president. Both of those towns were relatively close to a place where Mantle was to spend the 1950 season. It wasn't but a year later that Mantle was playing in the same park where Griffith and Truman had inaugurated the 1950 baseball season.

---

[313] Paul Stubblefield, *The Joplin News Herald*, column, July 3, 1950.
[314] The Associated Press, April 12, 1950.

Mantle was a late arrival to the Branson spring training camp. He had been working out with the Kansas City Blues at Lake Wales and after hitting a gigantic home run against the Philadelphia Phillies the Yankees rushed him out of that camp for they knew the Blues would want him in Triple A and the Yankees were determined that he was not ready to jump from Class D to that level after just 89 games in professional baseball.

The Joplin Miners were actually without form or substance by mid April and fast approaching the opening of the season. On April 12 the Miners sent out the only other shortstop in camp, Buddy Foell, to the Independence Yankees. Tom Gott reported from Quincy, Illinois, of the Three-I League to replace Foell, which made it almost a certainty that the now hard-hitting shortstop, Mickey Mantle, would stay with "Craft's men."

The infield was not settled for it was a toss-up as to whether Chuck Weiss or Cromer Smotherman, both on the Quincy roster, would get the Joplin job. Ron Burk appeared to be a "shoo-in" for the second base slot until he got hit on the elbow with a pitch.

By April 13 the Miners were less than spectacular. They had managed to lose to the Quincy Gems of the Three-I League five times, beat them once and then beat the Grand Forks, North Dakota Chiefs, twice.

The Miners broke camp in Branson on April 14 to make a trip back to Joplin to take on the Colorado Springs Sky Sox of the Western League. The team was not yet established so Joplin borrowed Charley Joe Fontana, Ray Haley and Chuck Weiss from the Quincy Gems of the Yankee Three-I League affiliate to fill three key positions.

The Sky Sox were managed by Buddy Hassett, the first cousin of St. Louis Cardinal All-Star second baseman Red Schoendienst. But Hassett turned the managerial reins of the Joplin game over to Paul Schoendienst one of Red's brothers. Paul also pitched that game and Mantle had his first base hit in Miner's Park in what would become commonplace during the regular season. He fell one hit short of the 200 plateau which was the goal he had set for himself at the start of the season.

That game with the Sky Sox established what every Joplin Miner knew. Mantle could not catch pop flies. *The Joplin Globe* reported on the win over Colorado Springs and commented, "The game was errorless and the fielding was spotless except for two fly balls lost in the sun. Mickey Mantle, Joplin shortstop, lost a pop fly in the second, and Tommy Gott, in center lost a hard drive by Marty Matella in the ninth which went for a double."

It may well have been that Mantle and Gott lost the ball in the sun against the Sky Sox. However, every member of that Joplin Miner infield throughout the season was given specific instructions by Harry Craft as to what to do when a pop fly was hit anywhere near Mantle. The standing rule was "run him off the ball."

The only birthday Craft spent with the Joplin was April 19, 1950, and his team was in spring training at Branson. *The Joplin Globe* reported, "This was Harry Craft's birthday and his team gave him a snappy present in the form of a 3-0 shut-out of the Grand Forks Chiefs of the Northern League. It was the first whitewash job of the training camp. A well-pitched six-hitter in which Lefty Steve Kraly, Lilburn Smith and Joe 'The Fireman' Crowder shared the honors." [315]

It was a bigger day for Bob Mallon, however. He held his former roommate from the 1949 Independence Yankees, Mickey Mantle, hitless. Although Mallon remembered nothing else about that game, he still relishes that feat.

Back to Branson for Further Training

By the time the Miners got back to Branson, following their defeat of the Colorado Springs Sky Sox, there was a first baseman in camp who was destined to fill that slot for the entire season. He was Cromer Smotherman who had won the batting title for McAlester, Oklahoma, in the Sooner State League in 1948.

Cal Neeman and Lilburn Smith were holdovers from a very good Joplin team in 1949 but before the spring training session ended they knew that a special breed of ballplayer represented the 1950 club. They had seen Mantle blast the ball out of the Branson stadium and the ball was never recovered since it landed in Lake Taneycomo.

Bunny Mick, who was slated to run the Independence club that season, watched in awe as Mantle "creamed" the same pitch that Neeman and Smith both watched soar out of the park during that eventful spring. Although Mick went on to play a lot more baseball, become a very successful businessman, major league batting instructor, and coach of the Russian baseball team at the 1990 Goodwill Games, nothing stuck in his mind more than the homer he saw Mantle hit at Branson in the spring of 1950.

Forty some odd years later, Mick could not rest until he figured out how far Mantle hit the ball. He took a tape measure and returned to the now-

---

[315] *The Joplin Globe*, April 20, 1950.

famous vacation playground of the Midwest. He dragged his tape from point to point. Curious tourists looked at him wondering if he was crazy or plotting a new development. Mick told all that would listen that he was measuring the distance of one of Mickey Mantle's homers hit back in 1950. In Mick's words, "The ball had to have gone over 500 feet."

That's right. Feats of legends don't die even after the legend maker is no longer among the living. Mick was never able to measure the exact length of Mantle's spring training home run, since he couldn't walk on water. However, it has stayed in his mind a half century as the longest ball he ever saw hit in any park at any time.

Harry Craft — Manager

Harry Ellis Craft had put six years in the big leagues as an outfielder for the Cincinnati Reds. His most notable feat was having played centerfield when Johnny Van der Meer pitched back-to-back no-hitters.

Craft was with the Kansas City Blues when WWII broke out. He entered the service and returned to the Blues and played there from 1946-48. When he was assigned to manage the Independence, Kansas, Yankees in 1949, he was slated to be a player/manager. After looking around at some of the speed and lack of control of the young bucks of the KOM League, he reportedly said, "There are arms as strong in this league as at the Triple A level and I am not putting my life in danger by batting against these guys."

Thus, in two years managing at the Class D and C levels, Harry Craft never once had the urge to pick up a bat and show the young guys how to hit.

Craft knew by early 1950 that there were some "real hitters" in the Joplin camp. It was never better demonstrated when the St. Paul Saints of the American Association pulled into Joplin to take on the Miners. St. Paul was one of two Triple A clubs in the Brooklyn Dodger farm system at the time. The other was the Montreal Royals.

Porter Wittich remarked, "One robin never made a spring and two home exhibition games do not make a baseball season, but what those who saw the Joplin Miners do against higher competition at Miners park Saturday and Sunday was heartwarming."[316]

What Joplin fans saw was that afternoon was something to which they would become accustomed during the season, home runs. The Miners hit 107 out of the park in 137 games. Steve Kraly, the crafty lefty on that club

---

[316] *The Joplin Globe*, April 17, 1950.

recalled, "We were called the Junior Bronx Bombers."[317]

George Brown pitched for St. Paul during that exhibition game and Mantle hit one over the Joplin scoreboard for his first homer in Miners Park and that was followed by Lou Skizas hitting one even further. A lot of speculation was bandied about regarding whether Brown threw a couple of fat ones to encourage the home-town customers or whether the blasts were legitimate. Joe Becker, the old Major League scout for the Boston Red Sox and four-time amateur wrestling champion from Joplin umpired that game and attested to the fact that Brown didn't ease up on the boys.

The Joplin club took on a major league flavor on April 17 when Lyle Westrum reported from Quincy, Illinois, of the Three-I League. Lyle's big brother Wes was catching at the time with the New York Giants. Thus, Joplin started the year with two good receivers. Along with Westrum was Cal Neeman who would go to the Major Leagues a handful of years later with the Cubs, Phillies, Senators, Indians and the Pirates. Westrum never made the big time as did his brother Lyle died of a heart attack while duck hunting in his native home state of Minnesota at the young age of 43.[318]

The Joplin club was one of those rare minor league outfits that didn't have constant turnover. Only 25 young men ever put on a uniform for that club and they were a solid group the entire season. Fellows like Bill Drake-pitcher, Ted Atkinson-catcher, Ronald Burk 2B, Melvin Wright-pitcher and John Krochins were the last players cut from that squad on April 18, 1950. Wright, although not making the Joplin squad in 1950 was nevertheless good enough to pitch in parts of four major league seasons with the St. Louis Cardinals and Chicago Cubs.

Surely, many of those fellows have looked back on that day and realized their chance for playing with a legend and also a great minor league team were so close to being a reality. Another fellow who had originally been signed by Tom Greenwade in 1947 showed up at Joplin at the start of the season and worked out with the team for a couple of weeks. Unfortunately, Springfield native Paul Nichols got shipped to Greenwood, Mississippi, in the Cotton States League. He wanted very badly to play for the Miners as his older brother, George, had done a decade previous.

There were a number of players who wanted to play for the 1950 Joplin Miners, while there was one catcher not pleased with the prospect of

---

[317] Steve Kraly.
[318] Cindy Self, daughter of the late Lyle Westrum.

another year in that town. The player not wanting to be on that club was Cal Neeman.

Neeman recalled, "My 1950 season actually began with the Yankee School during January of 1950 which was held at Phoenix, Arizona. Many of the players from that school went on to become the Yankees of the '50s and '60s, which I think won six straight American League Championships and maybe as many World Championships. There were many fine players like Jackie Jensen, Gus Triandos, Lou Berbert, Jim Finigan, Bill Renna, Bob Cerv, Al Pilarcik, Art Schulte and more who went on to Major League careers with other teams."[319]

Of all the players in that camp at Phoenix the one who stood out ahead of everyone was Mantle in Neeman's estimation. Neeman first noticed him when he ran off and left all others in his wake during sprint races. Neeman marveled that Mantle hit such long balls out of the park in batting either left or right and often hitting them to the opposite field with more power than other players did hitting them to their strong field.

Testimony to Mantle's name recognition was an incident when he, Jim Finigan, Denis Jent, Al Pilarcik and Neeman missed the players' bus to the park one day in Phoenix. As Neeman recalled, "Casey Stengel came along in a taxi and picked us up. After a short ride he wanted to know who in the cab had missed the bus. I believe we were all afraid to answer, but when he came to Mantle, Stengel called him, 'That mixed up kid who didn't know that players with great speed do not hit home runs, and that right-handed hitters are supposed to hit long ball to left field and to right like he does and then hit left-handed and hit balls over the left field wall.'"

Mantle's talent dominated the school. According to Neeman, "He was quiet and really didn't do much except play ball. At the end of the school most of us found out where we were going and I was very disappointed to find out from Bill Dickey that I was to return to Joplin again in 1950 after having a decent year there in 1949. Mr. Dickey did tell me thought that he wanted me to catch more games and that after a few weeks I would be glad to be on the team we were sending to Joplin."

As Bill Dickey predicted Neeman was happy to be a Miner for the second consecutive season. Neeman admitted, "It didn't take long to know that the 1950 Joplin Miners were special. We might have been the best Class C team in baseball as the Yankees were at the Major League level. While the

---

[319] Cal Neeman.

Yankees had great players we had some pretty good players for our league. I believe that Mantle made the difference between very good teams and extraordinary ones. He did make his errors at shortstop for us and he had games when he struck out two or three times, but he was always able to make up for whatever he did. One day in Hutchinson, Kansas he made two, three or four errors I don't remember exactly, but it was pretty bad, in the first inning. Leading off the second inning he grabbed the nearest bat and hit a line drive over the right field wall. What was so exceptional about this was the bat he used was broken and even a badly broken bat made not difference when he hit them."[320]

Neeman saw Mantle's ability from a broader perspective in that he played with and against the best of the Western Association talent for two seasons. This is his memory of the young slugger's power: "The ball did not carry well in Joplin at night to the centerfield wall, which at the time was 420 feet from home plate. During the 1949 and the 1950 seasons, the only player to ever hit it over the centerfield wall was Mickey. In the same game he hit two. One as he was hitting left-handed and the other one he hit from the right side."

A bit of falsifying the truth could have led to one of the longest home runs Mantle hit in 1950. Neeman said, "I remember we were in St. Joseph, Missouri when their starting pitcher Dan Lewandowski saw, I think Tom Gott, and a couple of our other players downtown the day he was to start. He asked if Mantle had a weakness. Our guys told Lewandowski, a hard throwing right-hander, that Mickey had trouble with change-ups. We all knew that Mantle killed off-speed pitching. That night Mickey hit a change up over the light tower. That was quite a laugher for the guys who had told Lewandowski of Mickey's 'weakness.'"

The Rev. Randy Sawyer of Mexico, Missouri recalled, "My dad used to take me to see the St. Joseph Cardinals play the Joplin Miners and watch Mantle. Even then, it was known that he was on his way up and I can still hear fans calling him, 'The Pride of the Yankees' whenever he came to bat."[321] The Mantle legend carried over into the 1951 Western Association season. Don Annen recalled, "I was with the Topeka Owls in the 1951 season, and every time we hit a home run in Miners Park, some fan would remind us that Mantle hit one farther."[322]

---

[320] Ibid.

[321] Randy Sawyer.

[322] Don Annen.

It seemed to the 1950 Miner club that no matter what they did, Mantle could top it. Neeman bragged on one of his hits in this manner: "One night, during batting practice, I hit a ball in left center that hit the top of the light standard about 370 feet away. Harry Craft wisecracked, 'You are about 20 hours late with that one.' I had popped up with the bases loaded in Muskogee the night before. The ball I hit was a pretty long shot, especially when the balls we used for batting practice were pretty beat up. However, Mantle hit a few minutes later and whacked a line drive over the same light standard. I had just hit what I thought was a real shot and he made mine look like a high fly ball."

Those who had to play catch with him didn't appreciate some of the Mantle talents. From Charles "Frog" Heavin, a Baxter Springs teammate from 1947-49, Mantle had developed a very good knuckleball. When his teammates got past the standard comments that, "There was no question that Mickey Mantle could run faster, throw harder and hit harder than anyone else on the field," they complained about the knuckleball. Keep in mind that Neeman was a catcher. But catching Mantle was not one of Neeman's favorite tasks. He recalled, "Mantle also had a great knuckleball. His ball would come at you in a circular path that made it impossible to know how it would break. He looked for the catcher or first baseman to warm up with before a game. I would duck his company at warm-up time and he usually found Cromer Smotherman or Lyle Westrum for warm-up throws. But I did occasionally catch his knuckler."

As he had as far back as the Gabby Street Pee Wee League in 1942, Mantle was regarded as a smart player. Neeman recalled how he used his baseball savvy to great advantage, "We usually had only two umpires, one behind the plate and the other somewhere behind the pitcher's mound when there were men on base. Mickey stole third one night in Joplin and was called safe because the umpire had a poor view and Mickey slid a foot or two past the bag. With the third baseman screaming at the umpire, Mickey called for time out, stood up backing even further from the bag and dusted off his uniform. What impressed me about this seemingly unimportant incident was that most ordinary players would have jerked their foot back to the bag and by doing so the umpire would have known that he was out and had over slid the base. Mantle had the presence of mind to overrule the natural instinct to reach back for the base and calmly called for a time out."

Like the majority of the 1950 Joplin Miners, Neeman's most vivid memories of Mantle were for the things he did on the field. Neeman knew he was from Commerce, Oklahoma; he had a high school sweetheart and didn't see much of him when they were not on the road.

On the road Neeman remembered they didn't do much but play ball, eat, sleep and go to movies when they could find one. His lasting visions of minor league baseball were, "We shared rooms with sometimes four or five other players, slept on cots, dressed in the hotel, waited for baths after the game and had all of $2.50 a day for meal money. I still remember dirty uniforms, wet sweat shirts and jock straps hanging from the ceiling fan or any other place to dry after games."

Of all the shortcomings of minor league baseball the amount of money for food was always at the top of the list. Unfortunately, neither good looks nor singing prowess, possessed by a few of the Joplin Miners would cover the cost of a meal. The return from a road trip to play the St. Joseph, Missouri Cardinals, on May 30 took the team down Highway 71 to the Kansas City area. The Miners had just lost a game by a 16-11 count as big George Schachle of Elk City, Oklahoma had clubbed two doubles and three RBI's and Ace Adamcewicz had contributed a two run homer in the St. Joseph onslaught. Steve Kraly lost one of his few outings and Joe Crowder in relief didn't stop the Cardinals that evening.

Although beaten soundly by the Cardinals' Class C affiliate, the Miners were basically broke and very hungry when they entered the restaurant. When Tommy Gott and Mantle were seated inside the restaurant they checked their combined wealth and neither had enough cash to cover anything more than a glass of water, napkin and a toothpick.

Driven to the edge by nagging hunger, Mantle and Gott mooched all the pennies and nickels they could from their not so rich teammates. After that collection they still didn't have much more in their bank account than when they started the fund raising. At that point Mantle said to the waitress, "Give me hamburger, an order of fries and a chocolate shake," as Gott recalled. He then admonished Gott to do likewise. Gott insisted they didn't have the money to cover the meal. However, "Mickey told me not worry," Gott chuckled in reflecting on that time of youthful verve.

After Harry Craft and the other 16 Joplin Miners had exited the roadside diner, Mantle scooped up all the change he and Gott had collected from their teammates. A discussion arose between the pair as to who would hold

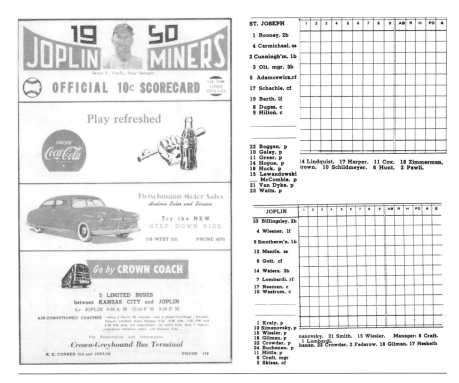

This scorecard provides the lineup for a 1950 game between the the affiliates of the St. Louis Cardinals and New York Yankees. In this game Joe Cunningham played first base for St. Joseph and was in the St. Louis lineup four years later. Both Mantle and Cal Neeman were soon to be "actors on the big league stage."

the door open and who would dump the change on the cash register. To Gott befell the task of handling the dough. Mantle was holding the door and when Gott put the "insufficient funds" on the countertop, he ran for the door that Mantle was holding open. Being the faster of the two Mantle was first to reach the bus but Gott was not that far behind.

As the old Yankee Greyhound bus sliced its way along Highway 71 in the Missouri darkness through the Western border towns of Peculiar, Harrisonville, Butler, Rich Hill, Lamar, Jasper, Nevada and Carthage it carried those two "fugitives." They must had been experiencing the same thrill that former outlaws such as Frank and Jesse James, Belle Starr, Bonnie and Clyde, Charles "Pretty Boy" Floyd and others had felt when they were in that part of the country pulling off another successful heist.

The problem back in those days was that outlaws didn't go around with their names painted on the side of their horses or Model A Fords. Baseball teams had a tradition in those days of placing their team logo on the bus.

So, the following day the Joplin Miners were home and it was payday. Mantle and Gott stepped up to get their "meager fare" and it was more meager than usual. On each pay stub was a deduction in salary for each of the boys in the exact amount of the money they had defrauded the cafe owner the previous evening.

Roy Beavers was the Joplin Miners Business Manager and the Kansas City cafe owner had contacted him regarding the episode from the night before. Beavers was typical of business managers of that era. Ballplayers were not prima donnas or coddled in any manner. They were charged for everything they did that cost the club money. If they wanted ice in their water in pre-game drills they paid for it. If a player gave a baseball to a fan it came out of his next paycheck.

Many was the time that batting practice started without an essential element—baseballs. When Mantle joined the Miners that situation was exacerbated for he would "lose" more than his share each evening in batting practice.

After Mantle would foul a ball into the stands or throw one over Cromer Smotherman's head at first, the public address announcer would say, "Bring the ball back to the backstop for a nickel." Then Beavers would clean off any dirty spots with condensed milk, let it dry and when the umpire needed more baseballs, Beavers would pass them to him through a hole in the fence behind home plate.

The Joplin Miners were cast to the four winds following the 1950 season. Neeman summed it up by saying, "Most of us were drafted into the Army. I was at Camp Chaffee, Arkansas when I read about Mickey's spring training season with the Yankees. The next thing I knew he was playing alongside Joe DiMaggio for the Yankees. We all knew he was good, but the Yankees and DiMaggio were legends. It just seemed impossible for anyone to jump form Class C baseball to the New York Yankees, the best in baseball. I kept seeing him trying to win a free game on the pinball machine at the old Keystone Hotel in Joplin. The New York Yankees, unreal. I was and am proud to have known Mickey Mantle and to able to say that I was once on the same team with him."

"I read one of his books," Neeman recalled, "and am also proud that he remembered and mentioned me, even if it was in some crazy stunt and I'm not sure he had the facts right. I do believe that in the early part of his career it was one of the happiest times of his life and it showed in the book in which I was mentioned. The simple things shared at Branson in spring training, just winning games, the pool hall on Main Street and especially Joe Crowder taking us out to snag fish and frying them up to enjoy with a cool six pack was great fun we shared. All of these things, plus other very talented players made the 1950 Joplin Miners a very good Class C baseball team. But there were other fine teams at Joplin and countless other places with equally good or better players, only the 1950 Joplin Miners had Mickey Mantle and that was special."

Baseball teams during the era of the 1950's were fortunate to have uniforms that fit, matched or in good condition. The Joplin Miners wore three different jerseys during that spring. The original New York Yankee jerseys were given to three players. Steve Kraly got one of them, #3, and he eventually wore the pinstripes of the Bronx Bombers. Guys like Lou Skizas and Tommy Gott and David Waters got the Joplin jerseys and the Kansas City jerseys were handed out to Len Wiesner, Cal Neeman, Bob Wiesler, Jerry Buchanan, Frank Simanovsky, Joe Crowder and Mickey Mantle. What no one could have guessed at the time was that #1 was given to none other than Mantle himself. That number did not adorn his jersey very long. Paul Stubblefield, writing two years later about the success of Mantle, stated, "We wonder if other Joplin fans listening or watching the World Series could 'see' Mantle in his Joplin Miners 'No. 12'? It's fine to see kids in your own park move up to the top and we couldn't help but think about the Joplinites who missed seeing Mantle and others who have or will reach the top. Also it brought to mind the remark of an employee in the K. C. office of the Associated Press as we pleaded for information about Mantle and Wiesler when they went to the Yank camp in Phoenix, in 1951, 'We can't cover every rookie who goes to camp—lots of them go to spring training.' But just a little dope, maybe a picture, was our plea. The kids are not ordinary rookies, was our pitch, and they proved we were right." [323]

---

[323] *The Joplin Globe*, the Sunday supplement, October, 1952.

A Joplin Miner scorecard listed these numbers for the members of the 1950 Miners:[324]

23	Al Billingsly	4	Len Wiesner
9	Cromer Smotherman	12	Mickey Mantle
6	Tom Gott	14	David Waters
7	Carl Lombardi	17	Cal Neeman
16	Lyle Westrum	1	Steve Kraly
10	Frank Simanovsky	15	Bob Wiesler
18	Dick Gilman	22	Joe Crowder
24	Jerry Buchanan	11	Dale Hittle
8	Harry Craft	5	Lou Skizas
17	Tom Hesketh	2	Emil Federow
21	Lilburn Smith		

Mantle's entry to the Joplin club was seen as something of a public relations coup for the Miners. A year earlier the Miami, Oklahoma, Owls didn't think he was that good nor did they think he would be a gate attraction. Porter Wittich reported, "Mickey Mantle, closest approach to a Joplin product to show up in years—he comes from Commerce, Okla — looks every bit a ball player, both afield and at bat, although he lost one popup in the sun which fell for a single and he delivered a hit only once in four trips."[325]

Mary Ann and husband Wylie Pitts attended a movie at the Fox Theater in Joplin in 1950 when Mickey was with the Miners. She recalled that Mantle and a couple of his teammates were standing outside the Keystone Hotel. Mantle and her husband exchanged greetings and spoke for a few minutes. Mary Ann recalled, "Wylie came back to me and said, 'I want you to meet a friend of mine.' When I extended my hand to Mickey he shook it and I was taken aback by the fact his hand was so soft."[326]

When we entered the theater Wylie said to me "I wanted you to meet him, for some day he is going to be famous." In response Mary Ann recalled saying, "No man with hands that soft will ever be much of a ballplayer." Mary Ann told her husband that he was a ballplayer and his hands were

[324] From the Frank Simanovsky collection.
[325] *The Joplin Globe*, April 16, 1950.
[326] Mary Ann Pitts.

hard and callused. However, Mary Ann admitted that her initial impression of Mantle proved that she didn't have perfect female intuition much less the ability to judge baseball talent.

17

1950: The Western
Association Pennant Race

T here wasn't a great deal of fanfare for a ball club that moved back to
Joplin, from Branson, on April 22nd to start the 1950 campaign a
couple of days later. Harry Craft introduced his roster of 20 players
to the Elks Club and *The Joplin Globe* ran photos of Harry Craft, Dave
Waters, Carl Lombardi, Len Wiesner, Lilburn Smith, Tommy Gott and Cal
Neeman. There was even a team photo on a full-page spread in the *Globe*
but the players were not identified.

Tom Greenwade had spent the spring watching a lot of the Miners'
games and their workouts. After an interview with Paul Stubblefield of *The
Joplin News Herald*, the sportswriter penned this statement, "Admittedly, the
grass always looks mighty green in the springtime, but now it would appear
that 1950 is going to bring many pleasant evenings under the arcs at Miners
Park in Joplin."[327]

Mantle didn't make the pictorial section of the *Globe* because no one

[327] *The Joplin News Hearld*, ca. April 20, 1950.

had bothered to take one of him in the Joplin uniform. A couple of days later a grinning photo of Mantle fielding a grounder was carried. It showed him in the pose that The *Independence Daily Reporter* had carried in their Independence Yankee Yearbook of 1949. Amazingly, after Mantle got off to a great start it was learned that a photo had been taken at Branson but was slow in arriving in Joplin.

It was time to start noticing Mantle. In the opening game against Springfield he had five hits in six at bats and drove in seven runs in a 21-6 route of the Cubs. He also stole his first base of the season. Most of the hitting was done against Walter Kohler, who two years later was killed in action in the Korean War.

A couple of days later Joplin racked up another 21-run outburst against Springfield but in the process gave up 15 runs of their own. So, it was evident the Miners had the power. It remained to be seen if they had pitching or defense in sufficient quality to win in the Western Association.

Mantle showed in one game at Joplin what had taken him many weeks at Independence the year before to do — swing at the ball instead of drag bunting all the time. Steve Kraly recalled, "We used to have to yell at the guy to swing at the pitch."[328]

Kraly was Mickey's teammate for both the 1949 and 1950 seasons. Kraly remarked, "The 1950 team had such tremendous talent and such great success on the field and off the field. We were from all parts of the country and we molded into many happy, successful teammates. I believe the credit for our success is because of Harry Craft. He had a way to guide us in the right direction on and off the field. There were five of us who made it to the Major Leagues. That alone speaks for itself. It just shows how great the Joplin team of 1950 was."

Due to the two seasons Kraly spent with Mantle at the Class C and D levels, he had insights that few others were afforded: "I was able to see this great individual blossom into a great ballplayer. He was also a personal friend. Mickey was a shy person off the field but on the field he was a tiger. I believe we all were similar to this; we had such a love for the game. When people ask me about Mickey, I tell them if you could have seen him play in 1950 you would be in awe to see him hit the ball over the lights at the age of 18. He became such a legend and I was fortunate to have had the opportunity to be associated with him as a teammate and friend."

[328] Steve Kraly.

Looking back over his shoulder Kraly remarked, "The climax of my association with the Mick was the 1953 World Series, and the thrill of a lifetime, receiving a World Series ring."

Late spring in the Ozarks can sometimes be akin to winter. The second game of the Joplin season was highlighted by the "low-lights." With Springfield leading in the eighth inning the lights went out. Cold, damp fans of the Springfield Cubs were staying around to see if the lights would ever come back on and the game could be resumed. The lights never came back on and after 45 minutes the game was called.

For most of the players the bus trips from Joplin to "wherever" were times for reading comic books, sleeping, counting Burma Shave advertising signs or in some cases doing something worthwhile. One of the scholars on that club was Dan Ferber. This was a memory that Dan Ferber shared with a college newspaper: "In 1950 Dan Ferber lived an astonishing story in the annals of Wabash College sports. A year earlier he had signed with the New York Yankees, but the organization would allow him to miss only one spring training. To meet both the Yankee and Wabash requirements, the dean let him take eight 3-hour courses in one semester. That following spring while others were enjoying Pan Hel and the liveliness of the campus, Ferber was studying for his comps while riding the Yankee bus to Joplin, Missouri. Mickey Mantle amused himself reading comic books on the long bus rides and referring to his teammate as 'The Professor' because Ferber was scrunched in a seat reviewing literature."[329]

Ferber's studying was successful, for his resume over the next five decades included:

- B. A. Cum Laude, English Literature and Philosophy, Wabash College, Crawfordsville, Indiana.
- M.A., Comparative Literature, Indiana University, Bloomington, Indiana.
- Ph.D., Higher Education Administration, Indiana University.
- Associate Director of Development, University of Pittsburgh.
- First Director of Development (Concept Invention), University of New Hampshire.
- Founder and Director, New England Center for Continuing Education.

---

[329] Dan Ferber, recalling a passage from a Wabash College newsletter in 1987.

- Dean of Academic Affairs and Vice President for Academic Administration, Gustavus Adolphus College, St. Peter, Minnesota.
- Founder, Commission on Minnesota's Future.
- Chairman, Minnesota Lifelong Learning Society and Intergenerational Education Consortium.
- Founding Chairman and CEO for the Minnesota State Board of Invention and Innovation, St. Paul, Minnesota.

There were some other pitchers on the team who didn't spend all the free time cramming for final exams. Tom Gott recalled, "When Kraly, Wiesler or Smotherman pitched, you knew you had a chance. When Jerry Buchanan pitched, you had a 50-50 chance of winning and when guys like David Benedict took the hill, you prayed for five innings out of the guy and hoped Joe Crowder could hold the opposition the rest of the way."

Buchanan had a very novel way of warming up. While hitters used weighted bats in their practice swings, Buchanan had a brick stationed in the Joplin bullpen and he warmed up by tossing that red piece of baked clay. Cal Neeman and Lyle Westrum were the two Joplin catchers, but none warmed up Buchannan when he heaved that brick. He may have thrown bricks but a Joplin newspaper described him thusly: "Buchanan is quicker than a panhandler snatching up a one-buck gratuity."[330]

During the same Springfield series when the lights went out on Buchanan's performance, Wiesler got the starting nod the next evening and caused the lights to go out once more. Electricians worked with the wires for over an hour before night vision was restored to the batsmen. It didn't do the Springfield batters much good, for Wiesler was on the road to his Western Association leading strikeout title that evening by whiffing 13.

There were a number of fellows who didn't pile up massive numbers with the Joplin Miners, but who nonetheless made a contribution. Dick Fiedler posted a 5-2 record and added some "maturity" to the young Miners ball club. He had been out of high school for six years and had seen some of the world that Mantle could only have experienced through a geography class.

Fiedler was a native of Union, New Jersey, who wound up graduating from high school in 1944 and joining the Merchant Marines. He served in the Philippines, where he contracted malaria, but returned to the States and

---

[330] *Joplin Globe*, circa July, 1950.

continued his educational studies, toward an eventual career as a Chemical Engineer. He attended the University of Southern California and he was on that 1948 the National College Championship that defeated Yale for the title. Also, that same year USC beat the Cleveland Indians in an exhibition game and the Trojans joked that since the Indians won the World Series that the Trojans by virtue of beating them were the real champions.

Fiedler played under the legendary Rod Dedeaux. Dedeaux had been injured playing minor league baseball and became content to coach one of the great powerhouse teams in collegiate history. Fiedler said that if you ever see a transport truck on the highway with the name DART as the logo, it belongs to Rod. He inherited that trucking firm from his father.

There was no intention on Fiedler's part to do anything but return to USC to play for the Trojans in 1950. However, due to having played one game in 1944, in college, he was ruled ineligible by the conference. Thus, he was signed to a Yankee contract for $5,999.99 and sent to Twin Falls, Idaho, in the Pioneer League. Had he signed for one cent more he would have had to have been placed on the New York Yankee roster.

When the call came to join the Joplin Miners, Fiedler was in for some things he had never seen as a New Jersey or California boy. His first encounter was with Miner relief pitcher, Joe Crowder. Crowder, an avid outdoorsman, served as Fiedler's nurse during a malaria attack.

Fiedler had contracted that disease in the Philippines during WWII. Craft put Crowder in charge of looking after him. Fiedler recalled, "I had this attack of sweating and chills and Crowder rounded up all the blankets he could find and put them over me. He then sat on top of me to keep them from coming off."[331]

Fiedler recalled Crowder and Mantle were alike in a lot of ways and had talents he had never witnessed as a city boy. He remembered the Joplin bus didn't have any toilet so manager/bus driver Craft had to stop many times by the side of the road. When Mantle and Crowder stood along the fence rows, doing what was necessary, Fiedler recalled, "They let out with some of the loudest and weirdest sounds I had ever heard. I was amazed to see all the varmints and fowl within earshot come to the fence row to see what was going on."

The next season Fiedler had the option of going to Kansas City with a chance of making the Blues club or going to Beaumont and getting a better

---

[331] Dick Fiedler.

shot in the regular rotation under his 1950 Joplin manager, Craft. Beaumont didn't work out and he wound up pitching for the Quincy Gems on the same staff with his "nurse" from 1950, Joe Crowder.

When Fiedler was suffering so much with the chills and fever in his hotel room, he recalled what Crowder told the nursing staff when he called St. Johns' Hospital in Joplin: "I don't know what he's got, but he sounds like a pig shitting a peach seed."

When Fiedler's former teammate, Mantle, was reaching his apex as a ballplayer his career was about to end. He hung around the Pacific Coast League due to the confidence Bill Sweeney, Portland's manager, placed in him. He told Fiedler that he would start the 1957 season as his opening day hurler if he would stay in shape. After a rather mediocre season with a bad ball club Fiedler wasn't sure he would show up in 1957. He did and Sweeney kept his word. He opened the season and lost 4-0 to San Diego. In his next start he lost 2-0 and was discouraged. Sweeney came up to him after the game and said, "Things will get better." As Fiedler recalled, "Sweeney died that night." Fiedler struggled on through part of the 1957 season winning two and losing seven. That hastened his career move into chemical engineering. As his career was fading into the halls of baseball oblivion his former Joplin teammate was continuing to be without peer on the Major League landscape with a .365 batting average and 34 homers.

Tom Greenwade took over the Joplin club on May 12 at Muskogee and all the games were rained out. By that time they had played 10 games. They were 7-3., and as a team were leading the league in hitting at .302. At that juncture the top hitter on the Joplin squad was Len Wiesner who was belting the ball at .400 clip. That put him sixty-five points behind Pete Maropis of Hutchinson, who led the league at .465. Mantle was the top RBI man with 16. The top home run hitter was William Wells of the Enid, Oklahoma Giants.

The late Billy Creech recalled the last time he ever faced Mantle was during the return trip to Muskogee, after the rained out series.. They had faced each other when Creech was at Iola, Kansas in 1949 and Mantle got seven or eight hits off him. Creech recalled, "Jim Bello and Lou Skizas were the guys who hit me the hardest."[332] Creech had some redemption and became the winning pitcher in the 1949 KOM League All-Star game when he defeated the Independence Yankees.

---

[332] Bill Creech.

This photo was taken at Miners Park in Joplin by a member of the *Globe* staff. Mantle was much bigger than he'd been just one season previous at Independence. [333]

Creech recalled the first game that Joplin played against Muskogee. He saw Wiesler and Skizas and went over to converse with them. He said, "I heard Mantle is with you guys this year." Wiesler replied, "That's right, Mick's out there at short." Creech recalled, "His back was turned to me and all I saw was this broad-shouldered young man, I couldn't believe he had grown that much over one winter."[334]

---

[333] Photo courtesy of Wendell Redden.
[334] Bill Creech.

By the summer of 1951, Mantle was sent back to the Kansas City Blues.
He wasn't demoted due to the lack of a great physique! Here he poses with his cousin,
Jerry Meyers.[335]

Like most everyone who remembered Mantle's youthful demeanor, Creech said, " I used to hang out on the street corner with Skizas, Wiesler and Mantle back then and he didn't say much, he would take in what was said and chuckle a lot."

By the time the season ended Mantle owned the batting title at .383 but he had lost the home run race to Elmer "Butch" Nieman, Topeka, Kansas Owl manager and former Boston Brave. Nieman also led the Western Association with 149 RBIs to Mantle's 136. In fact, Mantle finished third in homers. Harold Kollar of Enid pounded out 27.

The success Mantle experienced midway through the season had the sportswriters making some rather tongue-in-cheek remarks. Paul Stubblefield opined, "We're beginning to wonder whether we like the Commerce Comet. Mickey Mantle. Starting the season we had to figure out all the daily batting averages in the customary paper and pencil way. After searching we obtained a special book that was supposed to have all the averages. But come today and we find the book covering 121 hits doesn't cover Mantle. It starts off with 121 hits for 340 times at bat or an average of .356.

[335] Photo courtesy of Bobbie Crampton.

So we had to dig out the paper and pencil and find that 121 hits in 311 times at bat is good for a .389 average. Apparently, .356 is all a guy's supposed to hit. We're only kidding, Mick. Keep up swatting the old apple, we'll figure it out." [336]

Getting from the start of the 1950 season to the end was a task Craft was ready to tackle. He had seen Mantle for nearly three months during the 1949 season and knew that his baseball maturity depended upon having a teammate to keep him focused. Mantle was notorious for his mood swings depending on how the baseball gods were treating him on a given day.

Craft selected the veteran Cromer Smotherman to be Mantle's mentor and tormentor in his sophomore year of professional ball. Some have felt that influences of Whitey Ford and Billy Martin in later years hurt Mantle and his career in many ways. This author does not care to take that path or delve into that type of speculation. Most authors of sports books aren't qualified as psychologists and thus should steer clear of analyzing situations and outcomes. However, in discussing this issue with the author, Merlyn Mantle admitted that she finally came to the conclusion her husband did what he did because he wanted to and that outside forces such as Martin and Ford were not to blame for any of the negative things that beset him in his life.

Smotherman looks back on his 1950 season with great fondness and is generally conceded among the members of that club that he did a great deal to help Mantle cope with disappointments and successes. In understanding Mantle it must be kept in mind that he was not the average athlete and he demanded more of himself than he probably should have in some cases.

Smotherman recalled, "The 1950 Joplin team was a very special experience in my life, as brief as it was. After all these years I still recall those moments, which I continue to cherish." [337]

Smotherman had two years of professional baseball under his belt prior to joining the Joplin Miners. He was signed to a Yankee contract in 1948 by scout, Shaky Kain. His first year of pro ball was with the McAlester, Oklahoma Rockets. In his rookie season he led the Sooner State League in batting. In 1949 he was sent to Grand Forks, North Dakota in the Class C Northern League. In 1950 he was invited to spring training in Lake Wales, Florida by the Kansas City Blues. That was the same camp where Mantle started out before

[336] *The Joplin News Herald*, ca. mid-July 1950.

[337] Smotherman.

being sent to Branson and then drawing the Joplin assignment.

Smotherman recalled that time in history, "It was the 1950 spring training camp that I first met Mickey Mantle. He and other players were sent to their respective camps for training. Harry Craft was the manager designee of the Joplin Miners. He, along with many Yankee organization scouts and coaches, worked to put the team together. Scout Tom Greenwade, it seemed, followed us everywhere. Also, many named personalities traveled with the team—notably Burleigh Grimes.

As the team settled in and teammates got better acquainted, we became a team with great talent. I played first base. I was married, had one child, was a veteran of WWII and was in my 4th year of college at Middle Tennessee State. Being the oldest member on the team, other than manager Harry Craft, my nickname became 'Dad.'

Harry asked me to informally serve as a 'mentor' to several of the younger players, Mickey Mantle in particular. This is not to suggest anything other than age differences and talent development. There were a number of the players who had great talent and ability, the team 'bonded' well and excelled in all phases of the game.

Most of the players had hopes and dreams to make baseball their career. Several did continue playing for several years, including teams in the majors. I think it is fair to say, however, that the team did recognize the exceptional talent of Mantle.

Mickey, the young boy from Commerce, Oklahoma, was strong, gifted as a hitter, had tremendous speed and possessed a strong throwing arm. In other words, all the physical requirements to be a professional baseball player. His talents were exceptional by any measure."

The physical aspects of the game was not the reason Craft selected Smotherman to hang around Mantle during the game. Smotherman recalled, "He was very sensitive and easily discouraged if he failed to get a hit. He played shortstop, was impatient with himself and tended to err in fielding or throwing the ball to first base. My role as a mentor was to 'encourage' and 'pep' Mickey up during this lapse in attitude. There were moments in the dugout after Mickey failed to get a hit that he would become very emotional, I would help him to shake it off. Maybe he had already gone 3 for 4, Mickey was so driven to excel that at times he recognized a strikeout as a personal failure."

Mantle had broken down in tears the last night of the KOM League season and told the guys that they would never be together like that again. The same thing happened at the close of the 1950 playoffs after the Miners had lost the championship series to the Springfield, Missouri Cubs. Smotherman said, "I recall, at the conclusion of the regular season, we had boarded our bus. Mickey was sitting beside me and he broke down in tears. Even though he had led the team and league in every category he had fallen a few hits short of his personal goal in hits for the season."

Smotherman had a good sense of his young friend's background and spoke highly of all his family. He remarked, "Mickey came from a very small town and the Mantle family was a very typical rural family of the 1940s era. Just a hard working family with less than moderate means, as many of the players' families were. Just hard working 'blue collar' type families. Mickey's family seldom missed a home game, arriving early and staying late. Mickey's father, Mutt, and mother knew every player by first name. Mickey was very proud of his mother and father. By Mickey's account, and according to his father, he was born to become a baseball player. I know all these stories have been written about him but the 1950 team grew up with Mickey and knew him like no other team knew him or better than an sportswriter did. Mickey talked about his early childhood playing football in high school and dating the pretty cheerleader, Merlyn Johnson. Mickey told me about how he avoided most football injuries — by simply 'breaking clear' and showing everyone a good 'clean ass' by his speed."

The things that brought some empathy from Smotherman toward Mantle was the pain he endured. He said, "Mickey did have some type of injury to one of his legs. I observed on many occasions seeing him rubbing his leg after sprinting the base paths."

Smotherman didn't see Mantle in the same light as did Tommy Gott and others who were single young men. Smotherman observed, "Mickey was not a 'street smart' kid even among his same age teammates. He was very shy among strangers and avoided attention as much as possible. He was just a fun loving kid whose life was totally focused on hitting and playing baseball. Mickey, like most of his teammates myself included, had limited spending dollars. The team occupied itself primarily by going to movies and playing pinball machines in hotel lobbies. I don't recall Mickey or any of the players indulging in alcohol or other harmful behavior. Being married, and having a wife living with me in Joplin, most of my relationship with Mickey and teammates was on the field. But 'away' games I was Mantle's roommate many times. Mickey was very popular among his teammates and each knew and expected him to become a super-star player."

Smotherman and his teammates thought that something special was in store for Mantle after the season concluded. He recalled, "Near the end of the season Mickey learned that he was going up to Kansas City, a Triple A team at that time, and later to the Yankees. Everyone was excited. Mickey, like the other players didn't have 'dress clothes,' — sport shirts, etc. Just t-shirts and dungarees. Mickey asked me if I would go with him to buy a few clothes, including his very first new dress suit."

PHOTO COURTESY OF REBA JOHNSON

The young man from the 1950 Joplin Miners had many new suits once he hit the big-time. During the height of his Yankee career, three men's shops carried his brand name. Here he models the "threads" of the era.

Well, as a great epic story would have it, Mantle bypassed joining the Kansas City Blues that September and instead joined the Yankees during a doubleheader at Sportsman's Park in St. Louis on September 17th.

Smotherman left his mark in the field of business and education but knows that he was in a special place at a special time. He said, "I'm sure the team members of 1950 take great pride in having a part in developing, nurturing and associating with this fine young man, who was decent, respectful, and a humble young talent. I'm also sure every team member followed Mickey's career with the Yankees and was surprised to read all the 'wild' behavior credited to him. I can only credit his breakdown in behavior to the fact that Mickey was not prepared to deal with all the exposures that were thrown at him."

It was with great sadness that Smotherman summed up the Mantle years. He stated that the Mickey Mantle he knew compared to the Mickey Mantle he later became was tragic. A young man who started out so innocent and naive to the ways of the world became a victim in enormous proportions. Smotherman opined that Mantle was not prepared or conditioned to cope with such a way of life. The game of baseball made a model player of heroic proportions but it also set the stage for his destruction. A beautiful story of an All-American kid from a small rural community living every kid's dream ended so tragically. He lamented that the members of the 1950 championship team that sent this team member to baseball heights and glory now hangs its head in sorrow and regret that the great success of Mickey Charles Mantle came to such a sad and disappointing ending. Smotherman cautions all aspiring young talent that, regardless of their ability, they must also be just as strong and capable of withstanding the temptations that go with the spotlight of glory and fame regardless of the profession they choose. He spoke for all the Joplin Miners when he stated that the club's memories of that special year are precious to each former Mantle teammate.

The Three-Home-Run Spree

In a rather coincidental happening Mantle hit three homers for the first time in his professional career on the night of June 12, 1950. That was one day prior to the first anniversary of his professional debut as a member of the Independence Yankees at Chanute, Kansas. Just two years previously he had hit three home runs against Columbus, Kansas, in a Southeast Kansas Ban Johnson League game on June 13. In his two three-home-run games, he hit five of those homers off right-handers and one off a lefty. The right-handers were Ted Atkinson in Mantle's 1948 Whiz Kids game and right-handers Clarence Churn and Carl Gretline along with lefty Louis Tond in the Hutchinson game. Pete Maropis, who finished second to Mantle in the Western Association batting race in 1950 was playing centerfield for Hutchinson the night of Mantle's three home run spree. He recalled, "One night in Hutchinson, we beat Joplin 5-3 and Mickey had 3 home runs. I was playing centerfield, and one ball went over the centerfield light pole. Longest ball that I have ever seen hit."

Len Wiesner recalled that three-homer night most vividly. He was hitting fifth right behind Mantle. Len said, "As Mickey crossed home plate after the third homer, I said to the catcher, 'Let's not prolong the suspense, hit me with the first pitch.' I thought Mantle would fall down from laughing. No, they took pity on me and got me on the third pitch."

(The pitcher serving up that third homer was Clarence Churn who later pitched in the Major Leagues for the Pittsburgh Pirates, Cleveland Indians and Los Angeles Dodgers. The catcher who called for the knockdown pitch on Wiesner was Bill Hall, who spent parts of three seasons with the Pittsburgh Pirates.)

Dale Hittle had just been sent to Joplin from Twin Falls, Idaho, of the Pioneer League the night of Mantle's three-home-run feat. He didn't even dress for that game, but rather was watching the game from the grandstand. His recollection of the event was, "I sat there and watched Mickey hit three home runs and was awed by the power he possessed and how fast he could run." The Pioneer was another Class C League, but Hittle doesn't recall seeing anyone in that classification whose talents matched Mantle's. After a couple of weeks Hittle was headed back to Twin Falls and he never saw anybody as good as the Joplin shortstop until he observed the New York Yankee centerfielder the following October in the World Series.

Across town the evening Mantle hit his three homers in 1950 was the site of the annual Kansas Wheat Growers Association convention. So what was the significance of that event? The guest speaker was Herbert Clutter from Holcomb, Kansas. Nine years later Clutter and his family were the victims of a horrendous massacre that Truman Capote wrote about and won a Pulitzer Prize for, *In Cold Blood*.

Wiesner was involved in one of the greatest demonstrations of Mantle's base speed. He recalled being on third base and Mantle on second. On a fly ball to the outfield, Wiesner tagged up and scored easily. As he crossed the plate he turned around as Mantle was scoring just behind him. Len said, "Mick, there was only one out." Mick replied, "I know it."

Throughout the season Wiesner played left, Gott was in centerfield and Mantle was at shortstop. Wiesner recalled, "Tommy and I used to throw return throws at Mantle's feet to piss him off and he would laugh like hell. We had fun."

All young ballplayers were aware of the number on their jersey's and who wore that uniform with either the parent Major League club, with whom they were affiliated, or the person in the big leagues wearing that same number who was the best player. Wiesner wore #4, Tommy Gott #6 and Mickey Mantle #5. Thus, Wiesner remembered, "We called each other Ralph Kiner (#4), Stan Musial (#6) and Vern Stephens (#5)." Like his #5 counterpart, Stephens and Mantle were both shortstops. (An early season scorecard showed Mantle as #12 and Skizas as #5.)

The Joplin Miners were confident, probably a "little bit" cocky, young and full of life. As the old Joplin bus would roll into a new town for a road game the battle cry would be yelled from the window, "Mothers, call in your daughters, the chesty league leaders are in town."

Whether on the road or at home teams comprised of 18 players had to do various things such as coach the bases and throw batting practice. Wiesner remembered, "The Greek" (Skizas) and I use to throw a lot of batting practice. Never, ever did we throw a strike to Mantle. We threw nothing but inside stuff so he had to pull the ball. Nothing was thrown up the middle. We had to protect ourselves."

During the season there were various contests devised to draw a crowd. Home run hitting contests among the Joplin players usually involved Mantle, Skizas and Wiesner. As Wiesner recalled, "The Greek always won and T. G. (Tommy Gott) used to yell, 'Hey, Lenny, we are not going for doubles."

With the dynamic home run duo of Skizas and Mantle, they headed back to Independence, their old KOM League stomping grounds, in July of 1950 to take on Neil Holloway and Bill Virdon in a home run hitting contest. It was a Joplin Miner off day and the Independence crowd gathered to see the duo who had started there the year previous take on the "upstarts." Skizas and Mantle were the odds-on favorites to take the title, but the Holloway/Virdon tandem prevailed.

Virdon and Mantle had both been in the same spring training camp at

Branson, Missouri in 1950. Virdon recalled, "Mantle was doing things that I had never seen before. Everyone was talking about how he was a sure major leaguer and I'm thinking, if they are all like him in the majors, then I'm in trouble." Of course, they weren't like Mantle and Virdon, from a defensive standpoint, proved he was at least on the same level as Mantle and some experts rated him above Mantle in all-around outfield play once both

This is an original photo of the 1950 Joplin Miners and signed by each player. Notice that the team "hierarchy" did not sign the photo. Front row, left to right: Jerry Buchanan, Bob Wiesler, Frank Simanovsky, Dick Fiedler, Dan Ferber and Joe Crowder. Middle row, left to right: Cromer Smotherman, Len Wiesner, David Waters, Cal Neeman, Mickey Mantle, Tom Gott and H. R. Satterlee. Back row, left to right: Roy Beavers, Lyle Westrum, Carl Lombardi, Al Billingsly, Lou Skizas, Steve Kraly and William Wolfe.

of them reached the Major Leagues.

From 1950 to 1960 a lot of things changed. Virdon had gone from the Yankee chain to the St. Louis Cardinals in the Enos Slaughter trade. He was the National League Rookie of the Year in 1955 and he was later traded to the Pittsburgh Pirates. Virdon recalled the 1960 World Series, "It was game two and Mickey was hitting right-handed off Fred Green. I was playing deep centerfield. Mantle hit the ball on the line directly over my head. I turned and took several steps, looked up and said to myself, 'nobody hits the ball that far.' It was at least 50 feet over my head and going straight out. It traveled at least 600 feet. I was in awe. He was super-human."[338]

[338] Bill Virdon.

Mantle stayed at a rooming house at 405 South 10th in Independence during the summer of 1949. He started out rooming with Len Wiesner at Joplin in 1950 but in a move to save money he lived most of that season at his home in Commerce. His father, Mutt, came to each home game and thus Mickey would go back to Oklahoma after each home game and return the next evening with his family. Being spurned by Mantle, Wiesner moved in with Lou Skizas which he calls, "A stay in itself."

As the 1950 Western Association season opened, Fred Mendell of *The Hutchinson* (Kans.) *News* featured former Western Association players who were starting the 1950 season in the Major Leagues.[339] Fred had no way of knowing that the fellows the league produced in 1950 would compare favorably with the guys who had already made it to the top:

Boston Red Sox
Lou Stringer — Ponca City, Oklahoma

New York Yankees
Ralph Houk — Joplin Missouri

Philadelphia Athletics
Alex Kellner — Muskogee, Oklahoma

Boston Braves
Walker Cooper — Springfield, Missouri
Del Crandall — Leavenworth, Kansas
Buddy Kerr — Fort Smith, Arkansas

Chicago Cubs
Mickey Owen — Springfield, Missouri

Cincinnati Reds
Everett Johnson — Hutchinson, Kansas
Willard Ramsdell — Muskogee, Oklahoma
Harry "Peanuts" Lowrey — Ponca City, Oklahoma
John Wyrostek — Springfield, Missouri

---

[339] *The Hutchinson News*, circa May 1, 1950.

Philadelphia Phillies
Emory "Bubba" Church — Salina, Kansas
Blix Donnelly — Springfield, Missouri

New York Giants
Sheldon Jones — Fort Smith, Arkansas
Bill Rigney — Salina, Kansas

Pittsburgh Pirates
Pete Castiglione — Hutchinson, Kansas

St. Louis Cardinals
Joe Garagiola — Springfield, Missouri
Harry Brecheen — Bartlesville, Oklahoma
Stan Musial — Springfield, Missouri
Johnny Lindell — Joplin, Missouri

Only three of the Western Association players were post-WWII performers, namely: Everett Johnson, Del Crandall and Bubba Church.

Towns such as Ponca City, Bartlesville, Leavenworth and Fort Smith were out of the Western Association by 1950. The league in 1950 was grooming its own list of future Major Leaguers, such as:

Springfield
Robert Charles Speake — Chicago Cubs, 1955 and 1957; San Francisco
    Giants, 1958-59.
Donald Ray Elston — Chicago Cubs, 1953; 1957 Brooklyn Dodgers and
    Chicago Cubs; 1959-1964 Chicago Cubs.
Harry Chiti — Chicago Cubs, 1950-56; Kansas City Athletics, 1958-60;
    Detroit Tigers 1960 and 1961; and New York Giants, 1962.

Joplin
Robert George Wiesler — New York Yankees, 1951, 1954, 1955;
    Washington Senators, 1956-58.
Calvin Amandus Neeman — Chicago Cubs, 1957-59; Chicago Cubs and
    Philadelphia Phillies, 1960; Philadelphia Phillies, 1961; Pittsburgh
    Pirates, 1962; and 1963 Cleveland Indians and Washington Senators.

Louis Peter Skizas — Kansas City Athletics and New York Yankees, 1956; Kansas City Athletics, 1957; Detroit Tigers, 1958; and Chicago White Sox, 1959.

Steve Charles Kraly — New York Yankees, 1953.

Mickey Charles Mantle — New York Yankees, 1951-1968

Hutchinson

Clarence Nottingham Churn — Pittsburgh Pirates, 1957; Cleveland Indians, 1958; Los Angeles Dodgers, 1959; Kansas City Athletics, 1957-58.

William Lemuel Hall — Pittsburgh Pirates, 1954, 1956 and 1958.

St. Joseph

Joseph Robert Cunningham — St. Louis Cardinals, 1954-61; Chicago White Sox, 1962-63; Chicago White Sox and Washington Senators, 1964; and Washington Senators, 1965-66.

Most experts of that era agree that had Ray Cucchiarini, a member of the Muskogee team, not been killed in a car accident, he too would have made it to the big leagues. The Houston Buffaloes purchased his contract from the Fort Worth Cats of the Texas League. On May 25, 1954, Cucchiarini was driving to join his new team when he was killed near Huntsville, Texas.

By the middle of July of that 1950 campaign the talk of the Western Association was Mantle. Whether he would be as good or better than the best of the former Western Association alumni then playing in the big leagues was beginning to take focus. Only Stan "The Man" Musial, who played at Springfield nine seasons earlier, compiled better numbers than Mantle. His total production was better than Stan's since Musial was long gone to Rochester and St. Louis prior to the end of the 1941 season.

Porter Wittich summed up the consensus of Mantle's first ten weeks in the Western Association and was the first scribe to speculate in writing that he would probably be converted into an outfielder by the Yankees:

Some of the Western Association critics, being the sports writers of course, are guessing that Joplin's Mickey Mantle, at present stationed at the strategic shortstop position, is being fondled by the parent New York Yankees as an up-

and-going outfielder.

It will make no difference to Mickey, a Commerce, Okla., comet, what position they decide upon just so it is baseball.

Some of the sports writers have written about everything except his fielding of the job he holds, but this department, which gets telephone conversations on all details of Joplin's out-of-town games, can clinch the esteem in which the scribes hold him as a shortstop.

Mickey, being but 18 years old, is not sure of himself in the field, and the shortstop job is a tricky one to start with. But he is fleet afoot and strong of arm, and if the Yankees want anything more he is a switch hitter, an important matter these days in baseball.

What might be more important is the fact he hits hard from both sides of the plate, whether left or right. And what has the opposition worried is the fact that Mantle might as easily slam a triple to left as well as a home run to right regardless of where he stands at the plate.

Mantle, a natural right-hander, prefers to hit as a right-hander, but most of it has to be done from the left as he hits that way against right-hand hurlers.

"Just let me take a full cut from the right against a left-hander," he told us one day, "and that's where the power is."

Mickey wasn't bragging. He apparently was stating the fact, although the ball he belted out of Miners park right centerfield the other night might still be going. He also clouted one over the left center fence from the right-hand side of the plate, and it might still be rolling too.

Just how the writers in the rest of the league cities see the Oklahoman going up as an outfielder instead of an infielder could be explained by Mantle's speed. A shortstop does not need to be an Olympic dash man, but fast legs could be an important factor as an outfielder.[340]

Enid, Oklahoma, was a New York Giant farm in 1950, having been given

---

[340] *The Joplin Globe*, July 13, 1950.

that franchise which had in recent years been located in Muskogee, Oklahoma. The Giants counted on the town of Enid's ability to attract paying customers by estimating that a professional team in that city could draw as many people as the Enidaires and Enid Oilers had attracted when they were a semi-pro power that challenged for the National Baseball Congress titles in the late 1930s and early 1940s.

Horace Stoneham threatened the Western Association with withdrawal of the New York Giants participation in that circuit unless they allowed him the opportunity to move the Muskogee franchise to Enid. He got his way and installed his son Pete as the president of the club. What the Giants hadn't considered was that semi-pro teams played only a couple of games a week and there was a great rivalry among some of the powerhouse teams out of Wichita, Kansas, such as the Boeing Bombers, that would stir the passions of baseball fans. There were no such rivalries in the Western Association, and Enid was hard-pressed to even get 1,000 people for any game.

The Giants had signed a young phenom and Stoneham wanted him to play for his son Pete as well as gain valuable experience in the competitive Class C Western Association. Jerry Buchanan remembered talking about that possibility with some of his teammates the next year when they were members of the Army team at Fort Knox, Kentucky.

Some former Interstate League players related that since there were no blacks in the Western Association, Stoneham decided that Willie Mays should be sent to Trenton, New Jersey instead. What kind of competition the Western Association came close to seeing could only be speculated upon so many years after the fact. However, to have had Mays and Mantle in the same league at nearly the same age would have been remarkable.

One of the 1950 Joplin Miners who was close to Mantle up until the time he was elected to the Hall of Fame was Carl Lombardi. Lombardi was a WWII veteran who first broke in with the Newark Bears in 1947, or at least tried. He was farmed out to Amsterdam, New York, of the Canadian American League that year and then went to Norfolk, Virginia, in 1948 and also on to Butler, Pennsylvania.

Lombardi injured his thigh chasing a pop fly in the 1948 season and sat out the remainder of that year and also the 1949 campaign. In 1950 he joined the Joplin Miners, which he now calls the "greatest part of my life."

The Montclair, New Jersey, native may have been best remembered for his turn in the batting cage before a game Bob Wiesler was to start. Wiesler was having a great year and prior to batting practice one evening was standing beside the cage awaiting his turn to take some practice swings. Big Jerry Buchanan was throwing batting practice that July evening and was having a very good time taking target practice on the batters. He had nailed Lombardi a few times during his time at the plate and Lombardi was itching to retaliate.

On the last pitch Lombardi's intention was to let the bat fly out toward Buchanan. Instead the bat stuck to his hand and it headed straight towards Wiesler's jaw, which it found and put the big lefty on the disabled list for nearly a month. As Lombardi recalled, "I was on my way home after that act, I felt so bad over the incident."

Lombardi's time in Joplin was spent playing the game he loved and rooming with Steve Kraly, and sometimes Mantle. Mantle lived at home in Commerce during the season and his dad would drive him up to Joplin and back home after the game. Lombardi recalled they stayed in the home of an older couple and they gave the boys cooking privileges. Most of the time the fare was ham and eggs except the times that the boys had a good game the previous evening.

Lombardi recalled that after a few Miners games he, Mantle and Joe Crowder would take their carbide lights and go frogging on some pond or stream in the area. They were joined by other guys such as David Waters, who Lombardi called one of the funniest guys on the team. Being a Mississippi boy, Waters knew all about coon hunting and Lombardi remembered many a time they would go coon hunting around midnight.

According to Lombardi, some of the city boys, like Lou Skizas from Chicago, had enough of the coon, frog and snake hunting after one trip to last an entire season. However, the mantel of being the most mischievous fellow on the Joplin team went to Mantle, hands down. Lombardi recalled that Mantle had a fear of an early death and he intended to live life to its fullest.

Like the rest of the Joplin Miners and even the Independence Yankees from the previous year, Lombardi recalled the influence of Mutt Mantle on his son. Time after time Lombardi heard this same message delivered by Mutt to his eldest son, "If you think you can't play in this league, go home and work in the mines."

Mantle learned the game well while playing at the Class D and C levels and he carried the memories of those guys who "tolerated" his practical jokes, right on to the New York Yankees. Lombardi is just another of the Miner players who remember him being such a likeable young man and a great talent.

When Mantle set up his first residence after joining the Yankees, his home was located in North Jersey. He and Lombardi were close friends in those early years. Mantle would always provide tickets for Lombardi to any game he and his wife Anna wished to attend. The Lombardis had children around the same ages as Mickey and Merlyn's children, so they had a lot in common in that respect as well as their "prankster" year at Joplin. Even following Mantle's baseball career, he and Lombardi would see each other fairly regularly when Mantle was working at the Claridge Hotel in Atlantic City, New Jersey.

Those first couple of years in New York were times that Mantle did a lot of reflecting on his minor league career, as short as it was, and he would tell Lombardi, "Those years were more fun than anything. Now it's a business."

After the close of the 1950 Western Association season it was first thought that Mantle would join the Kansas City Blues to work out with that American Association team and possibly get into a few games. Bill Virdon had been sent to Kansas City after the close of the KOM League season and it was anticipated the pair would be worked into the Kansas City lineup.

However, there were a number of people in on the "secret" that something other than watching high school football was in the works for Mantle after the close of the Joplin season. Greenwade had confided in Joplin sportswriter Paul Stubblefield that the Yankees were interested in having the Western Association phenom join the big club for the last two weeks of the season. Thus on the morning of September 17, 1950, Mantle got on the train at Baxter Springs, Kansas and joined the New York Yankees in St. Louis. He worked out with the Yankees prior to their game with the Browns.

The trip to St. Louis was somewhat reminiscent to returning to the Joplin Miners clubhouse of a few weeks prior to that time. Wiesler lived in St. Louis and Neeman lived nearby. Jerry Buchanan was attending Drury College in Springfield, Missouri and he took that opportunity to drive up old Route 66 recalled to see Neeman. They went out to Sportsman's Park to see not only a St. Louis Browns/New York Yankee game but to determine what their teammate for the entire 1950 season looked like in a big league uniform.

During the period of time Mantle traveled with the Yankees during the fall of 1950 was the first time he had really "seen the world" outside the four-state area of Kansas, Arkansas, Oklahoma and Missouri. After the Browns game on Sunday September 17, the Yankees boarded a train to the Windy City, Chicago, and Mantle's first look at Comiskey Park. That would be the site of his first Major League home run the following season on May 1st against Randy Gumpert.

After a travel day on the 18th, the Yankees and White Sox played two games before the Yankees went back home. It provided Mantle with his first glimpse of Yankee Stadium. As a young man playing imaginary games with Nick Ferguson and Leroy Bennett, Mantle had always been partial to the Boston Red Sox. So, there he was looking onto a field that contained the likes of Walt Dropo, Bobby Doerr, Ted Williams, Jim Piersall, Mel Parnell and a host of others. These were the same men that Mantle pretended to have been when he and his buddies played baseball with a broomstick, tennis ball or cork from dawn to dusk.

Upon Mantle's arrival in New York, he was a fish out of water. The older players were mostly married men and there wasn't any way that the single guys were going to accept a young ballplayer from the "sticks" into their inner circle. With a good case of homesickness and boredom setting in, he called Carl Lombardi, with whom he had spent the bulk of the 1950 season. As Lombardi recalled, "He had an expense account so we went to more shows and ate more food than you could ever imagine."

But as Lombardi viewed the "Lights of Broadway," he couldn't help but recall what he and Mantle had just left a few weeks earlier. There were the memories of the long bus rides, never enough meal money to fill the belly of a young man, pillow fights in most hotels and Skizas, who had no wardrobe and whose pants were worn so long that they would stand in the corner, unassisted. However, "Lou's never smelled," according to Lombardi. And as far as money was concerned, "Skizas had every paycheck from the start of the season up to the last one," Lombardi mused. "I remember the night the season ended. We lost to Springfield in the playoffs. Lou came into the dressing room and tore that uniform to shreds. He wasn't mad at losing, he was just happy to have the season over. However, when Roy Beavers, team treasurer, found out about the uniform caper he billed Lou for it and then the happiness was gone," Lombardi laughed.

Most things were fun to Skizas except Mantle's hunting trips and his practical jokes. One day Mantle brought a terrapin to the ballpark with him. "He took it and placed it under Lou's cap. And when that cap starting moving Skizas was on his way out of that clubhouse," Lombardi said.

There were great contests among the Joplin players, probably because they were not challenged very hard during the regular season. One of the most competitive contests was the "pillow fights." In that competition the infielders and outfielders were pitted against the pitchers and catchers. Lombardi remembered, "When Harry Craft would arrive on the scene the air was usually filled with feathers. Craft had a standing rule, if you pulled off any 'funny stuff' you slept in the bus. So, 4-5 times that year we slept in the bus." Lombardi recalled they slept on the bus for a pillow fight altercation in St. Joseph, Missouri and for a water balloon barrage launched from the 5th floor of their Muskogee, Oklahoma hotel. However, being banished to the bus didn't do anything to lower the noise pollution level that the 1950 Joplin Miners could generate. As Lombardi remembered, "You couldn't believe the racket on that bus during the times we had to sleep in it."

Now there are some things that Lombardi will not tell about his days around Mantle for they were very confidential times when he would pour out his innermost feelings. I wish that had been the case in another instance but, unfortunately, the story must be told. Lombardi had a bad back and to compensate he stood in the dugout step with one foot on the top rung and the other on the dugout floor when the Miners were at bat. Thus, he was in a vulnerable position while he was intently watching the action on the field. There was always something going on behind him. Lombardi recalled, "Mickey used to pick his nose. He would then take what came out and gingerly put it on the back of my shirt sleeve, during those times I was watching the action on the field in my standing position. When we would get on the field he would yell over to me, 'Hey, Carl, look on the back of your sleeve.' Of course, I would find his boogers there and Mickey would go into his classic laugh. He really got a kick out of such things."

As a former Navy veteran, Lombardi was some four years older than Mantle. However, he was amazed at the things Mantle knew. He was awed by the number of practical jokes the kid from Commerce had in his repertoire and could pull off flawlessly. What Mantle didn't handle that well was the attention he generated in New York. Lombardi recalled that the kids would follow him and hound him for autographs, incessantly. During one session of being harassed for autographs Mantle feigned kicking one of the kids and then saying, "Didn't I sign one for you yesterday?" Lombardi recalled, "I kept telling Mickey that all this went along with the fame."

Fame could have easily eluded the superstar of the Joplin Miners shortly after the 1950 season ended. Al Billingsly, who shared the second base position with Lombardi owned the only car on the team. At the close of the regular season the team had a party and some beer was consumed. Lombardi talked Billingsly out of his 1935 roadster and loaded a joyful bunch of players in it for a night on the town. The car had a canvas top which wasn't there for long. The jubilant Miner celebrants tore the top out of it and went down the street standing and waving to the adoring throng that didn't amount to more than a few late night stragglers on Main Street in Joplin.

As the car headed west on 7th Street, which was also old Route 66, Mantle developed a sudden urge for a long journey. He hollered at Lombardi , "Let's go to California." So, they were on their way. At least for a short distance. By that time the beer was talking and Mantle ordered Lombardi to stop. Lombardi recalled, "Mickey got out of the car and went up to the door of the motel room and urinated on it. About that time the occupant came out the door with the longest shotgun I had ever seen. Now Mickey was fast but I never saw him run as fast and jump so high in my life. He ran as fast as he could and took a leap toward the car and came in the top where the guys had ripped it out just minutes earlier."

That was only starters for the last outing of the Joplin Miners. If there was ever a case to be made that young men shouldn't drink it was indelibly etched on Lombardi's mind that night and for the rest of his life. As if riding through town like conquering heroes would at a ticker tape parade in New York, or being chased by an irate man with a shotgun wasn't enough, there was another aspect of the "joyride" that evening which could have been tragic. When Mantle got back in the car he was seated in the middle next to Lombardi. At that point Lombardi said Mantle blurted out, "Let's hit that semi." Lombardi could see the big truck headed east on Highway 66 as they were headed west. He was petrified as Mickey grabbed the wheel of Billingsly's soon to be ex-car, and was attempting to steer it into the path of the oncoming truck. Certain bodily harm was going to befall the entire group unless immediate action was taken. Lombardi recalled, "It took all the power I had to hold that car in the right lane as Mantle attempted to steer it into the path of the oncoming semi."

Well, thanks to a merciful God and/or the fact that no one had a lot of money for incidentals, the car ran out of gas. At that point Mantle took charge. He told the guys he would take care of things and he went out and attempted to fill the gas tank with the same substance he had showered on the motel door an hour or so earlier. What seemed like a good idea turned to be a bad one when all the guys had to chip in the next day and pay to get the "water" taken out of Billingsly's gas tank.

But those are the kind of stories that could have been told by most young men of the early 1950s. To hear them now and to relate them to one of the greatest players to ever don a baseball uniform makes one think what could have happened on the night of celebration the Joplin Miners won the Western Association pennant. Those types of incidents were few and far between for that 1950 Miners ball club. Craft was basically responsible for ensuring that not many of those types of things occurred.

Most of the memories of that era told by Lombardi and the rest of the team involved game-related incidents. He vividly remembered that Mantle made it tough on second basemen, for he was such a poor fielder at shortstop. With balls rolling away from him or up his arm, he was always making what throws he made to second coincide with the base runner's arrival. Lombardi recalled, "My legs looked like they had been through a meat grinder, but I don't regret a minute of it." Billingsly shared the second base position with Lombardi, since Mantle was causing them both to get plastered too often. Each time Lombardi would find himself on the seat of his pants due to a base runner taking him out of the play, Mantle would yell, "I'll get it over there in time the next time." But he usually didn't, Lombardi lamented.

As time went by in New York, the friendly get together's between Mantle and Lombardi grew less frequent. Lombardi saw Mantle graduate from having nothing to having more than he ever thought possible growing up in the mining region of Northeast Oklahoma. According to Lombardi, he used to go to the hotel to visit his former teammate. Mantle would check his socks by smell. If they smelled bad he would toss them out the window and get a new pair. Yes, the kid had made it. He was hearing the cheers from Bronx rather than the razzing of one irate Joplin fan who sat behind first base. Lombardi remembered this fellow who came to every home game and called Mantle "Superstar" in derision. One evening Mantle had enough of this guy and went over to Lombardi with a plan. He told Lombardi, "Look, when another guy gets on first and someone hits a grounder to me I'm not throwing the ball to second. What I am going to do is hit that big 'fat ass' in the grandstand." So, true to his word, the next ball that was hit to Mantle he took aim at the heckler. As Lombardi recalled, "All you see is that fat guy running for his life and knocking down two folding chairs during the process." So, all the errors that Mantle made at Joplin weren't necessarily a lack of throwing ability. At least one was for the immediate gratification of the eradication of an unappreciative fan.

Lombardi had a great vantage point of Mantle's career from nearly the start to the finish. He saw him early in his Major League career and listened to the young man tell the stories of his fondness for his minor league team-mates. Then came the influences of the older and more "mature" Yankee teammates. Then Lombardi began to see the change in the Mantle he once knew as the practical joking, fun loving future Yankee prospect. He recalled being at the Mantle home after the 1952 All-Star game in Philadelphia: "I went over there and the kids are outside fungoing stones with this bat. I grabbed the bat and told Mickey that they were knocking the hell out of his All-Star game bat. All he said was 'Carl, take it home with you.' I did and it's still in my closet. It is so meaningful to me I won't even take it out and show it to anyone."

A lot of things that transpired between the kid from Commerce, Oklahoma, and the older fellow from Montclair, New Jersey, were special. Lombardi recalled the times Mantle would get mad at him over something that happened and then he would come up later with tears in his eyes saying, "I'm sorry."

The years went swiftly and one day Mickey Mantle was standing at Cooperstown, New York. He was there making his induction speech into the Baseball Hall of Fame. Lombardi remembered it as one of the great days in his life. There was a man whom he had known for so many years accepting the plaudits as one of the games greatest. He was there because Mantle had invited him to be a part of the festivities. That was an honor for him to have been affiliated with Mantle when they were both Class C performers and then to be with him when he received the greatest tribute any baseball player can receive couldn't be topped.

Lombardi was the only person affiliated with the 1950 Joplin Miners to be in attendance at the Mantle's induction into the National Baseball Hall of Fame. In Mantle's own words, [an actual transcript of his speech follows]the highlights of his career from 1947-50 are "mostly" correct:

I think the first real baseball uniform – and I'm sure it is – the most proud I ever was when I went to Baxter Springs in Kansas and I played on the Baxter Springs Whiz Kids. We had – that was the first time – I'll never forget the guy, his name was Barney Barnett, gave me a uniform and it had a BW on the cap there and it said Whiz Kids on the back. I really thought I was somethin' when I got that uniform. It was the first one my mom hadn't made for me. It was really somethin'. [Ed Note: Actually, Mantle was not recalling the composition of that uniform correctly. The hat had the WK insignia on it rather than BW and the Whiz Kid jersey at the time had a B over the heart. In later years Baxter was written across the front of the jersey. The only Whiz Kid item that ever had any writing on the back was the jacket from 1948.]

There is a man and a woman here that were really nice to me all through the years, Mr. and Mrs. Harold Youngman. I don't know if all of you have ever heard about any of my business endeavors or not, but some of 'em weren't too good. Probably the worst thing I ever did was movin' away from Mr. Youngman. We went and moved to Dallas, Texas, in 1957, but Mr. Youngman built a Holiday Inn in Joplin, Missouri, and called it Mickey Mantle's Holiday Inn. And we were doin' pretty good there, and Mr. Youngman said, 'You know, you're half of this thing, so why don't you do something for it.' So we had real good chicken there and I made up a slogan. Merlyn doesn't want me to tell this, but I'm going to tell it anyway. I made up the slogan for our chicken and I said, 'To get a better piece of chicken, you'd have to be a rooster.' And I don't know if that's what closed up our Holiday Inn or not, but we didn't do too good after that. No, actually, it was really a good deal.

Also, in Baxter Springs, the ballpark is right by the highway, and Tom Greenwade, the Yankee scout, was coming by there one day. He saw this ball game goin' on and I was playing in it and he stopped to watch the game. I'm making this kind of fast; it's gettin' a little hot. And I hit three home runs that day and Greenwade, the Yankee scout, stopped and talked to me. He was actually on his way to Broken Arrow, Oklahoma, to sign another shortstop. I was playing short-stop at that time, and I hit three home runs that day. A couple of them went in the river – one right-handed and one left-handed – and he stopped and he said, 'You're not out of high school yet, so I really can't talk to you yet, but I'll be back when you get out of high school.'

In 1949, Tom Greenwade came back to Commerce the night that I was supposed to go to my commencement exercises. He asked the principal of the school if I could go play ball. The Whiz Kids had a game that night. He took me. I hit another home run or two that night, so he signed me and I went to Independence, Kansas, Class D League, and started playing for the Yankees. I was very fortunate to play for Harry Craft. He had a great ball club there. We have one man here in the audience today who I played with in the minors, Carl Lombardi. He was on those teams, so he knows we had two of the greatest teams in minor league baseball at that time, or any time probably, and I was very fortunate to have played with those two teams.

I was lucky when I got out. I played at Joplin. The next year, I came to the Yankees. And I was lucky to play with Whitey Ford, Yogi Berra, Joe DiMaggio, Phil Rizzuto – who came up with me – and I appreciate it. He's been a great friend all the way through for me. Lots of times I've teased Whitey about how I could have played five more years if it hadn't been for him, but, believe me, when Ralph Houk used to say that I was the leader of the Yankees, he was just kiddin' everybody. Our real leader was Whitey Ford all the time. I'm sure that everybody will tell you that.

Casey Stengel's here in the Hall of Fame already and, outside of my dad, I would say that probably Casey is the man who is most responsible for me standing right here today. The first thing he did was to take me off of shortstop and get me out in the outfield where I wouldn't have to handle so many balls."[341]

It thrilled Lombardi that during Mantle's speech he said, "We have one man here in the audience today who I played with in the minors, Carl Lombardi." And the pages of this book are much the richer because Carl Lombardi shared his memories of his teammate and friend, Mickey Mantle.

After witnessing one of the most impressive Class C teams of the 20th century, Porter Wittich of *The Joplin Globe* gave the following summation:

The man in the grocery store stepped up to congratulate this department on Joplin winning the Western Association championship and we had to confess our only part was trying to keep the hits and errors segregated and the standings as correct as possible. And that we still had doubts about some of the hits and errors, just guessing at the doubtful one, like the umpires do about their decisions.

Then he asked a question which practically floored us, and would have been a knockout punch had we not been looking at the price of wieners, which already had landed a knockout blow.

The question went something like this: "You know what the Miners lacked this year?"

We mentioned the team led the league in team batting, team fielding, had the ranking batter and most of the others, and that two pitchers were leading the circuit in that capacity. Also that Manager Harry Craft was rated as the best in the league.

"You know most of the answers," he said, "but you know what the team lacked?"

We thought to our best ability while trying to decide on wieners or spareribs and finally shook our head.

"It lacked color," he said.

Well, just what does that term color imply?

There certainly was no George Sawyer on the squad. Nor a Bennie Bengough.

---

[341] Mickey Mantle, induction speech, Baseball Hall of Fame, Cooperstown, N.Y., Aug. 12, 1974.

This department made a weak effort: "There was Lou Skizas."

"Sure," was the reply, "and if the season had gone for another month he might have outhit everybody on the club, including Mickey Mantle. The same for Cromer Smotherman and Len Wiesner."

So we took the six wieners and had a sudden thought and said: "No color is needed when a team finishes as far ahead as the Miners did this year. The individuals furnished the color themselves by good, steady play. Color is no substitute for a bunch of champions."[342]

The 1950 Joplin season started with a 21-6 rout of the Springfield Cubs and wound up on September 9 with a 10-9 loss to the same Springfield Cubs in the playoff championships. That was to be Mantle's last taste of minor league baseball, except for the time he spent with the Kansas City Blues after being demoted by the Yankees for part of the 1951 campaign.

The Joplin Miners (1950):

Jerry Buchanan, Lou Skizas, Cal Neeman, Carl Lombardi, Tom Gott, Harry Craft, Bill Drake, Dave Benedict, David Waters, Cromer Smotherman, Dan Ferber, Lilburn Smith, Dick Fiedler, Frank Simanovsky, Dale Hittle, Tom Hesketh, Lyle Westrum, Bob Wiesler, Steve Kraly, Dick Gilman, Emil Federow, Joe Crowder, Al Billingsly, Carl Sellers and Mickey Mantle.

---

[342] *The Joplin* (Mo.) *Globe*, September 6, 1950.

Epilogue

Where does one begin to write a story of a legend? Everyone wants a "piece" of a legend and each of them makes claims about their contributions to the life of the legend that are not always grounded in fact.

Legends are oftentimes very different from what they perceived as being. Mickey Mantle was not the urbane New Yorker, although he was the "Toast of Manhattan." Mantle's cousin Max recalled that he was most at ease when he could get away from the limelight and head home to Northeast Oklahoma to hunt and fish with his closest relatives and friends.

There were many "fair weather" friends in Mantle's life. Max contends that his cousin would have been quite content to have lived out his days in his hometown. However, the ever-present knock on the door or a telephone call at any time of the day or night were constant interruptions to his private life. Max recalled that all of his cousin's "old buddies" felt no compunction in asking Mantle for a favor. Those favors may have been the "loaning" of money or asking for some of his memorabilia. Max said that no matter what someone requested, Mantle would give it away. And that, according to Max, was why the Mantles finally moved to Dallas. It was his way of getting away from a problem without making his old friends mad.

Max said that Mickey was nothing more than a poor old country boy who probably enjoyed playing baseball with Baxter Springs, Kansas; Joplin, Missouri; and Independence, Kansas, more than at any other time in his life. For those who knew the Commerce Comet only as a New York Yankee, this book is an attempt to depict *Mickey Mantle: Before the Glory.*

It was indeed an exciting life crammed into a few years. In looking back over those early years, none of Mickey Mantle's pals or teammates around Commerce and Baxter Springs ever expected him to have the success he did. He once confided to his lifelong pal Nick Ferguson after his retirement from the Yankees, "I can't believe this happened to me. It seems like I was somebody else."

Appendix 1

A Day with Merlyn Mantle

September 9, 1999 was a day filled with anticipation and equal amounts of apprehension. Tommy Gott had arranged for a visit with Merlyn Mantle, the wife of the late Mickey Mantle. Tommy, Lilburn Smith and Yours Truly met at Lilburn's Springfield, Missouri home to make the final leg of the trip to Joplin.

None of the trio knew what to expect when we arrived to speak with the young lady Mickey Charles Mantle had first met on a double date in 1949. Mickey and Merlyn had different partners on that first date but shortly thereafter Mickey called Merlyn for a date and that was the beginning of a long and sometimes stormy relationship.

Motoring along I-44 between Springfield and Joplin, the trio comprised of two former teammates of Mantle's, Gott and Smith and a former batboy were a little anxious about telling Merlyn we wanted to write a story of her husband as a minor league player. Each of us were convinced she had heard everything there was to tell and that we would just be putting an added burden on her life at worst and putting new wine in old bottles at best.

On September 9, 1999, the author and Merlyn Mantle fight the bright sunlight to pose in front of the Mantle residence at Loma Linda, just outside Joplin, Missouri.

Like the idealist each of us was 49 years before, we finally made it to Joplin — still a little hesitant to go barging in on the wife of a Hall of Famer. The first hour or so was spent in Joplin, which consisted of a trip down 4th Street to Miners Park (now called Joe Becker Stadium), where Gott and Smith had been integral parts of the awesome 1950 Joplin Miners. Smith didn't last the entire season, having being sent to the Cotton States League in mid-season. However, Gott was there all year, batting behind Mantle. As Gott recalled on the trip, "Mickey told me after the season that I only failed to get a hit one time, when the opposition walked him to get to me." He mused, "That sure made me feel good."

Smith had first seen Mantle in 1949 when he came to Joplin for a tryout. As Smith re called, "Tom Greenwade wanted Johnny Sturm, our manager, to have a look at Mickey to see what he thought of him. I was pitching batting practice that day and didn't think he was anything very great."

"His notable hitting came around very shortly. It was his speed and his arm that got all the attention," Smith observed. Mantle's first cousin, Jimmy Richardson, attributed the speed to running to the outhouse and back. He commented, "You froze to death in the winter and the flies ate you alive in the summer, so you had to be fast."

What Smith had observed in a tryout at Joplin a year earlier was again standing in the batters box in spring training at Branson in 1950. Smith recalled, "I was once again throwing batting practice. Mickey joined us from the Kansas City Blues training camp. Again, he popped up most of the time and I didn't see him as a great hitter. How foolish and mistaken I was. The next day we played a spring training exhibition game against St. Paul of the American Association. Mickey hit one out right-handed and one out left-handed."

Smith's time with the Miners didn't last as long as he would have liked he recalled, "We broke spring training camp and went to Joplin for the season. In our opening game the Springfield Cubs came to Joplin. My fondest memory of that game, once again I was the winning pitcher and we won 21-6. Mickey went 5 for 6 and I had 4 hits in 5 at bats. My chest sure did swell since I was from Springfield. Shortly afterwards our manager, Harry Craft, had to leave town to attend a funeral. He left me to manage the team. We went to Muskogee, Oklahoma for a three game series. When we reached the ballpark a heavy rain came and all three games were rained out. Tom Greenwade arrived on the second day to relieve me of my managerial duties."

Although a tough competitor and fine pitcher Smith had advanced no further than Norfolk, Virginia, of the Piedmont League by the spring of 1954. Smith had spent two seasons in the military and was trying to get back on track. He recalled that Mantle came through Norfolk with the Yankee parent club for an exhibition game. We did a lot of visiting. In that visit Smith remembered, "Mickey was very interested in my Army baseball career and we caught up on our lives from 1950-54. I told him about winning a bet with my Sergeant when he hit the winning home run to beat the Brooklyn Dodgers in the 1952 World Series. He assured me that I would always be a winner since I was placing my bets on him." That spring Smith asked Lee McPhail, head of minor league operations, for his release, "I knew my arm was bad and would not get any better. So, it was time to go home and get a college degree." Smith lamented.

Mantle and Smith kept in touch over the years and when Harold Youngman built the Holiday Inn at Joplin and put Mantle's name on the marquee it was a time for some celebrating. Smith recalled, "After the close of the baseball season in 1960 Mantle invited me and a group of baseball friends to come to Joplin for golf and to stay in his hotel."

The visits between Mantle and Smith were not that frequent but always meaningful to Smith. "One of the most vivid memories was in the summer of 1979 when Mantle was invited to Springfield to speak to the Life Underwriters Association. It was a tribute to Tom Greenwade. I picked up Greenwade and his son Bunch and took them to hear Mickey's presentation. In Mickey's speech he bragged on me and my pitching in front of my fellow insurance underwriters. It was a great night." Smith recalled.

That was a very emotional occasion due to Greenwade's failing health and since he, Mantle, and Greenwade had not seen each other for some time. Smith recalled, "We spent a long time visiting about baseball and the memories of Mick's early days with Tom in Willard, Missouri. Mickey had spent much of his recovery after surgery in 1951, by Dr. Daniel Yancey of Springfield at the Greenwade home. Tom and Mickey would go up Main Street and they would visit with the locals. My father-in-law who also lived in Willard recalled how comfortable everyone felt visiting with a great base-ball star."

Smith and Mantle last crossed paths in February of 1995, when Smith and his wife Joan were in Las Vegas. Mantle was at the Riviera for a sports signing event. Smith recalled, "I went just before it ended to have him sign a couple of baseballs. He looked so good, just like the old Mickey. While I was standing in line he looked up and saw me and said, 'Hello Lilburn, what are you doing here?' I held up my two baseballs and he gave me a big grin. We visited a short while and he asked me about some of the fellows back in Springfield. I'll always remember that handshake. I was one of the best and he was sincerely glad to see me as I was to see him. It brought back a lot of good memories in a hurry. It made my trip to Vegas extra special. In just a couple of months we heard that he was gravely ill and then of his death shortly thereafter."

According to Smith, "Mantle had a good knuckleball and he showed me how to throw it. He wanted to pitch just like I wanted to be a good hitter. We soon gave up on those ideas, however, we did a lot of pitching and hit-ting to each other. In fact, one day I took extra batting practice with the position players and wore a blister on my pitching hand. Harry Craft was not impressed and was very upset with me. That is probably what hastened my departure to the Cotton States League."

Some of the greatest memory were off the field antics. Smith recalled one of those incidents: "We could always come up with something to have fun about. We were staying at the Jayhawk Hotel in Topeka and with nothing to do so we got water pistols and fired them at girls as they walked through the lobby. The young ladies would jump and turn around. We would hide the guns behind a newspaper we pretended to be reading, I'm sure it was the sports section. We really thought this was funny. I think Mickey was our leader. I always reflect on those days as the fun time in my life."

As the trip to Joplin to meet with Merlyn progressed, the trio of Smith, Gott and Yours Truly felt the need to spend a few minutes in the Joplin

Public Library. After researching some of the games from the 1950 season so that their minds would be fresh with their boyhood exploits, a call was placed to Merlyn at her Loma Linda retreat, announcing that the two former Joplin Miners and the batboy were in town. She provided directions to a truck stop on Interstate 44 and said, "I will meet you there in ten minutes."

Off to the truck stop we headed looking for a black Lexus. Shortly upon our arrival, a beaming petite blonde lady with a big smile showed up and said, "Follow me." We followed for a couple of miles until we were in the community called Loma Linda. After winding through an area built around a golf course, Gott was completely lost and Smith and Yours Truly were attempting to figure out which house belonged to the Mantles.

Gott parked his white station wagon behind the black Lexus and Merlyn invited us into the "home on the hill" that was once a place where the Mantles lived and entertained some of the biggest names in the sports world. It was as though we were being escorted into a hallowed sanctuary, where you should hold your tongue and not say anything unless spoken to and then reply only briefly.

On the journey to Joplin, I had promised myself not to ask dumb questions. I recalled a story that Jack Hasten of the 1949 Independence Yankees had related. Hasten was at the 1979 function in Springfield that paid tribute to Tom Greenwade. A lady newspaper reporter asked Mantle for an interview and he replied, "Only if you don't ask dumb questions. If you ask three that I think are dumb, this interview will end." As Hasten recalled, "This lady asked Mickey a question that he thought was dumb and he warned her that she only had two remaining." When she got around to asking the third one, which was inevitable, Hasten said, "Mickey gave her an answer that embarrassed me to death and then walked off, proclaiming the interview was concluded. I had to plead with her not to print his response in *The Springfield News Leader.*"

My fears of speaking with Merlyn on a forthright basis were immediately assuaged when she broached the subject of how the Mickey Mantle name had been latched onto by so many people that the family couldn't even get a Mickey Mantle website on the Internet. The name "Mickey Mantle" has been adopted by everyone from wax museum owners to people selling every item imaginable. It finally resulted in the family getting the name trademarked.

As Gott, Smith, Merlyn and I spoke, we were seated on an stuffed sofa surrounded by the trappings with which all baseball fans would be familiar.

Above the fireplace was a large reproduction of a *Sports Illustrated* cover that featured a very young Mickey. While Merlyn was in the kitchen preparing each of us a drink — diet colas — Gott turned to Smith and remarked, "That is just how we remember him, isn't it?"

Conversations are difficult to conduct when your eyes keep traversing the scenery around you. Behind the overstuffed sofa was the real Mickey Mantle picture collection. They were the photos like those found in most homes but in most homes the man of the house is not an American icon.

The home where Mickey and Merlyn spent many of the holidays and get-away times sits on the highest point in the Loma Linda development. It was a home that Harold Youngman had built for the Mantles. According to Merlyn, "Harold was like a father to Mickey and I. He and his wife had no children and for all intents and purposes he adopted us."

Youngman was a builder and had hired Mickey to go around the country and represent him. He knew Mantle's great name recognition wouldn't hurt his business, but he genuinely liked the young couple and wanted to do what he could to ensure that they would be financially sound at the end of Mantle's playing career.

Merlyn remembered that her husband wanted to get rich a lot quicker than that and thus he was tempted by a lot of flim-flam hustlers. She recalled an old fellow coming to the door one time with dog hair all over him and telling Mickey that he ought to get in on the ground floor of an insurance company he was starting. Harold Youngman had the guy checked out and found he had pulled those types of con games previously. However, the dog hair covered pitchman convinced Mantle that the deal was a good one and that he already had signed up the world's greatest rodeo performer at the time, Jim Shoulders of Henryetta, Oklahoma. Merlyn said, "Mickey went down and withdrew $3,000 from the bank and gave it to this guy and that was a whole lot of money for us. And as I recall we liked to never got that money back."

After listening to Merlyn talk for a while I realized that she had some things that she wanted to share with a group of guys who either knew her husband personally or by reputation, as in the case of this writer.

Five years previous to the meeting with Merlyn I had begun writing about the old Kansas, Oklahoma, Missouri (KOM) League where Mantle had started in 1949. I wanted him to know about that the old league was being remembered and a lot of his Independence teammates from 1949 had urged that I contact him and let him know about the effort. A large number of those newsletters were sent to both Mantle's New York and Dallas addresses but nothing was ever heard from him. Actually, I had not expected it. However, as the discussion with Merlyn continued she said, "Someone used to send this little newspaper to us in Dallas." At that moment I didn't say a word. Then she went on to say, "My boys just loved reading it." I asked, "Why?" She concluded, "Because it told stories about their dad they had never heard before."

At that juncture I was emboldened and said, "That sender was me." I felt pretty good that I had told a kid of Mickey Mantle's something they didn't know about their dad. Then Merlyn talked about the early days of their marriage and the great love Mickey had for hunting. For a while she accompanied him but after a rabbit-hunting trip where the quarry was tied to the front grill of the car Merlyn proclaimed that her hunting days were over.

Mantle took his young boys hunting for a few years, but they came to dislike the aspect of killing an animal, and not long afterward, so did he. In defense of her late husband's love for hunting she asked, "But what was a young boy to do in our part of the country back then if he didn't hunt and fish?" There wasn't much else except athletics, and that is where Mantle excelled.

Mantle's hunting trips took him to places such as Kerrville, Texas where he was when his son Billy was born. Not liking the taste of deer the Mantles would donate the meat to orphanages. Then the hunting turned toward pheasant and Mickey took a few trips into Nebraska before gradually giving it up entirely.

Our conversation was interrupted by the ringing of the telephone and one could hear the voice of a concerned mother speaking to a son on the other end of the line. Gott, Smith and I engaged in conversation, walked through the house and waited for the conversation to conclude. Upon returning to the group, Merlyn told us that Mickey, Jr. was on the phone and he was getting out of the hospital the next day. She said that he had a form of skin cancer and was not doing too well. This led to his death within two years.

At that point I felt like we were now imposing on her time since she would have to leave in a few hours to head back to look after Mickey, Jr. and his 10-year-old daughter. However, she wanted to know more about what we had in mind regarding a book about her late husband. Gott explained that he just wanted people to know what a great kid and tremendous athlete Mickey was when he played with the Joplin Miners. Merlyn replied, "I will do anything in my power to help you guys do that."

The time at the Mantle home was running short for we had plans for a trip back to the old "stomping grounds" within a short period of time. Merlyn told us of the plans to auction off some of Mickey's items such as the Ford Bronco in the garage.

On my lap during the entire conversation was the manuscript I had prepared for this book, up to the point of the interview with Merlyn. I was beginning to feel that I might just as well drop it in the trash can and start over. I knew that no book, about Mantle's early days would be complete without her input and cooperation. The only thing that I felt even worthy of asking was about the part where Mickey once talked the legendary Bob Wills and the Texas Playboys into taking him to Joplin one evening. As I told that story, Merlyn seemed to be enjoying it. When I asked if she had ever heard it, she admitted she hadn't but retorted, "It sounds possible."

Merlyn was facing toward a pile of large boxes when I mentioned country music legend, Bob Wills. She pointed to a stack of four huge boxes and said, "That was Mickey's country music collection. He loved Hank Williams and Patsy Cline but his favorite was Roy Clark." Clark recorded, "Yesterday When I Was Young," one of the songs sung at Mickey's funeral.

The conversation was just getting started with Merlyn and I was already beginning to like her and Mickey in ways that I couldn't have imagined. Merlyn remarked that Mickey loved Stan Musial as a ballplayer and when Mickey went to the Major Leagues the Cardinals and Yankees both trained at St. Petersburg, Florida. Merlyn said, "We both became very close to Stan and his wife Lillian." This author could have imagined as a young man writing a story about Stan Musial but never Mickey Mantle. Stan was my idol.

Merlyn provided a tour of the home and it was time to head toward the hometowns of her and her late husband. She stopped to pose for pictures with three old guys and then the party loaded in Gott's van and away we went. Merlyn served as tour guide. When we came to the fork in the road that led to I-44 and old Route 66 a decision had to be made. Merlyn asked, "Do you want to take the scenic trip to Miami or do you wish to see where Mickey and I grew up?" Should the reader have to guess the answer to that question they should stop reading at this juncture.

From the last home Merlyn and Mickey ever shared, Highway 66 takes the traveler from Missouri into Kansas and over into Oklahoma in about 15 minutes. However, that trip covered 49 years and a lot of memories. From Joplin to Baxter Springs, Kansas is the reverse order of Mickey's baseball career. He was playing for the Baxter Springs Whiz Kids the day he was signed to a Yankee contract by Tom Greenwade. From Baxter Springs to Commerce, Oklahoma is a short trip with the town of Picher lurking on the horizon. Picher does have landmarks. They are called "chat piles" and they were born out of the lead and zinc mining that occurred there in the latter part of the 19th and early part of the 20th centuries.

Following Mantle's second year with the Yankees, a sports writer attempted to explain Commerce, Oklahoma to a readership from coast to coast, very few of whom could imagine such as great baseball player originating from an obscure place. The author summed up the town very succinctly, "Commerce is a rather drab town in Ottawa County, the extreme northeast square on Oklahoma's map, showing a population of 2,412 in a 1950 census and now claiming up to 3,500, which must be on a busy Saturday with all the farmers and a visiting football crowd in town. It resembles several hundred other small communities in Oklahoma and the Southwest, with stores and filling stations and a couple of vacant buildings strung for five or six blocks along a main street which is also U. S. Highway 66. Beginning with the city limits, and particularly along the four miles to the northeast to Picher, Oklahoma, a slightly larger town, this region is marked with huge gray mounds, 'dumps' of waste material from the lead and zinc mines." [343]

Merlyn's parents had come to Picher from the small town of Treece, Kansas located just a few miles north. As we passed the chat piles, Merlyn looked at them and said, "Billy Martin nicknamed me 'chat pile' Annie, because I came from here." Silence then engulfed Merlyn for a few moments. Then the conversation turned to Martin. This author asked her what it was like to have Martin around for a couple of winters. Merlyn measured her words and said, "If Mutt would have still been alive at that time he would have sent Billy packing his second day in town."

Mantle's cousin, Jimmy Richardson, recalled visiting with his cousin after the '56 season. During that visit, a *Kansas City Star* reporter knocked on the Mantles' door in Commerce. Mickey's mother, Lovell, answered and

---

[343] *Inside Baseball*, August 1953, Volume 1 Number 10, "The Mickey Mantle Nobody Knows", Clyde Carley, Page 13.

she was asked by the reporter if she was the maid or the mother? She, replied, "I sure as hell ain't the maid."

"At that time Billy was growing his hair a bit longer and it was hanging in ringlets and he was a bit pale from an overnight drinking binge," according to Richardson. The reporter was telling Mantle how he was sure that he would break all of Ruth's records, and the told him to go get into his Yankee uniform so he could take a picture. Richardson recalled Mantle looking at the reporter and saying, "I wouldn't put on that uniform if Dwight Eisenhower asked me." At that moment, Richardson recalled that Martin jumped up and got in the face of the reporter. "I thought he was going to bust the reporter in the chops," he said. Instead Martin said, "You don't want to take a picture of some 'damn' drag bunter. If you want a picture of a real slugger take one of me."

Merlyn knew that Martin would always show up each winter and he would either be between wives or about to be. Martin really enjoyed the simple life of the Midwest and the way he was taken in by Mantle's mother. Merlyn recalled that Martin told stories about being the son of a Portuguese fisherman and that his mother ruled her domain with a flag attached to the front of the house. If the flag was up visitors were welcome to stop by for a visit. If the flag was down they were to just keep on going for they were not welcome in her home. Martin's last name was one he took later in life. His last name at birth was Pesano.

Merlyn recalled that her husband chastised her for not doing Martin's laundry on one occasion. She recalled, "I got mad and said wash his clothes eh? I got a whole bottle of bleach and put it in the wash water and then dumped in his underwear. When the washing came out the only thing left of the fabric was the elastic tops of his undershirts and shorts." As Merlyn chuckled, "That was the end of doing Billy's washing." Later in life she buried the hatchet with him, but in those early day he was not the influence that she wanted around her family. That "hatchet burying" happened when the Mantles lived in Dallas and Martin managed the Texas Rangers. Merlyn had him over for dinner many times and she and Mickey were very fond of Billy's son, Billy Joe.

Back to the trip from Joplin to Miami. Nearing the city limits of Commerce, this author asked Merlyn what one thing about Mickey would she most want to be made known, or what misconception about him would she like to see cleared up. She replied, "I would want people to know that he was the most generous person I ever knew." She then recited how he had done so much for her mother and always remembered her on birthdays and other special occasions.

Johnny LaFalier said that after Mickey's father-in-law died that he sent his mother-in-law $100 each time he got his Yankee paycheck.

Mantle was greatly affected by his father's death. As Merlyn saw things, "The Mantles loved each other, but they were not an affectionate family." When Mutt passed away, it became the turning point in his eldest son's life. Merlyn said, "Mickey was expected to step forth and take care of the family." Merlyn added, "It hurt Mickey greatly, for he never got to say goodbye to his dad."

Taking care of a young family was difficult enough for the newlyweds, Mickey and Merlyn, in 1952. From Picher, Oklahoma, to New York City was quite an adjustment for the young lady who three years previous had dated Picher's left halfback, Jess Bogard, before falling in love with the Commerce Tiger fullback/halfback, Mickey Charles Mantle.

Merlyn arrived in New York to see ladies dressed up as she had only seen in magazines back home. Arriving in the Big Apple, there was no money with which to buy anything and the only accessible and affordable place for "struggling" baseball players and their wives to live was the Concourse Plaza Hotel, which was located near Yankee Stadium.

Merlyn recalled they had a sleeping room but not enough money for a kitchen or a TV set. The kitchen was an additional $10 a month and a TV was out of the question. So, the life of a baseball wife was pretty boring. Merlyn recalled that when the Yankees used to take two-week road trips, the wives would get together and pool their money so they could buy food. They would take it over to one of the players' apartments that had a kitchen, and they would eat and maybe watch TV once in a while. Mantle was paid the astronomical salary of $7,500 to start the 1952 season, but he would get another $2,500 if he lasted through June. As Merlyn mused, "We lived for bonuses and World Series checks."

Most of the "bonus" checks came in the form of World Series winning shares. Merlyn recalled the first time Mickey's mother, Lovell, came to New York to see a World Series game. They went to the game by subway and Lovell thought the people were following them so that they could get to Mickey and break his legs to ensure he couldn't play against Brooklyn.

Merlyn recalled that they were seated in a box next to Humphrey Bogart and Lauren Bacall during the 1952 World Series with the Dodgers. Merlyn warned Mickey's mother not to say anything or react to any of the comments that the rabid Dodger fans would hurl at the Yankees in general and Mickey in particular.

New York was a long way from 1949, the year Mantle signed with the Yankees and got a $1,150 bonus for going to Independence to play in the KOM League.

When Mantle got all that 1949 bonus money, a few of the prices of goods and services to be found in Independence, Kansas, were as follows:[345]

- Movie tickets, 35¢ Adult, 10¢ Children
- New US Royal tires, $9.32
- Khaki pants, 2 for $1.50
- Neckties, $2.00
- Manhattan shirts, $3.95
- Ladies slips, $1.00
- Pup tents, $3.00
- Sports Jackets, $25.00
- Men's suits, $35.00
- Lettuce, 10¢ a head
- Brake job for car, $1.19
- Ground boneless chuck, 49¢, a pound
- Good used tires, $1.50
- Men's dress straw hats, $3.95
- Ladies' cotton dresses, $2.98
- Mrs. Tucker's 3-lb shortening, 69¢
- 1933 Chevrolet used car, $60.00

Most minor league games were 50¢ for adults and 25¢ for children. Miami, Oklahoma tried to raise the price to 60¢ and they soon had to back track on that policy. People hollered too loud. They were not even prepared to pay to see local boy Mickey Mantle perform when the Independence Yankees arrived for a visit.

Mickey met Merlyn during the fall of 1949. Mickey took his bonus money and bought a Chevrolet with Air-Flo drive. Merlyn recalled the night he got it: "It was cold and snowing and we went to the movies. When

---

[344] From various sections of the June 13, 1949 edition of the *Independence* (Kansas) *Reporter*.

he pulled up to the theater Mickey said that he would leave the car running so it would be warm when we came out." Well, what happened was that he left his keys in the car. Mickey turned to Merlyn and said, "That's okay, I'll call my dad."

Merlyn recalled that they were sitting in the Coleman Theater in Miami when Mutt arrived a few minutes later. He tapped his son on the shoulder and asked him what he needed. Mickey replied, "I locked my keys in the car." Mutt retorted, "Well I'll be damned." At that point Mutt walked out and didn't offer any assistance. Merlyn recalled, "When the movie was over Mickey had to get a policeman to get the car unlocked."

That car was Mantle's pride and joy and the only music he ever played on its radio was country. Merlyn said that on every date we heard Little Jimmy Dickens singing, "Take an Old Cold Tater and Wait" or "Sleeping at the Foot of the Bed." She came to dislike Little Jimmy's singing because of Mickey's constant playing of it.

As the group entered the City of Miami, Oklahoma, on September 9, 1999, we were on a mission. Tommy Gott, Lilburn Smith and this author wanted to know more about Mantle's high school athletic career. As we drove down Main Street, Merlyn pointed out the theater where she and Mickey had gone on the date when he left his engine running with the key locked inside. Merlyn pointed to a building at 1st and Main Streets that was once Dawson Jewelry and said, "There is where Mickey bought my wedding ring."

There were a lot of memories for all of those in the caravan that went in circles for a couple of blocks attempting to locate *The Miami News-Record*. But thanks to the size of the town, it was located and we were soon scrolling through some old microfilm on a reader that was about as ancient as the files we were viewing. It had long since ceased operating mechanically and so I ran through the film by winding it with my finger. With the help of sports editor Jim Ellis, we were soon looking at the exploits of a 16-year-old football star. Highlights read, "Mickey Mantle broke loose and ran 65 yards to the 1-yard line before he was tackled. Mantle then plunged over to score. Mantle plunged off tackle for six yards to score after recovering a Fairland Owl fumble."

During the first three games Commerce played in Mickey's senior year, they lost each of them but Mickey scored 10 touchdowns during those losing ventures. The October 29th edition of *The Miami News-Record* stated that Commerce won their first game but, "The win was costly for the Tigers, with Mickey Mantle, their star fullback, being forced out of the game with a seriously sprained left ankle. It was not known exactly how seriously Mantle's ankle was injured nor how long he would be out of action." The conference in which the Commerce Tigers were affiliated was "The Lucky Seven." No one at that time realized what that magic number would mean to the life of Mickey Mantle, the baseball world and, eventually, the Baseball Hall of Fame.

That reported ankle injury was a recurrence of the injury Mickey suffered in his sophomore year. That initial injury plagued Mickey for the rest of his life. As this author stood at that microfilm machine and replayed Mantle's school boy heroics Merlyn was seeing things about her late husband she had never known. Mantle played football for Commerce for the last time in the fall of 1948. However, the idol of all the girls from that club was the handsome quarterback, Bill Mosley. Mantle told his 1949 Independence Yankee roommate, Bob Mallon, that the best athlete at Commerce High was Mosley.

Of course, Merlyn was a Picher High School cheerleader when Commerce played them in 1948 and she wouldn't have paid any attention to the opposition's fullback/halfback, Mickey Mantle. The microfilm scanned 1948 as Merlyn looked at the advertisements of the day which featured full-length mink coats for $650 but you had to travel as far as Tulsa to purchase one. Other items caught her eye such as the town gossip from Picher. Often she would stop the microfilm to see if her mother was mentioned in the news of the Baptist Church. It was apparent that Merlyn was interested as much in the social aspects of her family's life as she was of the sports pages that chronicled the accomplishments of her future husband. Finally, working up the courage, this author asked, "Did you really like baseball all that much?" Without hesitating Merlyn replied, "Baseball was my rival."

At one point in the scanning of the microfilm the image of Oklahoma star quarterback of 1948 appeared on the screen. Merlyn said, "That's Darrell Royal. In Mickey's senior year Oklahoma University tried to recruit him to play football. When he went down to look over the campus Darrell drove him around. A few years later when Mickey joined the Yankees he met Darrell at a golf tournament. He asked Darrell if he remembered driving him around the OU campus. Darrell said that he didn't. Mickey asked him how he could have forgotten and Darrell replied, 'You weren't Mickey Mantle then.' "

Departing *The Miami News-Record* office Merlyn was excited to have learned that Mickey had scored 10 touchdowns in three games in 1948. She expressed that her sons would be just as excited to hear another of their dad's accomplishments. After that another big decision had to be made. Should the group return to Joplin by retracing the route back up old Highway 66 or on the modern Oklahoma Turnpike. The decision was easy. We had made the trip 50 years into the past earlier in the day, via Route 66, and it was now time to return to the present "going home" on the Oklahoma Turnpike.

Our group of four had gone back for a few fleeting moments and resurrected a small segment of Mantle's past. He was with us now as we made the trip from the Commerce-Miami area to Joplin, one that Mickey had made countless times. Merlyn told some stories about how she could be brought to tears by some of her husband's antics when he had gone too far with booze. She told about the time he pulled a chair from under her as she was about to sit down at a fashionable New York restaurant. At that moment Merlyn recalled that she could have killed him. She said that she wrote about that in her book and Clete Boyer who was at the same table at the time of that embarrassing incident saw her later at a New York Yankees reunion. He told Merlyn he couldn't believe she wrote about that incident. Merlyn, said that she wrote about it because it was one of the most embarrassing times in her life. She told this author that Clete was acting as peacemaker in that original situation and had Mickey come out that door instead, "I would have run over him, I was so mad."

She verified, as true, the story about the loaded gun that he fired in her presence after swearing it wasn't loaded. It was a time that Merlyn said it scared him so badly that he was as "white as a sheet." But Merlyn recalled Mickey never was without a gun. She recalled taking the family car in for repairs one time and the mechanic called to tell her to come and pick up the pistol.

The tabloids notwithstanding, the Mantles remained friends. Merlyn recalled that following their separation in 1988 Mickey would still come back for her mother's birthday. Although Mickey was one of the most generous people Merlyn ever knew, she recalled that after he took "the cure," his son commented, "Mom, since Dad quit drinking, he sure has a lot more money."

The last days of Mantle's life were difficult times for his fans, friends and family. Merlyn recalled that her son Danny went into his hospital room in his final hours and said, "I love you, Dad." Merlyn recalled that Mickey smiled but didn't say anything. Merlyn had prepared a letter and went in to see Mickey. She told her first love that she wanted to read it to him. Mickey replied, "I am in so much pain, can you hold it until later?" Later never came.

Appendix 2

A Day with Johnny LaFalier

Johnny LaFalier knew Mickey Mantle as long and as intimately as any person outside the immediate family. Mantle and LaFalier married the Johnson sisters. Mantle graduated from high school in 1949, Merlyn did likewise from Picher High in 1950 and LaFalier graduated from Picher High in 1952 and his wife Pat followed in 1953.

The games of Mantle's youth, along with those he played in the minor and major leagues, were done so with LaFalier around most of the time. The only part of Mantle's baseball career that he missed out on was the 1949 season at Independence. That summer the mining jobs were in short supply and LaFalier followed the wheat harvest starting in western Kansas and then heading northward until all the grain had been cut and put into the large grain elevators that are the skyscrapers of the plains.

During Mantle's second season LaFalier watched a few of the Joplin Miner games since the drive up from Picher was less than a half-hour.

When Mantle was shipped out by the Yankees to their Triple A affiliate, the Kansas City Blues of the American Association, he was always wanting the guys he knew to come up and visit. LaFalier and his buddy Don Walker drove up to Kansas City after another of Mantle's requests.

He recalled Mantle taking them to Municipal Stadium where they both got to shag balls for the Blues during batting practice. Municipal Stadium in Kansas City was a far cry for the old wooden grandstand at Baxter Springs. Mantle had arranged for LaFalier and Walker to have box seats behind the Blues dugout. In keeping with Mantle's humorous nature he told the Blues officials that LaFalier and Walker were his twin brothers. Of course, the Blues knew that Mantle had twin brothers and having never seen them they took his word on the matter. LaFalier said, "I was French/Indian and more Indian than French." He never thought for a moment that the Kansas City officials bought Mantle's story, hook, line and sinker about them being his brothers but he and Walker did get choice seats for each game during their time in Kansas City and access to the field during pre-game warm-ups.

Mantle didn't start telling his "tall tales" after signing a professional baseball contract. By accounts from most of his grade and high school buddies, he could tell stories with the best of them. The *Inside Baseball* article that appeared early in his career stated, "Mickey was always a 'big tease' in school Mrs. Miller recalled, although seldom if ever to the extent of trouble-making. As a lad he was given to the Arkansas style of 'telling whoppers' to any gullible bystander who would listen; he would deadpan the farfetched yarns until the listener realized his leg was being pulled to the breaking point."[346]

During Mickey's time with the Blues, he was residing in a rooming house on Troost Avenue, as was a young third baseman on the team, Andy Carey. Carey had shown up that season with the Blues driving a convertible, which made him an instant pal of many of the players. Following each game, Mantle would load LaFalier and Walker in the car and they would get a ride home and stay in the same rooming house where many of the Blues players spent the summer. LaFalier looked back after a half-century and recalled that Carey was his chauffeur.

Some of the more "exciting" times that Mantle and LaFalier shared were not baseball related. LaFalier recalled that after his marriage to Pat Johnson, he went to visit the Mantles one day. Upon arriving, he found Merlyn and Mickey in a mood that he hadn't witnessed in either of them previously. He recalled that Mickey was a bit shaky and Merlyn was very quiet. He assumed

---

[346] *Inside Baseball*, August 1953, Volume 1 Number 10, "The Mickey Mantle Nobody Knows," Clyde Carley, Page 56.

he had walked into a family fight. However, it wasn't anything that had gone on between Mickey and Merlyn, but an incident involving five-year-old Mick, Jr. and two-year-old David. The silence was broken when LaFalier asked what had gone on prior to his arrival. Mickey stated that Mick, Jr. had found one of his pistols and he and David were playing in the front room. Mick, Jr. pulled the trigger on the weapon and it blew a hole through the front door that Johnny had just entered. Of course, both parents were visibly shaken and they couldn't figure out where David was positioned when "Little Mick" discharged the weapon.

LaFalier recalled that pistols were a constant companion of Mickey's. Once, when Mantle got a new car he told LaFalier to take it for a spin. He recalled that when he looked down there was a revolver on the floorboard beneath his feet. He went back and told Mantle about the gun and he replied, "Ya' I know it's there, ain't nobody ever gonna hijack me."

A lot of things were common threads in the lives of Mickey and Johnny but none so unlikely as the evening Johnny took his wife Pat to Freeman hospital in Joplin to give birth to their first born. As Johnny was entering the facility he ran into Mickey who was bringing Merlyn in for the same reason. Thus, on December 26, 1955 Mickey and Johnny both became fathers and their children were born within four hours of each other. That photo was "special" enough to have made it onto the Associated Press wire photo service and seen across the United States.

After Mantle arrived on the Major League scene to stay, LaFalier became very important to him. After the conclusion of the 1955 season Mantle had purchased a new Oldsmobile, with all the accessories, from a local dealer in Baxter Springs. When spring training rolled around in 1956 Mantle talked LaFalier into driving down and bringing along the wives and the two babies who by that time were not quite three months of age.

Once the baseball season ended for Mantle it was back to Commerce. By 1954 he and Merlyn were able to build their first home at the corner of 4th and Maple Streets. The house was just across the street from Seymour Field. The field was named in honor of Bob Seymour, who was Commerce's first great athlete. He was a star performer for the Commerce High School Tigers and then with the Oklahoma Sooners before graduating in 1939. He later spent six seasons with the Washington Redskins of the National Football League and finished his career with the Los Angeles Dons of the All American Football Conference.

The new home that the Mantles moved into in 1954 served a number of purposes. One of the more functional features of the home was the roof. It did more than just keep the snow, wind and rain outside. When Mickey's twin brothers, Ray and Roy, were gridiron performers for the Commerce High Tigers, Mickey had already received a lot of acclaim and preferred not to cross the street to attend the football games. So he, LaFalier and whoever else came over for the football game had the privilege of standing on Mantle's roof and watching Commerce play whatever Lucky Seven opponent happened to be in town that evening.

However, that home being so close to the old cinder block football field was too alluring for Mantle to ignore. Each October and into early November, the Mantle All-Stars from Commerce and the Alba Aces (which were basically the sons of Vern Boyer — Cloyd, Kenny, Cletis, Lynn and Wayne), would travel all over the four-state area to play baseball just because they loved the game. Never did that group attract very many spectators, regardless of when or where they played. When it became too cold to play baseball, the urge to play football was ever-present with Mantle. LaFalier recalled that there were frequent six-man football games. The football was of the miniature variety, and Mantle always insisted upon being the quarterback. The pairings for the games were always the same: Mickey, his brother Roy, and LaFalier were on one team, and Mantle's other brother Ray, and cousins Ronnie and Max were the opposition.

The football being played on Seymour Field without a soul watching from the sidelines or grandstands was not flag football or the "sissy" touch version of the game. Without helmets and padding, it was all-out tackle football. Had the Yankees known what Mantle was up to at the time, they would have had Tom Greenwade or some other Yankee representative in town before the game concluded with orders to throw a penalty flag for unnecessary roughness.

While the Yankees were never aware that Mantle played football during the off-season, they did know about the Southwest Chat Company basketball team. The "Chat" team was sponsored by Harold Youngman. Mantle dearly wanted to play for the team, but the Yankees strictly forbade it. That team was populated by the likes of Jimmy Judd, Johnny LaFalier, Leonard Brown, and Ray, Roy and Max Mantle. Ah yes, there was another member of that squad who saw limited action — Billy Martin. On occasion, fellows like Billy Mosley took the court, as did Mantle himself one evening. LaFalier recalled that the urge was so great that Mantle suited up for a game at Fairland, Oklahoma and due to a lack of press coverage the Yankees never found out about it—until now.

LaFalier recalled that Youngman did everything in the world he could for Mantle, even building a Holiday Inn at Joplin that carried his name on the sign out in front of the facility until Mantle decided to move to Dallas. LaFalier recalled that Youngman looked after Mantle as much as his own father would have.

There were always rumors going on in Southwest Missouri about anything for which a "juicy" story could be started. Many of the locals in towns such as Webb City, Carthage and Neosho were under the impression that the Kansas City mob had fronted the money for the construction of Mickey Mantle's Holiday Inn. Whenever a large black Cadillac limousine was seen on the lot located at 2600 South Range Line in Joplin, the rumor would bubble up again that the mob was at Mantle's place. Of course, Youngman financed the entire affair and he was as far from being a mobster as Mantle was from being a ballet dancer. LaFalier does recall a tale Mantle related to him about his "brush" with the New York mob mid-way through his career. During the off-season, Mantle was on a transcontinental from the east to the west coast. On board the same plane were some mobsters who immediately recognized the Yankee great. According to LaFalier, "When they arrived in Los Angeles, the mobsters asked Mickey where he was going. Mickey told them he was going to the hotel. When Mickey told them that they said, 'c'mon and ride in our limo.'" Mantle confided in LaFalier that he was sure glad to get out of that limo when it reached its destination. In LaFalier's recollection, Mantle said, "I was scared to death someone would see me with those guys."

Mantle's first home in Commerce at 4th and Maple had basically been built by the lumber from Giles Johnson's lumberyard in Picher. Giles was Mickey's father-in-law. Due to his ties to his father-in-law's lumber business, that house was built for $15,000. When Giles passed away the Yankees were on a road trip to Detroit. Harold Youngman knew the telephone number of every place Mantle stayed. He gave it to LaFalier and he got hold of Mantle and told him of his father-in-law's passing. According to LaFalier, "Mickey said, 'I'll be there.'" That was even before he checked things out with Ralph Houk. When Mantle approached the Yankee manager, LaFalier said, "Houk told him to take as long as he wanted for we aren't doing anything this year."

Mickey Mantle loved his mother-in-law, Reba Johnson. In 2002, at the age of 90, Reba posed for this photo in nearly the exact spot where her daughter and Mickey were married on December 23, 1951.

LaFalier was again there when required in a time of need for the family. He called a friend of Merlyn's in Dallas to break the news of the death of her father. Then, LaFalier headed to the Tulsa Airport to pick up Mantle who was flying in from Detroit. From there LaFalier drove to Dallas, picked up Merlyn and the boys and brought them back to Picher for the funeral.

In touring the city of Commerce to obtain material for this book, LaFalier was the chief scout. He had known Mantle since he was 12 years old and LaFalier was nine. LaFalier pointed out three places where the Mantles lived. He also got to know Mantle even better when the two later married the Johnson sisters of Picher. Mickey married Merlyn and Johnny took Patricia as his lifetime companion.

During the day the author and Johnny LaFalier were together, he made all the rounds. Here he delivers the "meals on wheels" lunch to Reba Johnson's home. This is the same house where Merlyn Johnson and Mickey Mantle were wed.

The visit that day with Mrs. Johnson was quite interesting. Inside the front door was a large notebook containing glossy 8"x10" photos of the life of her daughter and son-in-law from the time of their marriage until the day Mickey Mantle retired from the New York Yankees. It was the most comprehensive pictorial collection of his career that this author ever witnessed.

Mrs. Johnson remarked, "Take that notebook and do what you would like with them." For the better part of an hour the photos were taken from their plastic sleeves and captured by a digital camera. The following is one of the early photos taken of Merlyn and Mickey.

PHOTO COURTESY OF REBA JOHNSON

This photo was taken of Mickey and Merlyn as she packed for their honeymoon trip to Hot Springs, Arkansas.

Mantle and LaFalier were very close during and after his baseball career concluded. Anytime LaFalier would be laid off at the B. F. Goodrich Tire manufacturing plant in Miami, Oklahoma, a call would come from Merlyn for him to bring Pat down to Dallas so they could baby-sit the boys, Mickey Jr., David, Billy and Danny while she went to New York to be with her husband for a few days. On other occasions, before the boys were born and when Merlyn was in New York with Mickey, he would call Johnny and say, "If you and Pat don't come up here Merlyn is coming home."

According to LaFalier, the relationship between Lovell and Mutt changed when it came to sporting events. They never sat together at ball games. Mutt was embarrassed at what she might say or do. After many of the games in which Mickey or the twins, Ray and Roy participated, Mickey would ask, "Who did you hit or fight with today, Mom?" During a football game at Afton, Oklahoma Lovell beat up Lawrence Barton with her purse when she determined he had tried to injure one of the twins. Jim Bole of Bartlesville, Oklahoma was on the wrong end of Lovell's purse one evening after a baseball game. Jim was twice the size of Lovell but she was not deterred. Although Bole and Mantle were on opposing teams, Mantle recognized Bole many years later and remarked, "You're the guy my mom whipped up on with her purse." Bole claims he didn't play "dirty" against Mantle. All he can recall was sliding hard into second base when Mantle was making the pivot to throw to first on a double play attempt.

Some of the things Lovell did as the mother of five boys, in standing up for them, may have had an impact on her thinking a few years later when her son had graduated to the New York Yankees. Merlyn recalled the 1952 World Series when Lovell came up to New York. Going into Ebbets Field was sheer terror for Lovell. She kept telling Merlyn that the Dodger fans were going to, in some way, get to Mickey and break his leg or inflict some other type of harm on him so he couldn't play. Merlyn kept telling Lovell to pay no attention to the rowdy Dodger fans, and above all, not to say anything back to the hecklers. As Merlyn recalled, that October day in Ebbets Field they were seated in the box seats directly next to Humphrey Bogart and Lauren Bacall. It was difficult for Lovell to focus on the game with "Bogey and Bacall" seated nearby. The only time she had ever seen real movie stars was at the Coleman Theater in Miami, Oklahoma.

On the flights to and from New York, the Mantles and Johnsons were served liquor in the small bottles. Lovell informed her son that he didn't need that stuff and that she wanted the little bottle for her collection.

The Fame of the Whiz Kids

It is difficult to find anyone, 65 years and older, who lived in the Northeast quadrant of Oklahoma who doesn't have their own memory of Mickey Mantle. That also holds true for Southeast Kansas residents in the area of Baxter Springs and Galena.

In researching this book, at stops like Jack Dinger's radiator shop or McDonald's in Baxter Springs, it was not long before someone would come up and tell about playing high school basketball against Mantle or the daughter of the local undertaker in Commerce who was grabbing a hamburger and fries telling about her daddy who had transported a very ill Mutt Mantle to a Denver, Colorado hospital in 1952 for cancer treatment and then going back a short time later to pick up his lifeless body.

The presence of the heroes of Southeast Kansas and Northeast Oklahoma is never forgotten. If you care to eat steak in Miami, Oklahoma, you have to walk past the images of Heisman Trophy winner Steve Owens, a Miami native, and Mickey Mantle, from nearby Commerce, as you stroll through Montana Mike's Steakhouse.

Even when it appears your day is finished it probably isn't. Checking into the Super 8 Motel in Miami, a very nice lady handed me the registration slip to sign. Jokingly, I remarked that she should keep the autograph for someday I would be famous. She inquired as to how that might happen and wouldn't take no for an answer when I told her that it was just a flippant remark.

As it turned out, the receptionist was Mary Ann Crawford-Culver who had a brother, Lowell, who played with the Whiz Kids prior to Mickey's days with the team. Nonetheless, Lowell Crawford was a friend of Mantle's and even helped him with his golf tournaments some twenty years later

Crawford, like so many of the men who worked the mines, died of lung disease. Around the time he was playing with the Baxter Springs Whiz Kids, he also worked for the Price Department Store in Miami. Crawford's primary duties were to sweep the floors after school for spending money. One evening he was about his normal tasks when a holdup man entered the store and demanded money. When the bandit left with the loot, Crawford ran for the gun that was in the back of the store. He had a good aim and shot the man as he was fleeing. The bandit managed to get to his car and drove a short distance before crashing into a tree. He died before reaching Miami Baptist Hospital. Crawford was arrested and charged with manslaughter. Mary Ann recalled the telephone call that came to the house shortly afterwards. The police informed Mrs. Crawford that there had been a robbery and that her son had killed the robber in his attempt to flee. The charges were eventually dropped prior to a trial, but it was a difficult time for the Crawford family.

Crawford told his sister the story of Mantle visiting in Baxter Springs after the 1956 season. He was driving and in the front seat with him was a foreman for the Eagle-Picher Mining Company. The miner's son was in the back seat with Crawford. From there the young boy could see this rather large belt beneath Mantle's seat, and there was a name on it. The kid asked Mantle what it was and he replied, "Oh that is something they gave me this year." Of course, it was the Hickok belt, signifying the most outstanding athlete in America.

This belt was not something that anyone would expect to see stuffed under the front seat of a 1955 Oldsmobile. The young mining foreman's son obviously saw it as a special item. This is the description of the belt: "The S. Rae Hickok Professional Athlete of the Year Award, this trophy was established in 1950 by the Hickok Manufacturing Company of Rochester, N.Y., in memory of the company's founder. The trophy, an alligator-skin belt with a huge buckle of solid gold, an encrusted 4-carat diamond, and 26 gem chips, was valued at $10,000 to $15,000. It took 250 man-hours to produce it at the Hickok plant, which manufactured upscale belts, wallets, and other men's accessories. For the first 21 years, the Hickok Belt was presented at the annual children's charity dinner given by the Rochester Press-Radio Club."[347]

Crawford was another of the Whiz Kids who was good enough to be inked to a professional ball club and was signed by the Cincinnati Reds at a Bentonville, Arkansas, tryout camp in 1949. He was slated for a Class B assignment. When he called his mother with the good news, she cried and told him that he would be a long way from home. So, the obedient son returned home to Baxter Springs, according to his sister Mary Ann Crawford-Culver.

---

[347] www.hickoksports.com/history/hickbelt.

Appendix 3

Some 1950 Joplin Miners Reminisce

Appendix 3 is significant in that 1950 was the year that the baseball experts for the first time recognized that Mickey Mantle was a special ball player.

From September of 1950 until July 24, 1999, there had never been a gathering of Joplin Miners of more than two to three fellows. But on that day in July 1999, Bob Wiesler, Tommy Gott, Lilburn Smith, Cal Neeman, Cromer Smotherman, Steve Kraly and Al Billingsly shared their memories of a special time in their lives. Alvin Long, who had played with most of these fellows at Independence in 1949 and had been on the Joplin spring training roster, also joined in with his memories of Mickey Mantle.

A couple of days later Tom Hesketh joined the parade and his recollection of that year added a humorous touch to most of the stories the nine Miners recounted on July 24, 1999, and from there the stories of all surviving members of the 1950 Joplin Miners were located and each had a story to tell.

This writer was fortunate enough to have sat through the entire "hap-

Five former teammates who played with Mantle gathered in Columbia, Missouri, to tell their stories. From left to right: Lilburn Smith, Bob Wiesler, Al Long, Tom Gott and Cal Neeman.

pening" and to see the expressions on the guys' faces and to listen to the chuckles as stories were rehashed and you knew that it was a special time that they were savoring, almost as much as the choice rib-eye steaks with which they were feted following the afternoon-long interview.

Cromer Smotherman, Steve Kraly and Al Billingsly shared their recollections of that Joplin Miner club from their homes in Lawrenceburg, Tennessee; Johnson City, New York; and Venice, Florida respectively. Through the great facilities of KFRU radio station in Columbia, Missouri the interview was done in the studios with a three-way conference call with those who couldn't make the trip back to the "Show Me State."

This chapter hopefully gives an insight into the type of young man Mickey Mantle was as a second year farmhand of the New York Yankees.

Tommy Gott's reason for sharing his thoughts were to dispel the idea that Mickey Mantle was only a drunken bum. That seems to be the message that a lot of the media portrayed about Mickey subsequent to his death. The second message is that professional sports should better indoctrinate young kids in the things that they will face in their careers. That goes for all sports, and with those remarks, we are here for one reason — to talk about Mantle.

Kraly: What you are asking, if I understand it, was Mickey Mantle an alcoholic? I believe that is a bunch of hogwash in the first place. All of us who were with Mantle first at Independence and then at Joplin knew he wasn't that type of person. What Mickey was, was a good athlete who came from the small town of Commerce, Oklahoma, and then he went into the limelight at Joplin. He had changed from the previous season in Independence and became a tremendous ballplayer overnight. The Mantle I knew from lodging with him was an outstanding individual on the field and off.

I think once in a while he went into tantrums, and Cromer would know that. Cromer would hit line shots that they were catching and Mantle would hit line shots for outs and kick the cooler down. But that was his way of acting sometime. I think that as a ballplayer and as an individual I knew him, as well as anyone in this group even though some of you lived closer to him. He was a great ballplayer and great individual. And I knew even back then that all of us had a little taste of the beer and we couldn't handle it and neither could he *[Mickey]*.

Years later I had him here in Johnson City, New York, as a guest speaker when I was with IBM. He did a tremendous job of delivering the message to the young people. I think when you mention the name of Mickey Mantle to the youngsters they look up to him and I don't think they realize the bad press he received. I think the only reason he got that bad press was attributable to the people who had him to come to be a guest speaker.

I gave a group at St. Bonaventure, who sponsored a dinner, his name. He came and I cornered him after picking him up at LaGuardia Airport. My goodness he was stoned but then I talked to him and told him to remember to drink a lot of coffee for there were a lot of youngsters at a family oriented type of dinner. He did what I told him and I kept him with me after the dinner. In fact, I brought him back to my house and the kids admired him.

What we must do in this book is to relate what he was like as a youngster starting out in professional baseball like the rest of us. We came from different parts of the country and we went into a vast new world. Inevitably, as we progressed upwards in the classifications of baseball, things were changing and we were getting into more or less of a higher class of people who were fast as compared to those people we met while playing in Independence or Joplin. My take is that Mickey Mantle was admired by his teammates for his tremendous ability as a ballplayer and also as an individual.

That goes back to his father, who always came to all the Miner home games and would keep Mickey in line. I don't believe all that the sports writers wrote about Mickey was true. It is up to us to make sure the the press realizes this and that they rewrite the good things about Mickey Mantle and it was what he got in the minor leagues that made him successful in later years.

Laid-back Cromer Smotherman from Tennessee was just what the doctor ordered. Anything "Dr." Harry Craft would prescribe, Cromer was to do provide in the watching over of young Mickey Mantle. Smotherman had a college education and was a linebacker for Middle Tennessee State in his collegiate days. According to Tommy Gott, "This guy had muscles before weight-lifting was in vogue."

Smotherman: I, like Steve, kept in touch with Mickey over the years and at different times was able to go watch Mickey play. Mickey told a story one time in Nashville, Tennessee that he blamed me from his being moved from shortstop to the outfield for his first baseman didn't have long enough arms.

Of course, I don't know how many of you are there when Tom called me I was very excited. As I began to reflect on that period of time I remember what a great youngster Mickey Charles Mantle was and also how he was supported by a very strong family. I know all of you recall that Mr. and Mrs. Mantle never missed a home game. And the team felt very close to the Mantle family.

Each of us had experiences not only with Mickey but with each other and after all these many years I still think of that period of time and each of you as individuals for your strength and character. The 1950 team along with Harry Craft and those of you who played in 1949 with Mantle were special clubs.

I think the 1950 team who won the league by 13½ was special. Then I remember blowing the game for Bob Wiesler when I made an error and it cost him the game 1-0 in the playoffs and I want to apologize for that at this time, Bob. I never shall forget how helpful you were to me personally by excusing it and that showed what kind of person you were. All the people on the team were like that. I would like to see the book contain a profile of the different players and where they went, how they did in their career after leaving Joplin. It would show that baseball is an honorable type profession. I know many of you went on into various careers.

Now, back to Mantle. Harry Craft, as some of you may know, asked me if I would kindly help to keep Mickey pepped up and boosted. There were many occasions when maybe Mantle would have three or four hits in a game and would come back to the dugout and sit by me. He would grip his fist and be very emotional. Here I was probably batting 50 points less than he was and I was pulling out chewing gum and giving him a piece to pep him up.

When we would go out on the infield to take warms—I still have bruises on my shins—where Mickey would be throwing me knuckle balls and curve balls from his position at short.

I remember Mickey as a fun loving kid with tremendous skills and ability. I also remember him as a shy youngster especially around persons he didn't know and was not a street-smart youngster. I don't know that any of us were all that street-smart back in those days. But certainly Mickey was not a street-smart person. Unfortunately, when he went on to higher leagues then the stories were not only that was he a super athlete but he began to make headlines, which surprised all of us.

Billingsly: I got to know Mickey pretty close, for we roomed together on the road. Craft always put the shortstop and second baseman together. I played 70-80% of the time. Mickey was a straight shooter and never bad-mouthed anybody. He was strictly baseball. He lived breathed and talked baseball.

He was dating Merlyn Johnson at the time and otherwise wasn't interested in girls. As far as drinking, I don't recall him even drinking a beer for we never had any in the room. I wouldn't have allowed it anyway. I don't recall his drinking in those days.

His father was at all the games and ruled Mickey's emotions or cooled them down. I could relate a lot of experiences. But he was something special — we all knew that he was destined to be an outstanding athlete and baseball player.

I recall that he struck out in Salina one night and threw his back against the dugout and almost hit someone. Craft jumped him and asked him what he did that for and Mickey said, "I am going to hit three of them out of the park tonight." And he did it.

He was very emotional playing baseball and was very protective of me at second. When someone slides into me rough he would go after him. He would protect his fellow players. Even though Cromer had those short arms Mantle was quick and he could get to balls that most guys couldn't. He got charged for a lot of errors that shouldn't have been called.

Three years after he had been in the majors, he had an operation on his knees in Springfield. I went over to see him and the hospital wouldn't let me see him. They called Mickey's room and told him I was downstairs and Mantle said, "Send him up, I want to talk to him."

When I got up there I asked him what he was doing and he said he missed all the guys we had a great time at Joplin. He always remembered the Joplin Miners.

Tom Greenwade made some trips to the campus of the University of Kansas and found a boy who played quarterback for the Jayhawks in 1948-1949. Dick Gilman got off to a slow start in spring training and never fully recovered from a sore arm. The arm trouble first manifested itself at the spring training camp of the Kansas City Blues at Lake Wales, Florida, a month previous. He broke camp with the Miners and knew his role. With starters of the caliber of Wiesler, Kraly and Simanovsky along with the best relief pitcher probably in all of minor league baseball in Joe Crowder, Gilman had to come up with something to contribute to the team effort.

He was a great bench jockey and when the opposing pitcher would get shelled and removed from the game he would hum that famous funeral dirge, "The Funeral March of the Marionettes." Since he didn't pitch much he didn't have to worry about retribution. However, judgment day came. He was knocked out of the box by the Hutchinson club. The Hutchinson bench rose to the occasion by humming the same tune that Gilman had used so many times.

Gott: You sent a note stating that you recall Mickey having a bad knee at Joplin. I remember that too. In one of the books about him I remember that it talked about him hurting that knee for the first time in a World Series game.

Smotherman: I distinctly remember that, Tom; in fact he alluded to it on a number of occasions. He may have re-injured it in a World Series game but I know that he definitely had leg injury when he was with us.

Long: It was osteomyelitis

Wiesler: Cromer, I remember Mantle coming into the dugout and you telling him, "Gee, Mick, I have a wife and kid and you are going to kill me over there with those throws from your shortstop position." And I thought he was going to do it.

Smotherman: He had the throwing arm to do it, too.

Mickey was always experimenting with his throws from his shortstop position to first base. He would throw the knuckleball, curve or whatever came to mind. He just never threw it like a regular shortstop or infielder would was the consensus of the group.

Gott: Let's talk about Mantle's personality and some facts about his Joplin career.

Kraly: I remember a ball that he hit off the rightfield fence at Enid, Oklahoma and broke his bat when he hit the ball. Also, what I remember was his power to hit them over the lights in Joplin. I never had seen a youngster of his stature able to do things like that. Not only could he hit, he could run. Even with the bad leg! Not many people realized how fast he was. I saw him even bunt on 3-2 counts and beat them out.

Smotherman: I recall he was the greatest at laying down a pull bunt. He could outrun the "durn" ball after he laid it down and he would be at first base before the infielder could get to the ball.

Gott: If I'm not mistaken, he still holds the record from the left side of the plate to first base. I think it is something like 3.1 seconds. That's quite a feat.

Smith: I want to tell you about the spring training game we played against the St. Paul Saints. You remember he hit one out both left-handed and right-handed that day. That is a feat I will never forget.

Cromer: *[Chuckles, as though he was reliving the moment with Mickey.]*

Kraly: Cromer couldn't reach half of Mantle's throws. If you remember our business manager *[Roy Beavers]* wouldn't even sell the box seats behind first base because that was how strong Mantle's arm was. The other thing I remember was when David "Muddy" Waters was playing second we would yell at Mickey when there was a pop up at shortstop to get out of the way because he couldn't catch a pop up. *[A chorus of "that's right" echoed from those assembled in the radio studio and over the telephone.]*

Gott: Craft *[Harry]* said to chase him off anything I could get to. The next year I was in the service and Mickey was in spring training with the Yankees. In the *Stars and Stripes* magazine—I wish I had kept it—it was reported he was hit in the head with a fly ball.

Wiesler: I was pitching that day. It was in Phoenix.

Gott: That fall he was in centerfield for the Yankees.

Wiesler: No, he was in rightfield.

Gott: Anyway, that fall he could catch the ball and that showed what an excellent athlete he was. He learned to catch quickly. In spring training he became an excellent outfielder.

Neeman: *[Head down and sheepishly grinning]* I knew I sooner or later would have to say something. Steve Kraly, "Hello."

Kraly: Hello, Cal. I was lucky to have played with you for two years. You're my favorite catcher.

Neeman: Cromer and Al Billingsly, it is a pleasure to hear from you guys.

Smotherman: You were a great guy, Cal.

Neeman: We had a little birthday party at the house last night and I was telling them about the Lord and Al Billingsly and his seeing eye bat.

Billingsly: Yes sir, Mickey told me to ask the Lord. I can hear him today, he would say, "Don't you know that this is the Lord batting. Billingsly hits them where they 'ain't.'" I was the old Ty Cobb.

Neeman: Billingsly, you hit a homer one time that got stuck underneath the fence.

Billingsly: Yep, at Springfield.

Neeman: Playing on that team probably, well it is, the highlight of my baseball career. Especially, looking back and seeing some of the things that happened. I read Mantle's book and someone told me I was in it and so was Billingsly. He talked about Al's car, etc. and the convertible.

Reading that book of his, I really think some of the best times of Mickey's life was in those early days when he played in the minor leagues with all of us, his life in general and the fun he had at spring training in Branson, catching the fish and all that kind of stuff.

The drinking part — we would get a six pack and a few beers but I don't ever remember that anyone drank excessively. It was not a part of our lives. Most of our time, that I remember, was spent on the diamond. I don't really remember a whole lot of things that happened off the field.

Mantle, I couldn't believe reading about him after I went into the Army. It was spring training and he was hitting around .470 and so was David "Muddy" Waters.

I remember Mickey and I playing that pinball machine at the Keystone Hotel and putting our feet underneath so we could win a few games — you know, to make it a little leveler and easier to play. Also, we wouldn't have to keep putting nickels in it. Then, crying out loud, he is off playing in the World Series. But Steve's story about the broken bat is different from mine.

I think Mickey made three errors in the first inning of a game at Hutchinson, Kansas. He then led off the next inning. He picked up a bat, which was broken, and "roped" the first pitch out of the park.

I remember some of you guys going out with a pitcher in St. Joseph. I don't remember his name, but he was supposed to be pretty good. He wondered how to pitch to Mantle and one of you guys told him the best thing to do was to change up. You know that didn't work.

Mickey hit one over the lights in Joplin one night. It was 420 to dead center at Miner's Park. I was there in 1949 and no one hit it over that wall. It was kinda uphill and the ball didn't carry that well. In one particular game he hit one over the centerfield wall right-handed and later in the same game he hit one over left-handed. One thing we all knew was that he was better than the rest of us.

Of course, Cromer sometimes wouldn't throw ground balls to Mickey because he would go out there and pout and wouldn't pick up the infield grounders when they were thrown at him.

Anyway, Cromer, you were a steadying influence. You were an old man of 24.

There are a lot of memories. I didn't think I had any memories but I am beginning to see part of them, anyway.

Smotherman: I remember what a steadying influence, or I guess the best way I can say it is that it was always a thrill for a person like myself to have been associated with a group of guys like all of you. Cal, as I recall, was a great big old boy, tall and a built like a catcher.

Wiesler: He is still built like a catcher — he's thin.

Wiesler: Guys, remember how we used to sweat?

Smotherman: I used to be the same way. I know how Harry Craft used to try to talk me into drinking beer to replace a lot of the fluid I lost during a game. But I always liked a chocolate milkshake better. I just didn't like the taste of beer.

I also understand Lyle Westrum is now passed away. What a nice guy he was and his brother, as we recall, was a major leaguer.

Gott: I am going to throw one in here. I'm innocent, so I can throw this out. I think it was Kraly, I don't know, but one of you guys wrote a letter to one of the gals who stood out beside that gate down there at Joplin.

The gal was the one everybody avoided and whoever wrote the letter signed Mick's name to it and told her how much he loved her and all this 'n that. When we came off the road—remember they use to put our mail in the locker room? Mantle gets her return letter and— my goodness sake. Kraly, was that you who wrote that?

Kraly: Why do I get blamed for everything, how come? *[All attendees roar, seeming to indicate they think Kraly penned the love letter.]*

Gott: At any rate, he was such an athletic specimen. I remember this very clearly. Everybody is waiting to see what he would do because his folks and girlfriend *[Merlyn Johnson]* were out there waiting in the car. Here's this gal out there waiting for him also. We are all peeking through the fence telling him that she's all dressed up and giving him the business.

All the time Mickey is standing there not knowing what to do. Then he made his decision and just as quick as a wink he ran to the left field fence. He takes one bound, puts his hand on top of the fence and is over it and gone. He didn't realize that was some athletic feat that hardly any of us could possibly do. Probably no one else could have done it. He didn't even know he had done something special. Does anyone remember that?

Kraly: Oh, yeah.

Neeman: Seems to me I remember something about that letter.

Kraly: I remember, you are the one who wrote it.

Neeman: No, I didn't write it.*[At this point Lilburn Smith, Steve Kraly and Cal Neeman all expressed their innocence in this caper and Bob Wiesler claimed to have never heard about the story until the present time.]*

Gott: You guys remember Slick, who shined shoes at the Keystone Hotel? *[Silence.]* You guys might remember the story — It indicated the kind of person Mantle was. Don't you guys remember Slick? He shined shoes at the hotel, the black man.

Smotherman: I do.

Gott: Remember in 1953 when Joe Crowder drowned? Somebody put together a benefit game at Joplin. All the Boyers were there, Mike Ryba and Mantle came.

Most of the guys were standing out by the clubhouse and I'm out there with Slick. Mantle walked in the door by the clubhouse and Greenwade and the other scouts were all there—a lot of people.

The one guy Mickey went to immediately was Slick. "Hey Slick," he said, "how are you?" Now that meant everything to that man because Mantle was a superstar by then and the guy lit up. Mantle shook his hand and it showed how down-to-earth and unpretentious Mickey was. I thought he was a heckuva person.

Smith: All my experiences with Mantle were really great. He got six hits in the first game of the season at Springfield and I got four. *[Uproar from group. "You never did such a thing" was the general theme of the razzing. Ed. Note: Lilburn was in error on one count. Mantle only got five hits but Lilburn did get his four hits.]*

I bragged about that later and Bob Speake declared it must have been against a girls' team. I could always hit, you know.

Kraly: Are you trying to convince us you were a good hitter?

Smith: Well, I got four hits, do you remember that game?

Kraly: I remember that game, but the rest of the year you hardly got one.

Smith: I was only there the first two months and then got sent to Greenville, Mississippi, of the Cotton States League. I missed a lot of those good times.

That season opener in 1950 I remember. David Waters hit a line drive that struck the telephone pole in centerfield.

Gott: Mantle swung the toughest pillow in St. Joseph. We used to have those pillow fights. Man, when he hit you, you thought your head was coming off.

Wiesler: Water fights. Remember the water gun fights on the bus? We had water pistols and the guys in the front of the bus took on the guys in the rear. One day one end ran out of water and they attacked to take the water pistols.

Gott: And you *[Wiesler]* cut your index finger on your left hand and that was the end of it because you couldn't pitch for a day or two. And at that point Craft said, "That's all," and the water pistol fighting ended.

Wiesler: He stood for a lot of stuff we did, but we were winning.

Billingsly: Remember that drunk who was giving us the tough time over in Hutchinson? We positioned that guy underneath our room. Now Mantle didn't participate in that but I had some other guys help. I think that Cromer was one of them. We dumped water right on that guy and he called the police to come over. *[Everyone was silent at this point.]* Don't you guys remember that?

Gott: I think he's talking about those Shriners? *[In unison the group says, "I remember."]* And everyone waited for Mantle's word when to drop the water for they knew his timing would be perfect, and it was.

Kraly: And the Shriners thought it was raining.

Neeman: One of the big things about Mickey was that he could hit harder, throw better and run faster than anyone on the field and I think that was true no matter where he ever played. I don't think he really realized how good he was. I don't think we knew how good he really was when he was at Joplin.
Don't you remember that they used to run races and who won every race? *[United voices said, "Well, he won."]*

Neeman: If they did anything else, who would win it? You think about it. If an ordinary person would have had his talent they may have been hard to live with. Mickey never was.

Smotherman: No, Cal, he was a kid who had this nice little grin and he just kinda loved fun and most of that fun took place on the ball diamond. I remember one time he tried to steal third base and he was out. The umpire called him safe. The third baseman yelled to the umpire "Look, his foot is not on the bag." They only had one base umpire, he couldn't see that. Mickey never moved his foot. He just slowly got up, dusted off his pants and stepped on the base. The ordinary guy would have jerked his foot and put it on the bag and the umpire would have seen that he was off the base. But Mickey was smart enough not to do that.

Neeman: I remember the 1950 Yankee camp in Arizona. Me, Kraly, Mantle and Wiesler missed the bus to the ballpark. This taxi came along, stopped and the guys said, "Get in." He asked each of us our names but I didn't give him mine. When he came to Mickey and Mickey told him his name Casey Stengel said, "Oh, you're the kid who hits right-handed and homers over the right field wall, you hit left-handed homer over the left-field wall and when you race you win them all. Don't you know people who run like that can't hit with power?"

Neeman: I knew Mantle was different from the start. The ball sounded different coming off his bat. He was always looking for a catcher to warm him up. He wanted to throw a knuckleball. Mickey had a "circle kind," no one knew where it was going. Every time he started looking for a catcher I tried to hide from him.

Neeman: Mickey used to do the same thing to you didn't he, Cromer?

Smotherman: He never in infield practice ever just threw the ball normally. He was always trying something out *[knuckleballs, curves, sliders, etc.]*.

Neeman: It took me two years to get out of Joplin. After Mickey got out of high school he came to Joplin [1949] to try out. He took batting practice right-handed and they told him to turn around and hit left-handed. I protested it was my turn. I insisted that Mantle wait until all the other guys had hit. I kept insisting that you don't get double swings just because you want to hit left-handed. That's pretty good to have run that kid out of the batting cage isn't it? *[Laughs and chuckles from the group.]*

Kraly: In 1949 when Mickey came to us at Independence, all he did was bunt. We kept saying in the dugout, "Does this kid ever swing the bat?" He only weighed 160. I was awed the following year when we came to Branson. I looked at him and all of a sudden he weighed 190. It was like night and day. He became a man overnight.

The thing I liked about our Joplin team was wherever we went they called us the Junior Bronx Bombers. It was because of the sluggers we had with Mantle, Cromer, "Muddy" Waters and the rest of the guys. That team would go down in history because we won the pennant and had the whole month of August left to play.

Wiesler: Yeah, we lost in the first round of the playoffs.

Kraly: Yes, I know that.

Wiesler: Remember that?

Smotherman: I was responsible for that.

Wiesler: No, you weren't.

Billingsly: Who was?

Wiesler: I looked at records last night and I see where Cromer led the league in pitching.

Smotherman: Huh! Huh! You're right.

Wiesler: You were 1-0. I looked at that and couldn't believe it. 1-0 and he led the league.

Smotherman: I don't know who all was pitching but each of used pitched three innings, as I recall.

Neeman: I think Billingsly pitched.

Billingsly: I pitched three innings and I pitched shutout ball for three innings.

Gott: I know you kissed home plate. *[Smotherman heard laughing heartily in the background.]*

Billingsly: Yeah, I have done that too. You know about Mantle, I was around him all the time and I never heard him bad-mouth any of his fellow players.

Smotherman: I didn't either.

Billingsly: When someone made an error or did something wrong, or they lost a game or walked 3 or 4 guys in a row like somebody I knew that is in this group *[Wiesler].* He was a little wild, "Mr. Bob." Mantle never bad-mouthed anybody — do any of you recall?

Long: If you recall, if Mickey was never thrown at or if he was hit by a pitch he never charged the mound. He just saw that as a part of the game.

Gott: A while ago Cal was talking about Mickey pouting when "Smut" *[Smotherman]* wouldn't throw him ground balls during infield practice. But I never remember him getting mad at anyone but himself.

Billingsly and Gott *[in unison]*: That's right.

Gott: His expectations of what he should do for the ball club were so high that if we needed a run or base hit and he didn't produce it he was hard on himself. I never heard him criticize another player or saw him look down his nose at another ballplayers. He would only criticize himself and boy would he get upset with himself.

Long: And that was also true with the opposition too, wasn't it, Tom?

Wiesler: I want to tell you a story. I happened to be up there with the Yankees in 1951 for a short while. The letters Mickey was getting from people—mothers—about how can you run so fast and you are not in the service. My son is in the service.

You ought to have seen the hate mail he used to get from people. But he had that disease and people wouldn't believe he was 4-F. But the hate mail he got was terrible.

Smotherman: Is that right?

Gott: That's a new one on me but that's a shame. That hate spilled over into the grandstands; American League cities also.

Hall: I was going through some Joplin box scores recently and saw where Mickey was tossed out of a game. Do any of you guys remember the incident?

Smotherman: No, I don't.

Gott: But it was in the paper that he got run?

Hall: Yes. However, he was never chased from a KOM League game.

Gott: That surprises me, that he got tossed out of a Joplin game.

Hall: That was the only time he was chased in 1950.

Neeman: Well, no one could hardly get thrown out of a game.

Smotherman: I got thrown out one time.

Neeman: You did?

Smotherman: Yes, I was sitting in the back of the dugout and I was hollering "homer" at the plate umpire. *[Chuckles erupt from the group.]*

Gott: No wonder you got chased.

Smotherman: I knew I was getting under the skin of the umpire badly, for he kept looking over there at me. The next time I went to bat he made this big grandstand move and threw me out. It was the only time I was ever thrown out of a game.

Billingsly: We couldn't afford to be thrown out. It cost us too much money. It was a couple of months' salary, practically.

Hall: What was the average fine?

Billingsly: No, it wasn't that much. I don't know, maybe $20 to $25.

Gott: This is not about Mantle. This is about Smut [Cromer] Smotherman. Do you remember, Smut? I think it was Hutchinson that the manager had a knockdown pitch? We'd go over there and they would throw at us all the time. Wasn't that Hutchinson? I think it was.

Hall: Was the manager Wes Griffin?

Gott: I can't remember, he was an older fellow.

Hall: Yeah! that's who it was.

Gott: At any rate, we had a return series with them in Joplin and Smut was hitting the ball well. I guess he had his number dirty most every night *[from being knocked down]*. So, we come back to Joplin, never said a word and Hutchinson had a big redheaded right-handed pitcher. It seems like it was early in the game and this guy knocks you down again, Smut. You got up, grabbed the bat at about the trademark with that left paw of yours. You walked halfway to the mound and you said, "You can knock me down in your ballpark but you're not coming in my ballpark and doing that. And, if you throw at me again I'll come out there and straighten you out." Do you remember that, Smut?

Smotherman: Yeah! I remember getting real upset at him.

Gott: He didn't throw at you anymore.

Smotherman: I remember getting hit by him right in the back of the neck. That was before batting helmets. You know that could be a pretty dangerous league at that time.

Smith: You guys remember the time Harry Craft's partner up in Iowa was killed in a car accident and we were on our way to Muskogee, Oklahoma and he left me in charge of the ball club?

[Chuckles from many in the group who did remember and obviously knew some things they weren't telling. It seems that Lilburn was not as strict on the guys as Harry had been.]

Smith *(now pleading for affirmation)*: Don't any of you guys remember that?

Billingsly: I do.

Smith: You do? Wiesler does too. So does Tommy.

Gott: *[now chuckling]* Our new manager.

Smith: I was the new manager. Anyway, Tom Greenwade heard about that and got down to Muskogee real quick.

[A lot more chuckles. I knew at this point I wasn't going to hear all the story unless I pressed the issue.]

Billingsly: Yea! that was one of the major mistakes Harry Craft made, putting you in charge.

Hall: Can you elaborate on the subject a little bit, Steve Kraly?

Kraly: I think that was the time we were stranded in Muskogee when it rained five days.

Smith: That's right. It rained us out.

Kraly: Rained every game out.

Wiesler: Didn't play a game.

Kraly: So, Lilburn had a perfect record, no wins and no losses.
[More chuckles.]

Kraly: The Lord was with him.

Gott: What was the business manager's name at Joplin?

Neeman: Roy Beavers.
[The rest of the group, in mock derision, said, "Roy Beavers."]

Gott: Everybody was mad at him because we never had any balls with to take batting practice. Everybody hit them out of the park was why. Remember when we couldn't take hitting practice because the field was too wet?

We would stand down there in front of the clubhouse and try to hit them over the fence and get rid of them. And every time the guy would hit one it would go over the fence, almost—it was Mantle.

We had a lot of strong guys on that ball club. But nobody hit them out of there like he would. He would pitch them up and hit them over the fence like it was nothing. Smut would hit them over sometimes but Mantle would hit it over every time he would swing at one, almost.

Kraly: If you remember, Beavers was as tough as nails. We would shag balls in the outfield and there were kids on the other side of the fence. One kid never got a ball. I threw one over the fence to him and when I got my paycheck Beavers deducted the price of that ball from my paycheck.
[Laughter.]

Kraly: Remember, he charged for the ice water also. He was tough.

Smith: Roy Beavers was tight.

Long: We were making about enough money to send home for money. And as conceited as I must have been, I thought I made more money than Mantle in 1949. I didn't know until fairly recently, when John Hall put it in his newsletter after getting a copy of Mantle's contract, that I found out he was making $10 a month more than I was.

When I used to see Mick in Kansas City, when the Yanks came to play the A's, you could always kid with him. He was always laughing and cutting up. I kidded him the first time he got to $100,000. I said, "One time I made more money than you did, Mick." He just went 'hush! hush!' But the kind of guy he was, he didn't bother to correct me. He just let me go on believing it.

Another time he was going in with a developer in Kansas City. The developer was going to use Mickey's and Whitey Ford's names to promote the project. I went to the promotional kickoff and Mickey brought along a couple of boxes of baseball. He and Whitey signed them and handed them out. Mickey turned around and said, "Hey, Al, would you like to have one of these balls?" I told him I would love to have one. And, of course, I still treasure that ball today.

Smotherman: Absolutely.

Gott: When my two sons were small we took a trip to Washington, D.C. I don't remember which year it was, probably '56 or '57. So, we went to New York to see a ball game and took my boys down to the locker room after the game. I always thought Mickey was handsome. To me he was the Tom Sawyer or Huckleberry Finn of baseball. Today I think of him as the Michael Jordan of baseball. But, even with his good looks he had such a low self-image that he didn't realize his body was sculpted like a Greek god. He was good-looking.

Smotherman: You're right.

Gott: When I got in the clubhouse, Mickey says, "Hey, Tom, how are you doing?" I said, "There's the Mick, as ugly as ever." And I mean, I crushed him when I said that. I thought it was a ridiculous statement. I thought he knew he was good-looking. He didn't know it, he didn't realize it, that is the way he was.

Kraly: I think that relates to what everybody said earlier. While we remember him as a shy Oklahoma boy that came out of Commerce, I know that when I joined the Yankees he didn't like to be in the public limelight. He hated to go and make speeches. That all goes back to how we knew him when he was with us in Joplin. He was shy but he also loved to play the game. He played with great skills and determination. He got angry when somebody would catch a long drive off him.

Cromer, on the other hand would hit line shots and not get any hits and he would go back and sit on the bench. Mantle, on the other hand would come back to the dugout and kick the water cooler. He would always sit next to Cromer. Cromer was like his father, really, on the team. We always wondered if these two guys "liked" each other because they were always sitting together. The rest of us moved away from those two guys, for we knew what Mickey was going to do when he came to the dugout.

But that's the way his lifestyle was. I think the way the New York press wrote him up as being a drinker and all of that is so false. Because in his playing days, even with the Yankees, drinking was taboo.

What hurt Mantle was when he got mixed up with Whitey Ford and Billy Martin. With those two guys he was in the middle. The New York press would write stories that the guys were a bunch of boozers. But I think that was all out of proportion and what hurt him after he retired.

Smith: That's when he really started drinking, wasn't it?

Kraly: That's when everything hit the bottom floor because he got with the wrong people, the wrong agent to handle him and everything else.

I talked with Merlyn for a long time, even when I came up with the Yankees and had that stint with them from 1953-57. He wasn't the way he was portrayed by the press. He would go home after the game. Sometimes you would read tabloids where he was connected with the call girls. That, too, was blown out of proportion. I was very upset when I read all that stuff and I think the guy who admired Mickey, Bob Costas, was upset too.

Long: Steve, you and I talked over KFRU radio back when John Hall arranged for us to talk on the radio in Columbia, Missouri, after Mickey's death.

Kraly: Yes, Al, you were our great piano player at Independence.

Long: Boogie woogie. It may not be macho but I am not ashamed to admit that I cried for several days after Mick's death. [*His voice cracked at this point and new tears were in his eyes.*]

Smotherman: Al, I think all of us cried.

Kraly: I've got the picture in front of me of all you guys. It's sad to see as time went on—as I look at this—but we were once one family. We had togetherness, we did a lot of prankster things and all that. Truthfully, I don't remember any of us, except my roomie, Bob Wiesler, the old German taking a drink. You know the Germans always loved beer. I think Bob is the one who got us started on trying beer. I don't think if I ever had more than one beer that I could have seen home plate.

Wiesler: Talk about a story. Excuse me, Steve. I got that beer taste from way back when I was a kid. I used to go to the store or a tavern and pick up beer. We had a beer pitcher for my father when he would come home from work. So, I would go and get that filled for a quarter. It was a big jug. In the early days I used to take a sip once in a while.

I'd come home and put it in the icebox, not a refrigerator. You know the icebox where we kept the 100 pounds of ice.

[Group in unison says, "Sure."]

Billingsly: We are old enough to remember that.

Wiesler: He would say, "The Polacks really cheat me, they used to put a big head on this beer."

[The group roars in laughter.]

Kraly: If you guys remember, one particular night, I don't know whose car we had, but we went out to that place…

Wiesler: That was Billingsly's car we had.

Billingsly: You always took my car, Steve.

Long: You were probably the only guys who had one.

Kraly: The place we went to was the hot-spot of Joplin. I guess it was the only one in town.

Billingsly: Oh, yeah.

Smith: Was it Hidden Acres?

Kraly: When we came back from that place Mantle wanted to drive. Mantle couldn't drive. [*Much laughter, obviously all had seen Mickey attempt to drive.*] He drove up on the sidewalk and Wiesler said, "I hope the cops don't come." We pulled up in front of the Keystone Hotel and parked the car. Billingsly, if that was your car I would have gotten rid of it after Mantle drove it.

Billingsly: I'll tell you a story about that car. We used to go on a road trip and be gone 10 days. That car sat right there at the Keystone. Remember? It sat right there in a no parking zone and the police didn't give it a ticket, they didn't tow it, they didn't do anything with it. It was an old '35 Ford and it was old. But, hell, everybody enjoyed it.
[*Laughs of the admiration variety filled the air as the old Ford was fondly remembered.*]

Neeman: Do you guys remember the restaurant, Fosters, was it? They used to give you a free meal if you hit a double. And that other one down the street from the Keystone gave you a meal for hitting a home run.

Billingsly: Oh, yeah.

Neeman: That was a pretty good deal. I don't suspect Mantle spent a helluva lot of money while in Joplin.

Long: Another point about Mick. Knowing he had this disease with his bones. To me it was pretty darn courageous for him to play. Did any of you guys ever see him fail to slide when it was required?

Smotherman: No.

Long: When it was required of him to slide, boy he would go in there "ripping and tearing" and whatever it took. I don't know that I would have had the guts to do it if I had been in his shape. In fact, I know I wouldn't.

Kraly: I think if young players today would look at what Mickey

Mantle did with the disease he knew he had and how he played with a bad leg, with endurance, and would never sit out a game, they would have to admire him. Players today get a hangnail and the want to go on the disabled list. Back in Mick's day you played even when you were hurt. He was a role model in that regard.

I tell my grandson that if you want to be like somebody, be like Mickey Mantle. I can tell you what he was when he was in Class D and Class C and later when he went to the Major Leagues. I tell them that what they are going to have to learn to do is to play hard, play with your heart, have determination, be a team man and if you get hurt, learn to play hurt. I think the young players of today don't do that.

Hall: Steve, didn't you name one of your sons after Mickey?

Kraly: Middle name.

Gott: I don't know if you guys remember this story or not but it just popped into my head. We were playing St. Joseph and it seems like we came south through Kansas City and ate in a restaurant on the south part of town. They had individual pies, as I recall. At any rate, we had finished the three-game series at St. Joseph and we were hungry and nearly broke.

The next day was payday and all you guys seemed to have enough money for a hamburger, but I didn't and Mickey didn't. We had blown all of our money. We had some pennies and a couple of nickels. So, we went around to all you guys mooching pennies and nickels or whatever we could get off of you. None of you were flush enough to loan us any so we went back to the table and sat down. I don't know what we had, maybe 50 cents combined. So, the waitress came over and Mantle said, "Give me a burger with fries and a chocolate shake." *[Much laughter goes up from the group; they were beginning to remember the event.]*

I thought, "We can't pay for that stuff but Mickey isn't going to do that to me." So, I told the waitress to bring me a cheeseburger, fries and a chocolate shake." *[The old Joplin boys are now cracking up with laughter at a story they lived 49 summers ago.]*

I said to Mickey, "You crazy nut, what are we going to do?" He said, "Here's what we are gong to do. We'll flip to see who goes up and pays the bill and the other guys will hold the door open. We'll let everybody else leave and go to the bus." The bus was about a half block away, on the corner, with the motor running.

I said to Mickey, "No, we're not flipping because you can outrun me." Mantle insisted, "No, no, we're going to flip." We flipped and I lost. So, I got all this handful of pennies, a few nickels, maybe a dime in there and head for the counter. All you guys were on the bus screaming because we're not there, of course.

Mickey gets up and goes and opens the door and I put all those coins on the counter and we "cut and run." *[Boisterous laughter now engulfs the group.]* We jump on the bus and being dumb, young and silly kids we didn't realize until next day we hadn't gotten away with a thing. When we picked up our check the next morning the amount we owed the restaurant had been deducted. The restaurant owner had merely called Joplin after we left and we paid for the meal, just one day after we ate it. *[Laughter continued.]*

Hall: I guess you fellows didn't realize your team logo was written on the side of the bus, did you?

Neeman: Did we get $2.50 a day for meal money?

Smith: Yes, that's what we got.

Gott: It was $2.25, wasn't it?

Smotherman: Is that right? I had forgotten.

Gott: I thought it was $2.25, maybe it was $2.50, but that's all we had on which to eat.

Kraly: I don't even know if it was $2.25. All I can remember was $1.50.

Hall: That was your KOM League money, Steve.

Gott: You couldn't eat anything, anyway, Kraly. You had such a strict diet.

Billingsly: At the start of a 10-day road trip they would give us our money up front. When we were five days into the trip, half us were out of money. *[Laughter, but not the kind that comes from amusement, was heard rippling through the room.]* Harry Craft would always loan you money.

Kraly: Let's face it, look at what our salaries were back then.

Billingsly: I borrowed money from Craft.

Kraly: I remember asking Mickey how much money he was making. He told me, and I think Wiesler was also there at the time, that he was getting $200 a month. I was making $190. So finally I go to Mr. Beavers and I said, "I want to talk with you." This was after I won a few games and I had to buy vitamin pills to get my strength. The rest of you guys were such big monsters.

So, I went to him and said, "I've got to have a raise, you know. Geez, everybody else is making this kind of money." He asked me why I needed a raise. I said, "Well, I'm buying these vitamin pills and they cost me." Beavers asked, "How much?" I said, "$9.99." He said, "Well, I think you deserve a raise. Let's see your contract." He opened it up and said, "Yeah, I'll give it to you."

I figured I was getting $200, right? He makes it out for $199.99. I never got to $200 a month. *[Much laughter.]* And Mantle laughed and I can still hear him — he, he, he. You guys know how he laughed. He laughed like that every time he played a practical joke.

Hall: Do you remember many of Mantle's practical jokes?

Kraly: Especially on Lou Skizas.

Hall: What did he pull on Skizas?

Kraly: He took Lou's rabbit's foot out of his back pocket. Remember, the way he hit? He always had that right hand in his back pocket before swinging. I thought he would go bonkers because Mantle took it. Lou was hollering, "Who got it, who got my rabbit's foot?" Mantle said, "Got what? What do you have in there?" Lou kept repeating, "My rabbit's foot."

Billingsly: Skizas and his blue jeans. He could stand them in the corner couldn't he?

Kraly: Yes.

[Cromer Smotherman laughs the heartiest at that memory.]

Long: Or anybody else's blue jeans, or shorts, or sock or underwear or whatever.

Billingsly: Those jeans were so stiff you could stand them up.

Wiesler: I thought Skizas had a cross in his back pocket because of the way he used to slide. He wouldn't hit the ground with the hind end. He kinda scooted in there. And I always though it was a cross and he was afraid of ripping himself up if he slid.

Neeman: That's what I thought, too.

Kraly: It was a rabbit's foot. And not only that, if you remember, Mantle took all the tissue out of Lou's spikes. Lou padded those with tissue because he wanted to be taller. He had also put some lifts on his heels to make him look taller.

Billingsly: I remember that.

Long: How about the time, Steve, you put a toy snake in Lou's locker? *[At Independence.]*

Kraly: Oh, God.

Long: And Skizas, being the kid from Chicago, probably had never seen a real snake in his life. Man, he about tore the clubhouse up in getting out of there.

Gott: You want the Skizas story we all ought to remember? The crab story. Remember? *[Everyone in unison said, "Ah, yeah."]* Remember what you told him, Cromer? You said, "YOU son of a buck, if I get those things 'Greek' I'm going to kill you."

Smotherman: I really did enjoy Lou. He was from a different part of the country than I was. But a youngster I really did enjoy. I don't think I ever saw Lou when he didn't have a big smile on and face and having a big time.

Hall: He was a pretty good ballplayer too, wasn't he?

Smotherman: He could flat hit.

Long: He could hit a fastball, I'll tell you. Remember the time in 1949 at Chanute when they had this left-handed pitcher? He had struck Lou out a couple of times on curve balls. Lou came up late in the game and this guy was popping off and telling him, "I've got your number." Lou said, "I dare you to throw me a fastball." The guy made a bad mistake. He threw him a fastball and before he could get his glove down, Lou hit a ball that got him on the knee. We thought he was killed. He went down like he was shot by an elephant gun. We got out there and he couldn't ever get the elastic in the bottom part of his pants up over his knee. The next time we went into Chanute he was still on crutches and we yelled at him, "Do you still have Lou's number?" He didn't think that was too funny.

Neeman: I knew if you ever talked about that team of 1950 that Skizas had to come up sooner or later. I just saw a note John Hall gave us earlier today. It was a newspaper assessment of the 1950 Miners club that said, "They had no color."

Hall: That was a newspaper story, guys. I laughed when I saw it also.

Neeman: You know, that's kinda weird, isn't it. I asked Bob Wiesler on the way down here about Skizas wearing three pairs of socks when he went on the road. Instead of changing he would take the top one off (kind of like peeling an onion) until he got down to the last one. Then it was time to start over again. *[Much laughter over that story from the guys.]* I think that's true.

Billingsly: I know he wore the same pair of blue jeans.

Neeman: Yes.

Hall: Who the blue jeans belonged to was always the question, wasn't it?

Neeman: Yeah! I heard he took the entrance exam at the University of Illinois and had one of the highest scores of anyone to ever take it. And he wound up being the chairman of the science department. I don't know if that's true or not.

Gott: I heard he got his doctorate in anatomy. He also did the color commentary for the Illinois State University basketball and football teams for a lot of years.

Smotherman: Is that right? That doesn't surprise me.

Gott: He is on the faculty still at the University of Illinois I just can't ever catch him at home.

Long: John, you correct me if I am wrong, but he might hold the minor league record for hitting in the early part of the season. I think he had 25 hits in his first 29 times at bat.

Hall: Until they threw him a curve ball. *[A lot of laughter from the guys.]*

Long: That was putting some wood on the ball.

Hall: I think he was hitting .862 when someone figured out he could hit a fastball.

Smith: Didn't he play for Detroit for a while?

Long: He played for Kansas City and I would see him and he was still the "Grinning Greek." But, I think he had his own clothes by then.

Gott: Don't bet on it. He probably had all his paychecks in his pocket, too.

Hall: I think I will take this tape and sent it to Lou and see if I can get a reaction from him.

Wiesler: Uh!

Kraly: Do you know that he graduated from the University of Illinois with the highest academic scores?

Wiesler: That's what Cal just said. Did you hear that?

Kraly: He also became the assistant hitting coach for the baseball team the University of Illinois. He was a smart guy. We wouldn't have known that when we looked at him back at Joplin.

Wiesler: He was smart. He would always borrow money the day after payday. He had checks in his pocket all the time.

Kraly: Oh yeah!

Billingsly: He was always hitching his pants, hitching his pants, hitching his pants.

Kraly: He always had to touch his hips with his elbows. *[In unison all the guys said, "Yeah."]*

Hall: Do any of you guys remember Jerry Buchanan? He was the big pitcher from Dallas.

Smotherman: I was just looking at him on the picture. Yes, I remember him.

Hall: Do any of you know anything about David Benedict?

Wiesler: Dave was at Boys Town in Nebraska. I just wonder if that was his son who caught for the Atlanta Braves? *[Ed Note: One week later I found Dave in Omaha and his son, Bruce, was indeed the former catcher for the Atlanta Braves and was a bench coach for the New York Mets during the 1999 season.]*

Neeman: I have often wondered about that, too.

Wiesler: We visited up there the last year I was with Dallas. We went out to Boys Town and I met with Dave. He was in the administration department.

Hall: Let's talk about the guys that aren't with us today. Joe Crowder drowned in 1953. Does anyone remember Dan Ferber?

Wiesler: He was a right-handed pitcher.

Hall: Dick Fiedler?

Wiesler: Yeah, a pitcher.

Hall: Tom Hesketh?

Wiesler: He was from Cincinnati.

Billingsly: Yeah, Tom, I remember him.

Hall: How about Emil Federow and Dick Gilman?

Neeman: I don't remember Federow, but the reason I told John Hall and Tom Gott to try to get hold of Gilman was because he was the guy who sat in the dugout. When we would knock the other pitcher out, Gilman always sang that funeral song. Remember that?
[In unison the group all uttered, "Yes."]

Neeman: He was one of these guys who talked a lot and he would probably remember some stories that would be worthwhile. I remember he finally started a game and he got knocked out. The other team all gave him the big funeral song. However, we were scoring a lot of runs and he got to sing his song quite a bit.

It seemed like Gilman knew where he was, on the ball club. He was a good athlete. He had a heck of a record as a college quarterback. He knew that Mantle and some of you guys were pretty good baseball players.

Kraly: How about Len Wiesner?

Gott: That's Wiesner.

Wiesler: He was supposed to come up here today but his daughter-in-law and son were down at Branson and she got a heat stroke and Len went down to take care of the kids.

Gott: I've got to say this, Cal, when you talk about Gilman not starting many games, you think of the three left-handers we had: Simanovsky, Kraly and Wiesler. I mean, mercy! It was tough to get to start a game.

Neeman: That Buchanan, I think he was a Dr Pepper addict, wasn't he? He drank 10-15 a day.

Gott: Yes he did, I forgot that.

Kraly: He always used a brick to loosen up his arm with before throwing the ball in the bullpen.

Neeman: Yeah, that's right, Steve. Yeah, he did that. He could throw hard.

Kraly: But he couldn't get the ball over the plate half the time.

Neeman: Oh, no.

Gott: On that team, six of you guys got to the majors. I think that is highly unusual. *[Ed note: It was only five. Gott thought Joe Crowder had made it.]*

Neeman: I think another two guys would have definitely been there—Crowder and Waters

Gott: Crowder had a cup of coffee up there.

Neeman: David Waters was bound to have been a Major Leaguer.

Gott: Did he ever get there?

Smotherman: He didn't make it.

Neeman: From what I heard he was beaned.

Smotherman: He was.

Neeman: Yes, pretty bad. He was a little like Mantle. He married his high school sweetheart. He had an operation after his first beaning and went back and played again.

Gott: I didn't know that.

Neeman: Then he got hit once more and his wife made him promise not to ever play anymore. If you look at David Waters, he could have played third base for the New York Yankees.

Kraly: He was a great ballplayer. I don't know what happened to Muddy after 1950, really.

Neeman: Well, I hear he went to Birmingham first.

Kraly: Is that where he was?

Smotherman: Steve, he was in the Southern League—Southern Association at that time, and of course, Birmingham played Nashville at that time. I went down and had lunch with him. He was playing third base for Birmingham. When he got hit in the head they were playing at New Orleans. He was also in the military service like most of you were.

Smith: I think most of us went into the service in the fall after the 1950 season.

Smotherman: Yes, I'm pretty sure you did.

Smith: I know I got my letter when I turned 21. Tom, you went too, didn't you?

Gott: Yes.

Kraly: I think we all went to the Korean Conflict and came out in 1953.

Smith: I was in Okinawa in 1952 when the Yankees were playing the Dodgers in the World Series. In the seventh game there was a sergeant there who had played with Pee Wee Reese, Carl Furillo and all those guys in World War II. He asked if there was anybody who wanted to bet $250 that the Dodgers won't beat the Yankees in that seventh game. I said, "You're on, I'll bet you." Mantle hit a home run in the 8th inning. I never will forget it. We fell out for Reveille around 5:00 a. m. It was afternoon back in New York, the game was over and the sergeant gave me the money.

Neeman: I wonder how far Mickey would be hitting the ball today?

Smith: How much money would he be making today?

Long: He'd hit them out of the county today.

Neeman: You know that every park he played in he had almost the longest ball ever hit in that park. Even in St. Louis, at old Sportsman's Park, he hit it out of the park in left field. And he didn't play there that much. [Mark] McGwire hits them a long way, but I think if anyone would come close it would be Mantle.

Long: I think so, too. I was living in Kansas City and I recall going out to Municipal Stadium one night to see Mantle play. If I recall it was about 335 to right. Then there was this embankment that went up a hill to another fence which was 10 feet high. Then there was a sidewalk, Brooklyn Avenue, another sidewalk, a front yard and a house behind that. Mickey hit one that landed on the roof of the porch of that house. I want to tell you that was a bus ride.

Hall: Someone asked me to compare Mantle and McGwire recently. How would you guys make the comparison?

Gott: Mickey brought four things to a ball club. He could hit home runs, he could hit for average, he could run and he could field. McGwire doesn't have those four things in his repertoire.

Neeman: Being from St. Louis, I am glad the Cardinals got McGwire. Being down on that field people show me where he hits balls in batting practice and it's unbelievable to think how far he hits them. I think if anybody could compare for hitting the ball for distance it would be Mantle.

Gott: Nobody denies McGwire has power, but Mantle could beat you four ways and McGwire beats you one way.

Long: You have to remember Mantle was before all this expansion was taking place and he was seeing some good pitchers every day.

Gott: They had the larger strike zone then, too.

Long: And they hadn't cut the mound down, they hadn't brought the fences in and a strike was a strike. You could still throw at a guy and knock him down if you wanted to. Today you see 150-pound shortstops checking their swings and hitting home runs to the opposite field, and you begin to wonder what is in that ball.

Kraly: We all know that we never saw opposite field homers like we see today. I agree that expansion has ruined major league baseball because it has watered down the talent. They are not facing the great pitchers like they were when Mantle played. He faced the best and hit them from both sides of the plate with muscle. The switch-hitters of today can't do it. They just slap at the ball.

Hall: *The Joplin Globe* reported that Mickey Mantle was one of the few switch-hitters in organized baseball in 1950. How many players did you see in the Western Association that year who hit both ways?

Gott: There weren't that many.

Neeman: I don't remember any.

Smotherman: I don't recall any.

Smith: I think it was only Mantle.

Neeman: That's what upset me in 1949, when Mickey wanted to take batting practice form both sides when he was trying out. I said, "I'll hit left-handed, too, then."

Long: Wasn't his dad behind Mickey's switch hitting?

Gott: When I talked with Merlyn she said that had Mickey's dad lived she didn't think he would have ever got wrapped in that "stuff" that he eventually did.

Wiesler: He was very close to his dad.

Long: It was almost reverential, wasn't it?

Hall: Bob, you and Steve were as close to Mickey for the first two years as anybody. Between you two, when did you know Mantle would be a star?

Wiesler: At Independence it didn't even dawn on me. But when he got to Joplin I saw where he was hitting those home runs to the opposite field with such power and he could run. I know Tom Greenwade got all the credit, but Johnny Sturm, the 1949 Joplin, manager, was the guy always telling Greenwade to sign him.

From 1949 to 1950 he developed his neck, shoulders and legs. It was unbelievable. The way he performed in the rookie league got him held over for spring training in 1951. That's when DiMaggio was considering retiring. The New York Giants and Yankees switched camps that year. The Yankees went out to Phoenix and toured the West Coast so the Californians could see their native son at the end of his career.

Every park we went to they had standing room only. That is when Mickey first played centerfield and he went right on to New York and stayed with them for a while. And then came down to Kansas City and went back up. It was unbelievable how he developed his skills.

Hall: Bob, you may not want to say it, but weren't you the Yankees' prize young hurler?

Wiesler: I don't know. They said when Whitey Ford went into the service I would be his replacement. I got a shot in 1951. I got up there. Me and Bob Cerv went up together and Tommy Morgan and Mickey were sent down. The next thing I knew, I was going down to Kansas City and Mantle was coming back up.
  [Laughter.]

Wiesler: I missed coming to St. Louis when the Browns were there. I was in Detroit when Casey Stengel told me I was being sent back down. I kinda missed that chance of being with the family in St. Louis.

Gott: The answer to your question, John, is, "Yes."

Smotherman: I know Bob won't remember this but the Yankees stopped to play an exhibition game in Chattanooga. I went out to the ball game and watched it. Bob was kind enough to get me an autographed baseball.

Wiesler: It's worth a lot of money; keep it.

Smotherman: I still have it. I also ate dinner with you guys that night since you stayed in town. I remember eating with you, Mickey Mantle and Enos Slaughter.

Hall: Bob Wiesler has a picture of that dinner. Have you seen it, Cromer?

Smotherman: No.

Smith: Bob, were you with the Yankees in 1953?

Wiesler: No, I was in the service.

Gott: I remember them talking about Wiesler and Vinegar Bend Mizell of the Cardinals. Guys in the Cardinal organization were telling us how great

Mizell was. I'd laugh at 'em. I said, "You guys haven't seen a left-hander until you see Wiesler."

Smotherman: I know I would not have wanted to bat against Wiesler.

Neeman: Of course, Kraly was the kind of pitcher who just kept getting you out.

Long: Of course, I saw both Wiesler and Mizell. I was in the Cardinal organization after I got out of the service. But to my eyesight it was not a contest between Mizell and Wiesler. Bob would have blown him away.

Gott: You have to remember that in 1950 Bob broke his jaw. How long were you out, Bob?

Wiesler: Three to four weeks. They didn't wire me up. They sent me home to heal. To this date, whenever I move my jaw back and forth, I can still feel it.

Smith: Did you get hit with a bat?

Gott: Yes, it hit the side of the batting cage and came around and got him. He was pitching that night.

Wiesler: I was pitching that night and the next thing I knew I was in an ambulance. I wonder if some of the names John Hall read off replaced me when I was on the disabled list?

Gott: I remember the first game you pitched when you came back off the disabled list. You started a game at Springfield.

Wiesler: I got rained out.

Gott: You had faced 15 batters and struck out 14 of them when the game was halted. Only one guy even got a piece of the ball.

Wiesler: That was a bad park because I remember you (Gott),

Lombardi and Skizas ran into each other.

Gott: I ran into Skizas.

Wiesler: Yeah, and you swallowed your whole chaw. You ran past Craft and said, "Get somebody to replace me," and you headed to the john.

Long: Kraly wasn't any slouch as a player either.

Smith: Yes, he was.

Gott: Don't blow him up like that.

Hall: Can you guys tell me something about the park in Springfield? A *Joplin Globe* reporter wanted me to pose that question to you and determine the source of the odor that hung low over that ball field.

Long: It was Nichols Park and the smell came for the sewage disposal plant.

Hall: How did you guys take that odor with the humidity and temperature both being around 100?

Wiesler: It seems like all the parks were close to a creek or something. Geez, we had more damn trouble with mosquitoes. Some biggies! It was mosquitoes and floods.

Long: Hutchinson, Fort Smith and a lot of other parks were built on rivers. I wonder why they did that?

Gott: Because it was flat.

Billingsly: We were talking about Buchanan. Remember when he whiffed 18 guys at Hutchinson for a record?

Gott: He always huffed and puffed when he pitched.

Smotherman: Kind of a hefty guy.

Kraly: As to an earlier question about my roomie, Wiesler. He was touted as the best-looking left-hander in the organization. I say that from the bottom of my heart. We roomed together on the road and even at Independence. I think the problem Bob had is the same one I had when I went up with the Yankees. The problem was Jim Turner. If you didn't do it Jim's way, you were out to lunch. I don't think they gave Bob enough of a chance to pitch. I'm looking at a list of seven lefthanders the Yankees had for 1954. Bob, do you remember that?

Wiesler: Yes.

Kraly: But back then I didn't care for Jim Turner because he would also haunt you to pitch his way and that is why they called him "The Milkman." Johnny Sain and the other guys would say, "Don't listen to him because he could steer you wrong." All Wiesler needed was more confidence and to get into the games and pitch more. I could never understand why they kept optioning him down.

Hall: Do any of you remember Denis Jent? [*"Ah yes, absolutely" was the consensus of the group.*] Denis told me he was in Phoenix in 1950 and Turner told him to go out and pitch. Denis told him that he hadn't warmed up, but Turner insisted that it was a warm day and he didn't need to warm up. Denis recalled that he hurt his arm that day and was never the same pitcher after that. He didn't have a high opinion of Turner, either.

Gott: Wasn't Denis at Joplin in 1950?

Hall: He was at Joplin in 1949. He led Independence hurlers in strike-outs in 1948, and Wiesler came along in 1949 and broke the record. Denis led Joplin in strikeouts in 1949, and Wiesler came along in 1950 and broke that record.

Long: Some of us old pitchers get together and one of the things we remember is that nobody in the lower minors ever told you anything about pitching.

Gott: Back then all the managers were "great hitters." They all wanted to help you hit.

Kraly: Well, we were good hitters. Us pitchers were anyway. But let's keep in mind that we lived the stories that have been written about Mantle. So, I think we can talk firsthand about all those things that have been written about him in his early years. We lived them and there are a lot of good things that can come of this attempt to set the record straight. I am tickled to death to be a part of it, especially it if will help the Mantle family.

Smotherman: Goodbye to all of you and I look forward to seeing you in Joplin.

At the end of this conversation, Billingsly, Smotherman and Kraly hung up and Gott, Wiesler, Neeman, Long, Smith and his wife headed to the home of the author for more conversation and food.

While the evening meal was being prepared, the telephone rang. It was Steve Kraly calling back to express the great time he had in renewing the friendships of his former teammates after 49 years of not seeing or hearing from many of them.

The guys hung around and told more stories before the long day of interviewing finally concluded. They were determined to go back to their respective homes and think of more "tall tales."

The session had been cathartic. It gave them the chance to talk about their buddy, Mickey Mantle, for the first time in such a forum since his death some four years previous. These former Joplin Miners carried a lot of great memories about their former teammate that many people had never heard. They did so amidst a lot of negative press that had hounded Mickey even after his death.

Appendix 4

Anecdotes from Ray,
Roy and Max Mantle

R ay and Roy Mantle were twin brothers of Mickey. Mickey had 41/2 years on the boys and was the "leader of the pack." Ray, in describing his older brother said, "He is the greatest person I ever knew."

Ray recalled watching a lot of Mickey's KOM League games and most of his Western Association home games played by the Joplin Miners. Harry Craft was the manager of both those clubs and when the season concluded in 1950 both Harry and Mickey thought they would be at Beaumont, Texas in 1951.

Ray and brother Roy both signed with the Yankees and played for McAlester, OK in the Sooner State League in 1954. Playing on that same McAlester team was a guy Ray claims had the greatest arm he ever saw. The fellow was from Springfield, Missouri and his name was Rod Kanehl. I asked Ray if he had a stronger arm than Mickey and he replied, "I am afraid I would have to say 'yes.'"

Ray was drafted after the 1954 season and went into the service. Roy wasn't and he went on to play in the Cotton States League. The only baseball Ray played after that was at Fort Lewis, Washington. He hit eight homers in his first eight games, but baseball was over for him, except for watching his older brother carve his way into the Hall of Fame.

The great memories for Ray revolved around the off-season when Mickey would come home to Commerce and Billy Martin would be tagging right along. Ray and Roy looked upon Billy as a brother and Mrs. Mantle looked upon him as a son. Ray recalled, "Mickey, Billy, Roy and I used to get up at daybreak and ride the country roads, looking in fence rows for quail. One morning Billy saw a covey and jumped out of the car and started shooting. Mickey yelled at him to give the quail a chance. Billy responded with 'I want quail and eggs for breakfast.' He knew my mother would cook him up a big breakfast when he got back to the house." Max Mantle recalled that Billy had never eaten quail before. When the platter of quail got to the table Martin started gobbling up those delicacies. Mickey advised him to slow down because quail were very rich. According to Max, Martin kept on eating the game bird l and within a short time he was heaving them up.

Ray recalled that Billy Martin was the best friend Mickey ever had with the Yankees and that Yogi Berra was the funniest. During winter months or the early 1950s, fellows like Ray, Roy and Max Mantle, along with Bruce Swango and a few other top-notch athletes in that Northeast Oklahoma area, played basketball. The team was sponsored by Harold Youngman, who owned the Southwest Chat Company. Thus, the team was known as the Southwest Chat Company Five. The coach was none other than Mickey Mantle. The team played all around the area, and would even take on Marques Haynes and the Harlem Magicians when they appeared in the Four-State area.

Billy Martin was still living in Commerce with Mickey during the winter months and would suit up for the games. Martin never thought Mantle was much of a coach because he would start his cousin Max ahead of Billy in every game. Martin felt in his heart that he was superior to Max. So one night, Mantle substituted Martin for Max early in the game. Martin confidently took the floor and took his first shot. It missed everything. Mantle called timeout and ran Max back into the game. When Martin got back to the bench, he approached Mantle and said, "What in the hell did you take me out of the game for?" Ray recalled that his older brother retorted, "You weren't hitting."

Mantle loved Yogi Berra and relished telling his twin brothers about the things Yogi would say. According to Ray, Berra was facing this kid pitcher. The boy threw one that was way outside and Berra swung at it and missed. He threw the second pitch into the dirt and Berra swung and missed it. The third pitch was a foot over Berra's head and he whiffed on that one too. When Berra got back to the dugout he looked over at Mantle and said, "That kid will never make it in the big leagues, he hasn't got any control."

Mantle's favorite "Yogism" was the time Berra and his wife Carmen were discussing their mortality. Carmen asked Yogi that when he died would he rather be cremated, have a regular funeral or be put in a vault. According to Mantle's version of the story, "Yogi thought it over for a few seconds and replied. 'Surprise me.'"

Myths arise from stories that get embellished by their frequent narration. Tom Greenwade was a Yankee scout doing what he could to please Lee McPhail by finding the best talent possible. Ray recalled that he never saw Tom more than a couple of times at most and when he first appeared in Baxter Springs he came scout to at a boy named Bill Johnson. Bill was deemed to be one of the hottest prospects in the area. However, it wasn't long before Johnson was forgotten and they latched on the number two guy on the team—Mickey Mantle.

Brothers of legends, as Ray Mantle surely was, had his own memories of guys he saw as a young man playing the game of baseball around the KOM League and Western Association. How many people have ever heard of Walter "Zeb" Snyder or Leonard Wiesner? Snyder was a slick fielding first baseman for the 1948 Miami Owls in the KOM League and Wiesner was a hard hitting member of both the 1949 KOM League's Independence Yankees and 1950 Joplin Miners. These were the two guys who impressed Mickey Mantle's younger brother, as great ballplayers or at least with the talent to become so.

How the Mantle twins were signed by the New York Yankees is remembered by Bunch Greenwade, the son of Tom Greenwade. He told this story: "After Mickey became a fixture with the Yankees his twin brothers were of signing age. The Yankees decided that they wanted an all-Mantle outfield and called dad to go down and sign them. Dad argued that he had seen the boys and they weren't in the same league as their older brother. The Yankees were still insistent and dad placed a call to Commerce to have the boys come up for a tryout.

"The tryout was held in our cow pasture where Dad raised prize beef cattle. Dad marked off 90 feet and timed the boys. Then he let them swing at a few pitches and throw. At the end of the 'tryout' Dad called the Yankees and without reservation said, 'Damn, Lee, they will never play major league ball.' McPhail's response was, 'Well, sign them whether you like them or not.'"

Years after that cow pasture workout and the Mantle twins were working as pit-bosses in Las Vegas, they always had a laugh each time they met Bunch about that day in Willard when Tom Greenwade announced they would never make it in the big leagues. However, they did survive a few summers in the Sooner State, Cotton States and Eastern leagues. Neither of the twins was ambidextrous as was their older brother. Roy hit from the left side and Ray the right and both threw right-handed.

Ray quit the game after his stint in the Cotton States League but Roy went on until tearing up a knee at Binghamton while playing in the Eastern League.

Cousin Max Mantle was signed about the same time the Yankees inked Ray and Roy to contracts. The twins had gone to New York immediately following their graduation from Commerce High School. Mickey wanted them up there for various reasons. One was that they could get his car to him and the other was that he genuinely missed his brothers. Upon arriving in New York they were outfitted in uniforms spent the entire month of June 1954 working out with the Yankees and enjoying the sights of the Big Apple. Upon their departure the Yankees had decided both boys had enough potential to be signed to a minor league contract. That is when they called Tom Greenwade and told him to sign the twins.

Max's signing was a bit different. The Baxter businessman, Harold Youngman, had his own airplane and on a trip from Joplin to Springfield the passenger manifesto included; Tom Greenwade, Harold Youngman, Mickey Mantle, Max Mantle and the pilot. The trip was the occasion for Greenwade to sign Max to a Yankee contract for 1954. Mickey was up to his usual practical jokes on this occasion. He had worked it out with the pilot to make it appear somewhere en route to Springfield that the plane was about to crash. Max recalled, "Mickey told the pilot to drop something on the floor and then act as if he had lost control of the plane. The pilot did as Mickey requested but as the event unfolded the pilot was more clever than even Mickey anticipated and Mickey was more scared than I was."

Max's memory of his cousin Mickey was that he was always doing things he later regretted. During the last season the St. Louis Browns were still in the American League Mickey invited his brothers and cousins up for a series. The group was comprised of Ray, Roy and Max. The designated driver for the trip was Mickey's high school baseball coach, Johnny Lingo. Max recalled there wasn't much to do during the day, "so we had to find things to keep occupied." On one of those slow days the group decided to go to a local amusement park. Small town boys of the Midwest didn't see large amusement park rides. The only thing similar was the traveling circus which would set up in a vacant lot in a small town and then pull out in a couple of days. So, the Commerce group decided to take their first roller coaster ride. That was Mickey's first time to take such an adventurous ride, even though he had played in a few cities prior to that who had such entertainment venues, such as Kansas City's Swope Park.

Max recalled he and Mickey sat in the front car a nd Ray and Roy were seated directly behind them. As the coaster slowly inched upward Mickey said, "This isn't bad." Then, as the coaster reached the apex of the incline it started downward very rapidly with Mickey yelling at the top of his voice, according to Max, "Stop this damn thing." Max said it was so terrifying to Mickey that, "I had to hold him in the seat to keep him from jumping out." After the roller coaster came to a stop Mickey was the first one off. Max recalled, "We let Mickey go his own way and the rest of us rode that thing the rest of the afternoon."

Max recalled what he called "fall ball." That was after the baseball season ended for all the Mantles and their buddies and when they returned to their respective home towns they would play anywhere they could get a game in the four state area of Oklahoma, Missouri, Kansas and Arkansas. That "season" lasted until it got absolutely too cold to play baseball.

Max played amateur baseball for about five years following his retirement from the professional game. During one of those fall games in 1954 the Mantle bunch went to Bentonville, Arkansas. Bentonville, according to Max, "Had this hotshot pitcher from Hollis, Oklahoma who was supposed to be something special and I went 4-5 against him." The "hotshot" pitcher was Lyndall Dale McDaniel who was regarded highly enough that the St. Louis Cardinals gave him a $50,000 signing bonus and he was in a Cardinal uniform the following year.

The success Max had against McDaniel, who was so highly regarded at the time, led him to question whether he had given up the game too early. Max played a number of years of semi-pro baseball for the Tri-State Miners, as did Ray and Roy Mantle. That team was actually out of Joplin, Missouri, but they called Treece, Kansas, their home site since it was easier for them to advance to the National Tournament at Wichita as a Kansas representative rather than a Missouri team. Jack McGoyne, another miner who had coached numerous amateur teams in the Miami, Commerce and Joplin area coached the Miners. After his mining days Jack went to work for the Junge's Bakery in Joplin and managed the Tri-State Miners due to his love for the game.

Bibliography

Books

Dixon's Oklahoma-Kansas Mining Directory — 1926. Miami, Okla.: O. T. Dixon Printing and Stationery Company. Reprint, undated.

Gibson, Arrell. *Wilderness Bonanza: The Tri-State District of Missouri, Kansas and Oklahoma*. Norman: University of Oklahoma Press, 1972.

Hall, John. *Majoring in The Minors*. Stillwater: Oklahoma Bylines, Inc., 1996.

Mantle, Mickey, as told to Ben Epstein. *The Mickey Mantle Story*. New York: Henry Holt and Company Inc., 1953.

Sporting News, The. *The Official Baseball Guide for 1950*.

_____. *The Official Baseball Guide for 1951*.

Suggs, George G. Jr.*Union Busting in the Tri-State: The Oklahoma, Kansas, and Missouri Metal Workers' Strike of 1935*. Norman: University of Oklahoma Press, 1986.

Articles

Carley, Clyde. *Inside Baseball*. August 1953. Vol. 1, No. 10. "The Mickey Mantle Nobody Knows."

KOM League Remembered, The, newsletter, Vol. 2, No. 6, (Nov. 1995), Vol. 2, No. 7 (Dec. 1995), Vol. 2, No. 8 (Jan. 1996).

Wabash College newsletter, 1987. Quotation by Dan Ferber.

Newspaper Stories

Advocate, Pataskala, Ohio, Chad Klimack article, Nov. 5, 2001

Associated Press, "Sports Roundup" column, unsigned, Jul. 30, 1940. Apr. 12, 1950.

Baxter Springs (Kans.) *Citizen,* May 19, 1949, Apr. 27, 1981.

Baxter Springs (Kans.) *Citizen and Herald,* Aug. 7, 1947

Carthage (Mo.) *Evening Press,* Aug. 29, 1949.

Cedar Rapids Gazette, ca. February 1951.

Coffeyville (Kans.) *Daily Journal,* May 26/28, 1949.

Hutchinson (Kans.) *News,* Jun. 13, and ca. Aug. 1950.

Independence (Kans.) *Daily Reporter,* Jun. 13, 15, 16, 18, 23, Jul. 19, 21, 22, 27, Aug. 2, 5 ("Strictly Sporting" column, Les Davis), 6, 9, Sep. 10, 1949. Aug. 14 (copy of Mantle's $1,150 bonus check), 15 (reproduction of Mickey Mantle's first baseball contract), 1995.

Joplin (Mo.) *Globe*: Aug. 3, 1948. May 2, 21, 23, 28, 29, Jun. 11, 1949. Apr. 16, 17, 20, May 5, Jul. 13, Sep. 6, 1950. Oct. __ (Sunday supplement) and Nov. 4, 1952.

Joplin (Mo.) *News Herald*, ca. Apr. 20, Jul. 3 (Paul Stubblefield column) and ca. Jul. 15, 1950

Miami (Okla.) *News-Record*, May 7, 1952.

New York World Telegram, March 25, 1939.

Tulsa Tribune, _____, 1963, "It Was the Hangout for Everyone" (article about the Black Cat Café, Miami, Okla.), by Mac Bartlett.

Internet Website Documents

"Campbell Killing," Frank R. Ballinger's Bonnie & Clyde's Hideout, retrieved Feb. 2004.
texashideout.tripod.com/Campbell.html

"Lead and Zinc Mining," Kansas Geological Survey, Geology Extension, retrieved May 17, 2002.
kgs.ukans.edu.Extension/ozark/mining.html

"Tri-State Mining District—The Jasper County Superfund Site Project," Environmental Division, U. S. Army Corps of Engineers. Retrieved May 17, 2002.
hq.environmental. usace.army.mil/minutes/p03.pdf

History of the building of Pensacola Dam and the impounding of Grand Lake, as described in *The Chronicle of Grand Lake*, Langley, Okla., Rusty Fleming, publisher. Retrieved Dec. 2002.
grand-chronicle.com

Interviews by the Author

Mantle family members:

Crampton, Bobbie (cousin), 2001-fall 2004, Catoosa, Okla.

Johnson, Reba (mother-in-law), fall 2002, Picher, Okla.

LaFalier, John (he and Mickey Mantle married Reba Johnson's
daughters), summer 1999-fall 2004, Picher, Okla.

Mantle, Elmer (second cousin), 2000, Columbia, Mo.

Mantle, Hallie (family historian), summer 2000-fall 2004, Linn, Mo.

Mantle, Harold (third cousin), summer 2002, St. Louis, Mo.

Mantle, Joy & Levi (third cousin), summer 2002, Brookland, Ark.

Mantle, Mark (third cousin), summer 2003-fall 2004, Columbia, Mo.

Mantle, Max (first cousin), summer 1999-fall 2004, Joplin, Mo.

Mantle, Merlyn (widow), summer 1999-fall 2004, Dallas, Tex.

Mantle, Ray (brother), summer 1999-fall 2004, Las Vegas, Nev.

Mantle, Roy (brother, deceased), summer 1999, Las Vegas, Nev.

Richardson, James (cousin), winter 2002-fall 2004, Bethany, Okla.

Richardson, Tom (cousin), summer 2002-fall 2004, Grove, Okla.

Boyhood pals in Commerce:

Barker, Joe, summer 2000-fall 2003, Commerce, Okla.

Bennett, Leroy, fall 2002-fall 2004, Ponca City, Okla.

Ferguson, Nick, winter 2001-fall 2004, San Diego, Calif.

Mosley, Bill, winter 2002-fall 2004, Topeka, Kans.

Shouse, Ivan, summer 2000-fall 2003, Commerce, Okla.

Teammates on the Baxter Springs (Kans.) Whiz Kids (1947-49),
in addition to Bennett and Ferguson:

Ball, Buddy, winter 2002-fall 2004, Duncan, Okla.

Barnett, Walter A., Jr., summer 2000-fall 2003, Lowell, Kans.

Craig, Ben, winter 2001-fall 2004, Overland Park, Kans.

Crow, Bill, summer 2001, Scales Mound, Ill.

Crow, Guy (batboy), summer 2001-fall 2004, Galena, Ill.

Garrison, George, summer 2000-summer 2004, Joplin, Mo.

Harbaugh, Duffy, summer 2003, Seneca, Mo.

Heavin, Charles, fall 2002, Topeka, Kans.

Heavin, Rex, fall 2002-fall 2004, Overland Park, Kans.

Johnson, Willard "Billy," fall 2002-fall 2004, Pataskala, Ohio

Kerley, William, fall 2003, Baxter Springs, Kans.

Lee, Bennie Maxwell, summer 2001-fall 2003, Derby, Kans.

Lovelace, Delbert, winter 2000-fall 2004, Welch, Okla.

* Mishler, Calvin, fall 2002-fall 2003, Baxter Springs, Kans.

Pitts, Wylie, fall 2001-fall 2004, Riverton, Kans.

Steele, Bob, summer 2003, Richardson, Tex.

Widows of Baxter Springs players:

Kenaga, Judy (Mrs. Jim), summer 2002-fall 2004, Ardmore, Okla.

Myers, Earlene (Mrs. Bocky), winter 2003, Baxter Springs, Kans.

Independence (Kans.) Yankee teammates (1949):

Belotti (Bello), Jim, summer 1999-winter 2003, Crowley, La.

Bennett, Ken, summer 2002, St. Louis, Mo.

Cobb, James, winter 2002-fall 2004, Washougal, Wash.

** Hasten, Jack, summer 1999-fall 2004, Springfield, Mo.

* Joyce, Arnold, summer 1995, Chattanooga, Tenn.

*** Kraly, Steve, summer 1999, Johnson City, N.Y.

* Long, Alvin, summer 1999-fall 2000, Lee's Summit, Mo.

Mallon, Robert, summer 1999-summer 2004, Highlands Ranch, Col.

** Moffit, Burl, summer 1999-summer 2004, Fagus, Mo.

Newbill, Bob, summer 1999-summer 2004, Windsor, Mo.

Rose, Kenneth Jack, summer 1999, Louisville, Ky.

*** Skizas, Lou, summer 1999, Champaign, Ill.

Speck, Keith, summer 1999-fall 2004, Loveland, Col.

Waska, Darrell (replaced by Mickey Mantle on the team), winter
2003-fall 2004, Temecula, Calif.

Weber, Charles, summer 1999-fall 2004, Belleville, Ill.

*** Wiesler, Bob, summer 1999-fall 2004, Florissant, Mo.

*** Wiesner, Len, summer 1999, St. Louis, Mo.

Whitaker, Jack, summer 1999, Hollywood, Fla.

---

* Now deceased.

** Left team shortly before Mickey Mantle joined it.

*** Also with Mickey Mantle on the 1950 Joplin team.

Joplin (Mo.) Miners teammates (1950):

    Benedict, Dave, summer 1999, Omaha, Neb.

    Billingsly, Al, summer 1999-fall 2004, Venice, Fla.

    Buchanan, Jerry, winter 2001-fall 2004, Dallas, Tex.

*   Craft, Harry, spring 1995, Houston, Tex.

**   Drake, Bill, summer 2002, Raytown, Mo.

    Ferber, Dan, summer 1999-fall 2004, Eagan, Minn.

    Fiedler, Dick, summer 1999, Altadena, Calif.

    Gott, Tom, summer 1999-winter 2002, Quincy, Ill.

    Hesketh, Tom, summer 1999, Cincinnati, Ohio

    Hittle, Dale, summer 1999, Lodi, Calif.

    Lombardi, Carl, summer 1999-fall 2004, Montclair, N.J.

    Neeman, Calvin, summer 1999-fall 2004, Lake St. Louis, Mo.

*   Simanovsky, Frank, summer 1999-winter 2003, Fallbrook, Calif.

    Smith, Lilburn, summer 1999-fall 2003, Springfield, Mo.

    Smotherman, Cromer, summer 1999-fall 2004, Lawrenceburg, Tenn.

    Waters, David, summer 1999-fall 2004, Betonia, Miss.

Others:

    Anderson, Don, summer 1999-fall 2004, Hemet, Calif.

    Annen, Don, summer 2000-fall 2004, Madison, Wis.

    Barnett, Cass, summer 2001-fall 2004, Baxter Springs, Kans.

    Brown, Denna, fall 2002, Tulsa, Okla.

    Buzzard, Max, summer 1999-fall 2004, Miami, Okla.

*   Childs, Robert, winter 2001-summer 2002, Tubac, Ariz.

    Daniels, Harry, winter 2002-fall 2004, Columbus, Kans.

    Greenwade, Bunch (son of New York Yankees scout Tom Greenwade), fall 2002, Willard, Mo.

    Greenwood, Val, winter 2002, Joplin, Mo.

    Haney-Getter, Joan, summer 1999-fall 2004, Dallas, Tex.

    Heiserer, Herb, summer 2002-fall 2004, Atlanta, Ga.

    Metcalfe, Wayne, fall 2001, Baxter Springs, Kans.

    Mick, Malcolm "Bunny," summer 1999-fall 2004, Odessa, Fla.

    Newkirk, Dave, summer 1999-fall 2004, Bethany, Okla.

Neighbors, Pat, summer 1999-fall 2004, Rickman, Tenn.

Pevehouse, Phyllis, summer 2003-fall 2004, Coffeyville, Kans.

Pitts, Wylie, winter 2000-fall 2004, Riverton, Kans.

* Pollock, Joe, summer 1999-summer 2003, Miami, Okla.

Sawyer, Randy, summer 2001, Mexico, Mo.

Schmidt, Don, 2000, Moline, Ill.

Self, Cindy (daughter of the late Lyle Westrum of the 1950 Joplin
    Miners), fall 2002, Bemidji, Minn.

Solenberger, Al, winter 2000-fall 2004, Bartlesville, Okla.

Speake, Bob, summer 1999-summer 2004, Topeka, Kans.

Terry, Ralph, summer 2002-fall 2003, Larned, Kans.

* Tole, W. A. "Cap," fall 1995, Independence, Kans.

Vallina, John, summer 1999-fall 2004, Belleville, Ill.

Virdon, Bill, summer 1999-fall 2004, Springfield, Mo.

Waldrip, Jerry, fall 1996, Pittsburg, Kans.

Documents

Mantle, Hallie, untitled, unpublished Mantle genealogy, 1990. This is a
collection of oral history and charts.

Mantle, Harold, "The Mantle Family History," unpublished manuscript,
undated.

Mantle, Mickey, speech, Baseball Hall of Fame, Cooperstown, N.Y.,
Aug. 12, 1974.

Tulsa, City of: "Clear & Cold, Pure As Gold; How the Waters of the
Spavinaw Came Down to Tulsa," Tulsa Metropolitan Utility Authority,
Community Affairs and Planning Section of the Department of Public
Works.

United States, Bureau of the Census, census reports for 1920-2000.

Commerce (Okla.) High School, yearbook, 1949.

Letters

Parkinson, Ted, to Lee Newman, Apr. 30, 1951; from the John Hall collection.

Sims, Dean, letter to the editor, "Inside Picher and Tar Creek," *The Tulsa World*, Jan. 5, 2003, p. G-2.

About the Author

John Hall was born eight years after Mickey Mantle entered this world. Each grew up in the Four Corners area of Southeast Kansas, Northwest Arkansas, Southwest Missouri and Northeast Oklahoma. Their early life experiences were strikingly similar.

Their paths first crossed in the summer of 1949, when Mantle was a shortstop for the Independence, Kansas, Yankees and the author was a wide-eyed pre-teen watching his first professional baseball game from the box seats at Carthage, Missouri's Municipal Park Stadium.

The lure of professional baseball affected the author to the extent that he was visiting team batboy for Carthage opponents in 1950 and home team batboy in 1951.

The KOM League folded after the 1952, but interest in the old league and the young men who performed therein, including Mantle, remained for by the author. In 1996, Mr. Hall wrote his first book, *Majoring in the Minors*, a history of the KOM League.

The author is a graduate of Carthage High School and attended Joplin Junior College, where a member of one of Mantle's Baxter Springs Whiz Kids teams was his physical education teacher. The author holds undergraduate and graduate degrees from Southern Nazarene University in Bethany, Oklahoma and Pittsburg State University in Kansas.

He spent a number of years in the active ministry before entering careers in state government in both Kansas and Missouri. For a number of years he was a Medicaid director in governmental entities and served in the public sector as a consultant to some of the largest data processing companies in the United States.

For over 10 years the author has published a monthly newsletter entitled "The KOM League Remembered," and in the summer of 2004 he wrote his second book, *The KOM League Remembered*.

The strength of all of Mr. Hall's writing is his documentation of Mantle's early life through becoming acquainted with family members, his closest boyhood pals and fellow players on kid baseball and minor league teams.

At the urging of many of Mantle's minor league teammates, the author took on the task of researching and writing the story of Mantle's early years, from his birth through the 1950 Western Association season with the Joplin Miners. With the assistance of threescore and ten of those most closely affiliated with Mantle, this book became a reality after five years of in-depth research

Mickey Mantle: Before the Glory is the definitive work on the early influences in the life of Mickey Mantle. This book is, in all manners, a coming together of people — from Mantle's friends and teammates, to the author and editor — who were all shaped in the crucible of the Tri-State Mining area of Kansas, Oklahoma and Missouri.

The Editor

Greg Olds was born in Oswego, Kansas, and grew up in Tulsa, Oklahoma. He loved reading the sports pages of *The Tulsa World* and *The Tulsa Tribune* as a young man and that was the inspiration that led him to graduate from the University of Texas with a degree in journalism.

Olds loved the atmosphere of the small town newspapers in Texas and Missouri and worked for a number of them before becoming the editor of *The Texas Observer*, a political journal in the state capital at Austin, where he still resides. After his recent retirement, Olds has kept busy writing a newsletter for the local University of Oklahoma alumni club.

In one of those moments that can only be called "great luck," Olds heard of the writing about the old Kansas-Oklahoma-Missouri (KOM) League. During one conversation he became aware that a book was being written about the early life of Mickey Mantle. That immediately got his attention, and his words were, "I'd be happy to help on this project."

The author as he appeared when Mantle was playing in the KOM League against Carthage, Missouri.

The author in the exact same spot, 55 years later. At Carl Lewton Field in Carthage, a plaque on the entrance to the stadium honors Hall's contribution to remembering those who played there between 1946-1952.

Index

Page numbers in italics (other than roman numerals) refer to photographs; the letter "c" refers to captions; and the letter "n" refers to footnotes, followed by the footnote number.